BOBBY SHERMAN
Still Remembering You

BOBBY SHERMAN
Still Remembering You

BOBBY SHERMAN AND DENA HILL

CONTEMPORARY BOOKS
A TRIBUNE COMPANY

Library of Congress Cataloging-in-Publication Data

Sherman, Bobby.
    Bobby Sherman : still remembering you / Bobby Sherman and Dena Hill.
       p.   cm.
    Includes discography.
    ISBN 0-8092-3206-5 (P)
    1. Sherman, Bobby. 2. Singers—United States—Biography.
I. Hill, Dena. II. Title.
ML420.S5372A3   1996
782.42164'092—dc20
  [B]   96-15551
                                                                                                 CIP
                                                                                                  MN

Cover design by Monica Baziuk
Cover photos courtesy of Bobby Sherman Enterprises, *Tiger Beat* magazine
Interior design by Hespenheide Design

Copyright © 1996 by Bobby Sherman Enterprises Incorporated
All rights reserved
Published by Contemporary Books
An imprint of NTC/Contemporary Publishing Company
Two Prudential Plaza, Chicago, Illinois 60601-6790
Manufactured in the United States of America
International Standard Book Number: 0-8092-3206-5
   10   9   8   7   6   5   4   3   2   1

Photo Credits

Photos courtesy of Patti Carnel: pages 173, 176, 178, 179, 180, 186, 189, 190, 191, 192, 193 (bottom), 194, 195, 196, 197, 198, 200.

Photos courtesy of Dena Hill: pages xvii, 209, 212.

Photos courtesy of Kathi Hoffman: pages 36, 37.

Photo courtesy of Fred A. Miller: page 211.

Photo courtesy of Bobby Sherman: page 193 (top).

Photos courtesy of Bobby Sherman Enterprises: pages ix (right), xiv, 3 (right), 30, 44, 48, 53, 64, 71, 72, 79, 92, 100, 116, 119, 125, 136, 152, 166, 184, 187, 202, 206, 207, 214, 217, 220, 223.

Photos courtesy of Nita Sherman: pages 4, 5, 6, 8, 9, 11, 12, 17, 18, 26, 41, 43, 46, 49, 50, 51, 54, 57, 59, 61, 63, 219.

Photos courtesy of *Tiger Beat* magazine. Copyright © *Tiger Beat*: pages vi, viii, ix (left), xiii, xviii, 2, 3 (left), 14, 22, 23, 28, 32, 35, 39, 58, 62, 65, 67, 68, 70, 74, 76, 77, 78, 80, 82, 83, 85, 86, 89, 91, 93, 94, 96, 98, 99, 102, 104, 106, 107, 108, 110, 111, 112, 113, 114, 115, 122, 123, 126, 131, 132, 135, 138, 140, 141, 142, 143, 146, 147, 149, 154, 156, 158, 159, 160, 161, 162, 163, 165, 167, 168, 169, 170, 174, 208.

An Open Letter to a Fan

This book is dedicated to you.

My fans are the ones who have made life such a joy for me.

If you were a fan, God bless you.

Because of you, I've been able to fulfill many of my dreams. You had the final vote. If I had been the greatest tenor in the world, unless you liked me, I might as well have stayed in the shower.

Through the years, I've had the good fortune to meet many of you personally. If our paths ever cross, I hope you'll always take a moment or two to come up and say hello.

For everyone who remembers Jeremy on "Here Come the Brides," or listened to "Easy Come, Easy Go," this book is for you. For everyone who watched "Shindig" or "Getting Together," or sang along at one of my concerts, this book is for you, too.

If you find something here to connect to, it may remind you of a good time in your life.

When you read about me, I hope it also sparks memories of who you were and what you were doing, thinking, and, most of all, feeling at those times.

I honestly believe that's the power of this story. It's your story as well.

Still remembering you . . .

Peace & Love
Bobby

Contents

An Open Letter to a Fan	vii
Acknowledgments	xi
Prologue	xiii
1 Shiny Dimes	1
2 Don't Let the Milk Bottles Rattle	15
3 The World According to Disney	31
4 Discovery	47
5 "Shindig"	55
6 The Monkees	69
7 "Here Come the Brides"	81
8 A Dream Date with Bobby	105
9 Concert Tour Tales	117
10 The Groovy Fans	139
11 "The Partridge Family"/"Getting Together"	157
12 Girls, the Press, and Patti	171
13 Christopher and Tyler's Dad	185
14 TAC-5 and the LAPD	203
15 What Now?	215
Discography	225
Bibliography	229
Index	231

Acknowledgments

Because this is my story, all the people who have been part of my life have contributed to this book. Acknowledging each of them would take another volume.

I have been blessed with a loving family and friends. My life and my careers in show business, emergency medicine, and the Los Angeles Police Department have been filled with people who were kind, encouraging, understanding, supportive, and eager to help.

To all of them, I am very grateful.

Bobby Sherman

Special thanks to:

Joy Dickinson, for creative consulting, unending accessibility, and the general ability to inspire; Nita Sherman, for opening her heart, home, and personal family mementos; Darlene Mack, for unconditional cooperation and congenial support; Debra Sailors for sharing a wealth of information from her personal collection; Kathi Hoffman, whose research abilities, fact-checking know-how, and genuine willingness to help deserve an "Encino Olympics" award; Roxanne Berry, without whom there would be no title of this book or joy in Mudville; Michael Bennett, for online uplinks and constant technical advice; Patti Carnel, for candor and graciousness above and beyond; Patricia Lee, for a call at the right moment; Marjorie Wilson, for the three breaths theory; Bridget Hanley, for grace under pressure; Susan Tolsky, for laughter and that laugh; Charles Laufer, who paved the way; *Tiger Beat* magazine for its generous cooperation; Linda Kruger and Evan Fogelman, for opening the doors; and Linda Gray, our editor, whose belief in this book made it all happen.

With heartfelt appreciation,

Dena Hill

Prologue

1969

This was work.

I had to keep moving. It was 110°F under the stage lights. The screams of the audience were so loud I couldn't hear my band. I'd been on the road so long that I couldn't remember what city I was in.

The only thing I could do was avoid any one spot for too long. It was that time in the show—the throwing time. I was performing for fifteen to twenty thousand screaming fans. The ones who had thought of it had brought something to toss to me to get my attention. They always started out throwing soft things like nice cuddly little bears. But they'd run out of them, and now they were throwing whatever they had to get me to look their way.

The fans brought cameras that had those attachable flashcubes. After a while, they would take their used flashcubes and throw them! It was just a way to make contact. Sure, they were plastic and lightweight. That wasn't a problem up close. It was a different

story if someone was hurling them at me from the balcony. From there, they had to get their arms into it. The flashcubes were coming pretty fast—and they stung!

On top of that, the sheer volume at the concerts was excruciating. My ears would ring for days. But it was fun. It was what I called "the love-in." It didn't matter what I sang. In concert, I literally could have been lip-syncing a Supremes record. The audience wouldn't have known the difference, because they screamed through the entire show.

All I could do to entertain was just keep moving around the stage. I'd play one side, and then I'd play another side, and point to as many fans as I could and say, "YOU!" They'd scream and say, "That was me! He pointed at me!"

1994

This was work.

I had to keep moving. The baby's head already had started to crown. Delivery was imminent. I opened one of the obstetric kits we carry and put it on the lawn near the curb. As an Emergency Medical Technician, I'd already delivered four babies on the job without any problems. And now, aside from the fact that we were on a public street delivering a baby in a car, everything was going normally. There was only one problem.

By instinct, infants know they have to rotate in order to clear their shoulders through the birth canal. In this case, though, the mother was bearing down, which was making it hard for the baby to turn.

Because the mother spoke only Spanish and my partner and I only spoke English, I tried to show her what to do. "Don't push. Don't push," we said, using gestures to make ourselves understood. "Take short, quick breaths. Puff, puff, puff. Do that." Fine. She caught on and started doing it, which relieved the bearing-down pressure.

The baby rotated beautifully. No problem. I suctioned. The baby started crying even before it was fully born. In no time at all, out came this beautiful little girl. The miracle of birth always astounds me.

I wrapped the child in a receiving blanket and put her to her mother's breast. In the meantime, the mother had managed to ask my partner what my name was.

"Robert," he told her.

After a few moments, she pointed to her little girl and said, "Roberta."

Thank God my partner didn't say "Sherman."

Dena

1971

I'm in the middle of a huge crowd of people. There are bright lights and blaring music. Bobby Sherman is nearby.

I am three days short of being fourteen years old, a woman by my standards. I have long, dark hair parted in the middle, and I am wearing my special, purchased-for-the-occasion outfit: blue hot pants and a white tunic that laces up the side. I decide I look at least sixteen and a half.

I have lived for this concert for months, and now I'm here and so is he. This whole experience is even better than I thought it would be. He's wearing a gold, sort of mariachi-inspired outfit. I have never seen anything like it.

He sings, dances, points, and yells, "You!" to thousands of hysterical pubescent girls. Everyone around me is screaming. I am annoyed. This is my first concert, and I feel screaming is impolite. After all, he's trying to sing up there.

I'm sitting in the middle of the second row with my mom. How she got such good seats, I don't know. Still, I wish I was in the first row. I wish that even harder as the evening progresses.

I know every word to every song that is on his albums. When Bobby launches into, "If I Were a Carpenter," the audience goes crazy. "Would you have my baby?" he sings. "Yes," they vow. They would marry him under any circumstances.

He never stops moving, pointing to as many girls as possible. It seems to me he keeps looking at me. I just know he can see me. But I am quiet. I'm convinced I'll get to talk to him, although I don't know why I think so.

The question-and-answer period of the show arrives. I raise my hand. He comes immediately to me.

"Hi. What's your name?"

"Dena."

"What's your question, Dena?"

"I'm here for my birthday. Could I have a birthday kiss?"

My mother slips into cardiac arrest. Other girls start waving their hands.

"Here come a lot more of those questions," Bobby says to the fifteen thousand or so other people rude enough to be in the room with us at the moment.

"How old are you?" he asks, returning his attention to me.

I can't decide quickly enough what age I can truly fake. I tell the truth and regret it.

"I'll be fourteen on Tuesday."

He eyes the distance from the stage to where I'm sitting.

"I don't know if I can reach you," he says, leaning out for that kiss.

The people in the front row move apart obligingly. Bobby nearly falls off the stage.

"I'm sorry, babe. I can't make it. Here." He kisses his hand, then touches mine.

"Happy birthday."

The rest of the concert is a blur.

1995

I'm in the middle of a huge crowd of people. There are bright lights and blaring music. Bobby Sherman is nearby.

We are standing on the private balcony of Club 33, the exclusive VIP club at Disneyland. We have dined in gorgeous surroundings and drunk champagne.

Prologue

xvii

I am wearing my special, purchased-for-the-occasion outfit. I am thirty-eight. I look at least thirty-two and a half, I decide. I have lived to write this book for months, and now I'm here and so is he. This whole experience is even better than I thought it would be.

We are standing on the balcony watching fireworks and the intricate light show that follows. Tinkerbell flies across the sky, and, from somewhere, the song "When You Wish Upon a Star" fills the air.

I begin to believe it.

 **Shiny Dimes**

"Are you Bobby Sherman?" the fire marshall asked.

"Yes."

"We have a problem. You'd better come with me."

It was 1968, and "Here Come the Brides" had just started appearing on television. I had gone to Buffalo, New York, with another actor from the show, Robert Brown, to appear on a telethon. We had been taking telephone calls, and kids were calling in to talk to me. After a while, the fire marshall walked into the studio and said there was a problem.

"Some kids want to say hi to you," he said.

I thought that was really nice. What was the problem?

He asked me to follow him, and we walked upstairs to the second floor of the building. I had no idea what was waiting for me. He opened a window overlooking the parking lot. There below us stretched a sea of kids filling the whole lot. Thousands of them. The minute they saw me, they started screaming, waving, and carrying on. I'd never seen anything like it.

Suddenly, almost overnight, those thousands of kids had become my devoted fans. I didn't know why, but they were. I couldn't believe it. I wanted to go out and talk to them, but there was no way I could risk it. The situation was out of control. The kids had surrounded the television station, and we couldn't leave.

To prevent a riot, I was taken to the very top of the station where we crept along a crawl space that connected to the fire

24 INTIMATE HOURS

Did you ever wonder what time Bobby gets up in the morning? If he brushes his teeth before he takes a shower? What he eats for lunch? Well, don't keep yourself in the dark any longer! Now YOU can find out all the intimate facts about Bobby! For he has invited YOU only to spend a day with him!

With the first click of the clock-radio, Bobby slowly opened his beautiful blue eyes. He eyed the face of the clock with a slight frown as the wake-up music suddenly burst forth. It was 6:00 a.m., time to rise and start another hectic day.

Bobby pushed his falling locks from his eyes and climbed out of bed to start the morning rituals. Flashing his lovely smile at his reflection in the bathroom mirror, Bobby yawned once and reached for the toothpaste. Vigorously he brushed his teeth until they gleamed extra bright! Then, he ran a soapy wash-cloth over his face to soften his beard. With a mound of shaving cream over his jaws and chin, he carefully shaved with his razor.

Shaving finished, Bobby turned on the shower and stepped out of his pajamas. Quickly he got under the needle-like spray. Bobby doesn't have to wait for the water to get hot because he always takes his showers lukewarm! Hot showers make him sleepy!

WHEN HIS WORK IS DONE on "Here Come The Brides," it's really not done at all. At night he often tapes guest appearances on other TV shows.

JUST ORANGE JUICE

Back in the bedroom, Bobby selects a blue shirt, black scarf and levis. Sitting on the edge of the bed he puts on his shoes and socks, then runs a comb through his hair and snaps off the radio.

Once dressed, Bobby fixes himself breakfast—a tall glass of orange juice. He never has anything else. A big breakfast just doesn't agree with him in the morning!

It was 6:45 now, and Bobby hurried outside to where his Rolls Royce was parked. It only takes him about 10 minutes to get to work. As usual, Bobby glanced at the sky to see what kind of day it would be, then paused to say a few cheery words to the elderly lady walking her dog! Then he got into his car and headed for the Columbia Ranch.

GROOVY IN THE MORNING

Bobby's first stop once at work is at the wardrobe room, where he undresses and dresses in his "working" outfit. From there, he makes a stop at the make-up department, then it's on to the set!

Before shooting begins, everyone exchanges cheery good mornings and smiles. What Bobby especially likes about the entire cast and crew of the "Brides" is that everyone feels groovy in the morning. There's not a grouch around! This makes everything start off on the right track!

Until around 1:00, Bobby is busy shooting and re-shooting scenes. Or, if he isn't in the part being shot, he watches the others work, or talks to anyone who is free. Sometimes Bridget comes over, and they have a cup of coffee together! She and Bobby always seem to have some time for each other between takes.

At 1:00 a halt is called in shooting for a lunch break until around 2:00. Sometimes if Bobby doesn't feel like going out he'll shoot a game of pool, or just stay in his dressing room playing the guitar or writing songs.

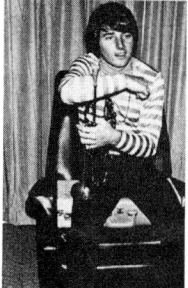

SOME NIGHTS BOBBY SPENDS ALONE in his recording studio at his parents home in the Valley. He plays 12 instruments, including trumpet.

16

DAYS ARE LONG AND HARD, but always fun on the "Brides" set. Bobby says everyone is always cheery in the mornings even though it's early.

---

station next door. When we got downstairs, they put me in the back of a hearse and covered me with a tarp. The hearse inched its way through the crowd that was still waiting for me to come out of the television station.

I lay motionless underneath the tarp, thanking God that I wasn't inside a coffin, and thinking, "This is show business?"

That was the beginning of the madness.

Once my career began to blossom, life took on a very unreal quality. Even the very facts of my existence seemed to change. At one point, after I'd had a hit with "Little Woman," somebody quoted my birth date as July 22, 1945.

I said, "It's not '45, it's '43." I was told, "Well, it's too late now." To avoid confusing everybody, I simply said, "Forty-five it is," and that's what it stayed.

But here are the facts.

I was born at 9:30 P.M. on July 22, 1943, at St. John's Hospital in Santa Monica, California. I was named after my father and,

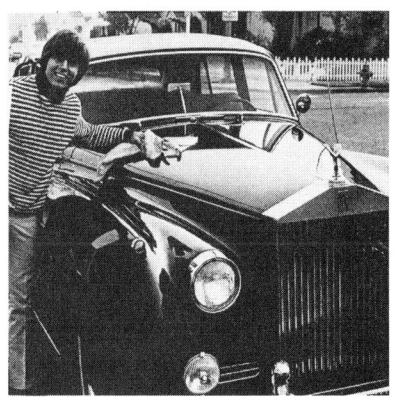

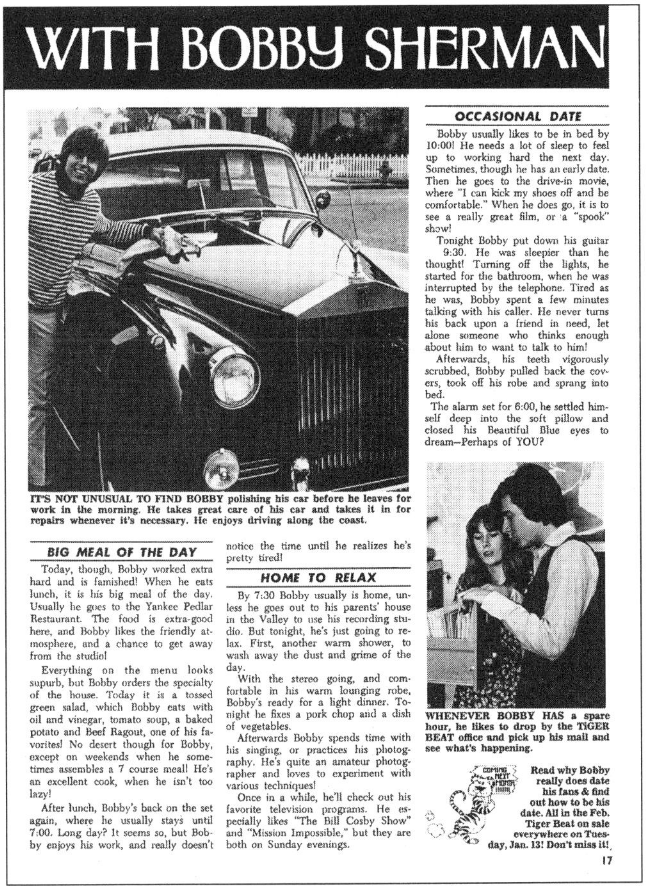

WITH BOBBY SHERMAN

IT'S NOT UNUSUAL TO FIND BOBBY polishing his car before he leaves for work in the morning. He takes great care of his car and takes it in for repairs whenever it's necessary. He enjoys driving along the coast.

BIG MEAL OF THE DAY

Today, though, Bobby worked extra hard and is famished! When he eats lunch, it is his big meal of the day. Usually he goes to the Yankee Pedlar Restaurant. The food is extra-good here, and Bobby likes the friendly atmosphere, and a chance to get away from the studio!

Everything on the menu looks supurb, but Bobby orders the specialty of the house. Today it is a tossed green salad, which Bobby eats with oil and vinegar, tomato soup, a baked potato and Beef Ragout, one of his favorites! No desert though for Bobby, except on weekends when he sometimes assembles a 7 course meal! He's an excellent cook, when he isn't too lazy!

After lunch, Bobby's back on the set again, where he usually stays until 7:00. Long day? It seems so, but Bobby enjoys his work, and really doesn't notice the time until he realizes he's pretty tired!

HOME TO RELAX

By 7:30 Bobby usually is home, unless he goes out to his parents' house in the Valley to use his recording studio. But tonight, he's just going to relax. First, another warm shower, to wash away the dust and grime of the day.

With the stereo going, and comfortable in his warm lounging robe, Bobby's ready for a light dinner. Tonight he fixes a pork chop and a dish of vegetables.

Afterwards Bobby spends time with his singing, or practices his photography. He's quite an amateur photographer and loves to experiment with various techniques!

Once in a while, he'll check out his favorite television programs. He especially likes "The Bill Cosby Show" and "Mission Impossible," but they are both on Sunday evenings.

OCCASIONAL DATE

Bobby usually likes to be in bed by 10:00! He needs a lot of sleep to feel up to working hard the next day. Sometimes, though he has an early date. Then he goes to the drive-in movie, where "I can kick my shoes off and be comfortable." When he does go, it is to see a really great film, or a "spook" show!

Tonight Bobby put down his guitar 9:30. He was sleepier than he thought! Turning off the lights, he started for the bathroom, when he was interrupted by the telephone. Tired as he was, Bobby spent a few minutes talking with his caller. He never turns his back upon a friend in need, let alone someone who thinks enough about him to want to talk to him!

Afterwards, his teeth vigorously scrubbed, Bobby pulled back the covers, took off his robe and sprang into bed.

The alarm set for 6:00, he settled himself deep into the soft pillow and closed his Beautiful Blue eyes to dream—Perhaps of YOU?

WHENEVER BOBBY HAS a spare hour, he likes to drop by the TIGER BEAT office and pick up his mail and see what's happening.

COMING NEXT MONTH

Read why Bobby really does date his fans & find out how to be his date. All in the Feb. Tiger Beat on sale everywhere on Tuesday, Jan. 13! Don't miss it!

17

indirectly, the Massachusetts senator Henry Cabot Lodge.

My paternal grandfather, Herbert John Sherman, and my grandmother, Esther, had lived in Wisconsin before moving to Chicago. Both their families had emigrated from Germany. My grandfather managed a hotel in Chicago and became friendly with Senator Lodge when he visited the city. During World War I, the family name, Schermeister, had been changed to Sherman.

American influences continued to shape the names in our family. My grandfather thought that Cabot Lodge was such a gentleman that he named my father after him. That name, in

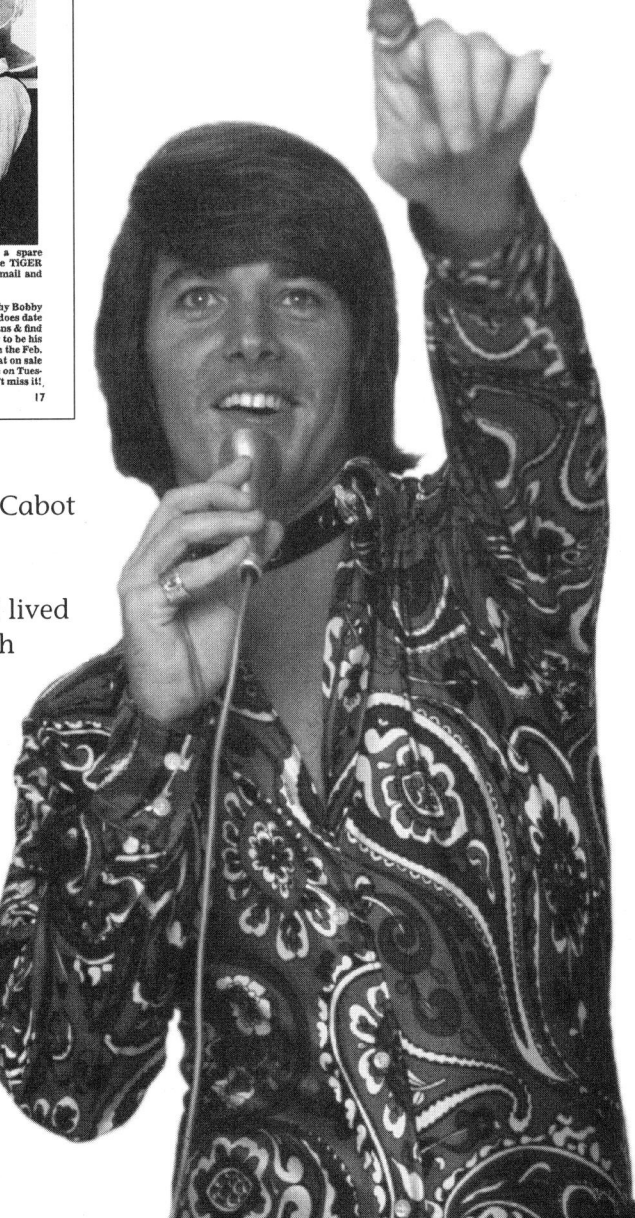

turn, was passed on to me. Robert Cabot Sherman, Jr., was a big name for a baby who almost didn't make it here at all.

Nita, Bobby's Mother

I almost lost Bobby. It was terrible.

We were living in Hollywood, and my doctor was in Santa Monica, about thirty minutes away by car. Bobby's due date was September 29. But, starting at the beginning of July, I was in the hospital more than I was out to avoid having him prematurely.

In spite of our efforts, Bobby was born early—about two months and fifteen minutes early. The hospital was going to celebrate the event of delivering its 1,000th baby by paying all the expenses for its birth. Bobby was the 999th. I guess he wanted to be born so badly, he couldn't wait another fifteen minutes.

He weighed just under four pounds when he was born. He was two months premature, and when I first saw him, he was so ugly. It's true! He had black hair all the way underneath his chin and all over his arms. Afterwards, I was crying, and my husband came in the room and said, "Did you see the baby? He looks like an ape."

But by the next week, all the dark hair was gone and Bobby just had blond fuzz. Thank God. Because I'd never have been able to explain it to the neighbors.

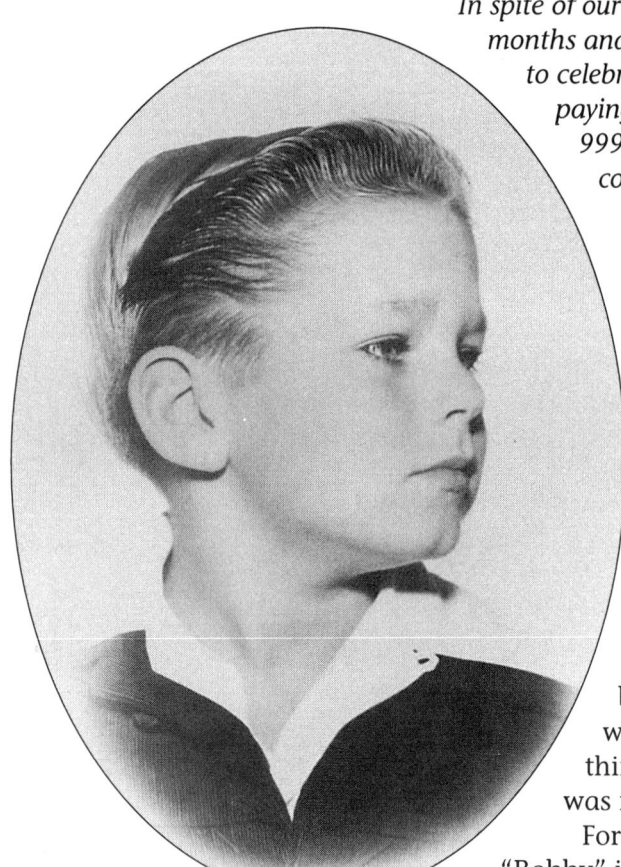

Me at age 6.

According to my mom, when my parents brought me home, they already knew they were going to call me Bobby. This created something of a problem for my sister Darlene, who was not much more than a toddler at the time.

For some reason, she called our dad (Robert, Sr.) "Bobby" instead of "Daddy." Apparently, while holding me in her lap on the ride home from the hospital, Darl, as I call her, decided once and for all how she would address my dad and myself.

Luckily for me, she wanted a baby brother.

Nita

All of a sudden, Darlene looked at her dad and said to him, "Bobby, I can't call you 'Bobby' any more."

"Why not?"

"'Cause now I've got another Bobby, so I guess I'm gonna have to call you Daddy."

She called him Daddy until the day he died.

Everybody called my husband Bob or Bobby. It was the same with Bobby, Jr. We never thought of him as "Robert." I called him "Robert" only if I was angry with him.

From the time he was born, though, he's been special—and God let us keep him.

My dad and mom were young when I was born. They married when he was seventeen and she was fifteen. Darlene was born almost a year later. I came along when Darl was five, and our folks grew up with us.

Their love for each other was an anchor in our lives. They were so much in love, they were married twice! The first wedding took place in Mexico, but they learned soon afterward that the marriage wasn't legal. So they had a second wedding on October 15, 1937, in Santa Ana, California. That's the date we always celebrated for their anniversary. Even though they had their disagreements, they were devoted to each other.

Robert Sherman, Sr., and Juanita Freeman met on New Year's Eve, 1936, in Los Angeles. He was working as an usher, making $8.50 a week at the Alvarado Theater. Mom has always said he accused her of marrying him for a free show ticket. She insists that it was his snappy uniform that caught her eye.

Nita

He was an usher, and my mother and I had gone to see the ten-cent show. He seated me on the aisle. He kept coming down and flirting with me. When I started to leave, he said, "I want to know your name, your address, and when I can see you." I said, "Go away."

But my mother, who was visiting me from out of town at the time, liked him. My mom ended up telling him where I lived, and he came to visit me every time he got off work. I wouldn't let

Mom.

Dad.

him in, but, every time, he'd come down and start pounding on the door.

Then one day he was standing outside in a downpour, and my mom said, "Well, at least invite him in out of the rain." I said, "I don't want him to come in." Actually, I was crazy about him, but I was playing hard to get—and I wanted that show ticket, too!

As my mom saw it, marrying my dad was an either/or choice. She could either wait until she was seventeen, old enough to qualify for training as a nurse, or she could marry my dad and start a family. I'm happy that the odds, and her heart, were in Dad's favor.

Unlike the carefree childhood she and my dad gave me, Mom was out on her own at an age when most girls are still having slumber parties. Tiny and blessed with striking features, Mom stood just four feet, eleven inches, and weighed eighty-nine pounds the day she arrived in Los Angeles.

Mom.

Born in Dallas, Texas, on January 27, 1922, Mom was adopted when she was only a week old by Willa Mae and Henry Choate. She has been told since that time that her birth mother was a sixteen-year-old Cherokee Indian who hated the idea of giving up her infant daughter, but was unable to care for her. After they adopted Mom, the Choates moved to Fort Worth, Texas. Unfortunately, they divorced when Mom was just five years old.

After the divorce, Mom lived with her adoptive mother, Willa Mae, in Texas. When Mom was nine, Willa Mae married my step-grandfather, Tom Freeman. The three of them then moved to Hemet, California, where Tom grew watermelons.

Only a few years later, as a teenager, Mom set out on her own from Hemet. She was armed with a fierce sense of independence, truckloads of charisma, and a reasonable nest egg. She had scraped together several hundred dollars by working at a watermelon stand owned by her folks. By the time she married my dad at fifteen, she already was supporting herself doing cleaning in a three-story rooming house.

Of course, the owner of the rooming house adored her. Mom has always taken care of everyone around her, and people are drawn to her. That's just the way she is. Naturally, she found an almost instant family in her employers. For a kid making her own way, she was doing pretty well.

Dad, on the other hand, moved to Los Angeles with his family shortly before he met my mom. He was born to Esther and John Herbert Sherman on November 28, 1919, in Oak Park, Illinois. The second of three sons, he arrived between his older brother, Herbert, and younger brother, Bill. As a boy, Dad suffered horribly from asthma, but he learned how to live with his physical challenge. Sadly, a treatment that was meant to help him ultimately did him the most harm.

Darlene

Dad had a really rough life growing up with severe asthma. He was very lucky to have survived infancy because, at that time, they didn't know what to do for asthma.

For as long as he could remember, he slept standing up and leaning over the back of a chair. Because of the asthma and the problems with his breathing, he started smoking. This sounds strange, but the doctors at that time gave him what they called "cubeb cigarettes" made from dried berries. They caused him to cough and bring the phlegm up.

So he started smoking at thirteen, which helped his asthma. But smoking is what gave him emphysema later in his life. He also had an enlarged heart because of the strain. Sometimes with every breath he took, you just thought, "It's got to be his last. I don't know how he can make it like this."

Because of his asthma, Dad couldn't get out and play as the other kids did. He was a good student, but he couldn't participate in sports.

Later, he wanted Bobby to be able to do the things that he couldn't do. When Bobby played football in high school, it was like a life's dream for my dad. He couldn't play, so he was going to live it through his son.

My dad died in 1990, just before my parents' fifty-third anniversary. I miss him. If it hadn't been for smoking, my dad would have lived longer. If I could go back now I'd pull the cigarettes out of my dad's hands. He was instrumental in so much of my success.

Both he and my mom helped me immeasurably by giving me so much freedom and encouragement as I was growing up. They allowed me to experiment and turn my daydreams into tangible projects. Their support for me never wavered. Our family life was like something out of "Ozzie and Harriet." How my folks learned to be such wonderful parents, I've never known. Even though Mom married Dad so young, she had already formed an idea of what a solid family should be like.

With Santa and Mom, 1953.

I feel grateful for the cohesiveness that my mom and dad brought to my childhood. They provided a good example of the way parents should handle themselves and their children. Yet they didn't spoil us. We were even a little afraid of Dad because he was very strict. I don't recall him ever spanking me, but his look and his voice when he was angry could make me shudder.

My mom always took my side when I got in trouble, and she was very loving. Even when I was young, she didn't have to do much—just give me a look—to discipline me. If I thought I was out of favor with her, I would feel devastated. She was my best friend.

Together, my parents were an attractive, dynamic couple. My dad was a handsome man, and my mom was gorgeous.

Darlene

When my parents walked into a room, people would stop and look. There was something special about them, and Bobby is that way, too. He has my dad's imagination and my mom's charisma.

In the first several years of their marriage, my mom and dad lived with my father's parents, sharing a house in Hollywood. My parents moved out on their own in 1942, to a large one-story triplex on La Brea Avenue.

That first year at La Brea proved eventful. The same week I was born in 1943, my dad received his first paycheck from Arden Farms, where he began his career as a milkman. Ten months later, Dad was drafted for World War II and was sent to train at an Army base in Texas. Soon after he was gone, I was injured badly in a life-threatening accident. A ten-foot fall broke my collarbone and knocked me unconscious. Although I recovered completely, I spent several months virtually immobile—boxed up and in a cast.

In the jeep—with Frank.

Nita

I had taken Bobby and Darlene up to the grocery store, and Bobby was in a stroller. Darlene was pushing him up this ramp where there were some bars and a railing. He was very active, and he reached up and went right through the railing and over the side of the ramp, falling about ten feet.

The fall knocked him out. Darlene was hysterical and I almost passed out, but a woman at the grocery store drove us home and we got Bobby to a doctor.

The doctor said Bobby had a broken collarbone. Once Bobby revived, the doctor told me I had to keep him awake all night. So I walked the floor with him all night long—and he was heavy!

He had just learned to walk, but then he couldn't walk any more because he had all this stuff on. He was trying to crawl, and when he did he cracked the plaster (on his cast), and we had to take him back to the doctor.

So that's when I sat him in a box for safety, and he wasn't happy at all. When he was awake, the only thing I could do was to sit and hold him straight up or walk the floor with him, but he never cried. He had the cast on for about three months, and they said he could never play football.

Ha! They said he couldn't do this, he couldn't do that. But he did.

During the years we lived on La Brea, we often saw my grandparents. I spent more time with my mom's family than I did with my dad's. My grandmother, Willa Mae, was a real sweetheart. We called her "Meemaw" because, as a child, Darl couldn't say grandma. We called Meemaw's husband, Tom, "Pop." I liked Meemaw. She was always a lot of fun and generous with hugs, a trait that passed on through my mom to Darl and me. When Meemaw wanted a hug from us, she'd say, "Give me some sugar."

Darl and I stayed with Meemaw during the summers in Imperial Valley outside Los Angeles. This area is known as earthquake country. The tremors are usually minor, but they occur frequently.

For fun, Darl and I played the earthquake game, which was a kind of land surfboarding. We'd ride out the tremors to see who could remain standing while the earth trembled, shook, and rippled. Thanks to the game, I've never really had a fear of earthquakes.

Darlene

It seemed like every time we went down to see Meemaw there was a tremor. My grandmother would say, "Well, here comes another earthquake."

There was a huge tree on her land and she used to say, "Now you put your arms around that tree. Hang onto each other's hands, and if the ground opens up, the roots will hold you. You won't fall through."

The ground was opening up and hot geysers would shoot out. Bobby would say, "Look," and I'd look and say, "Oh, isn't that pretty!" We didn't know to be afraid. We'd hold each other's hands and hang onto the tree.

The other thing I liked about being at Meemaw's was picking watermelon right off the vine. Nothing tastes better. We'd cut the melon and eat it fresh. Darl especially liked the fact that we could eat straight through the middle— no seeds to stop us. Summers were an odd combination: earthquakes and fresh watermelons. But that's how those times felt to us as kids.

In contrast to Meemaw, my dad's parents were more formal and standoffish when they visited. They were German and strict and didn't want to be referred to as "grandparents." I called my grandfather "Dad" and my grandmother "Honey." My grandfather also was known to be close with a dollar, although something happened that made me wonder.

One evening when I was about five, my parents planned to go out to dinner with Dad and Honey. My grandfather had brought me a gift, a plastic tube filled with marbles. I was happy with that.

Darl and I were sitting in the living room when I caught sight of a shiny dime on the floor. I picked it up without saying anything. I wasn't going to tell my sister about it.

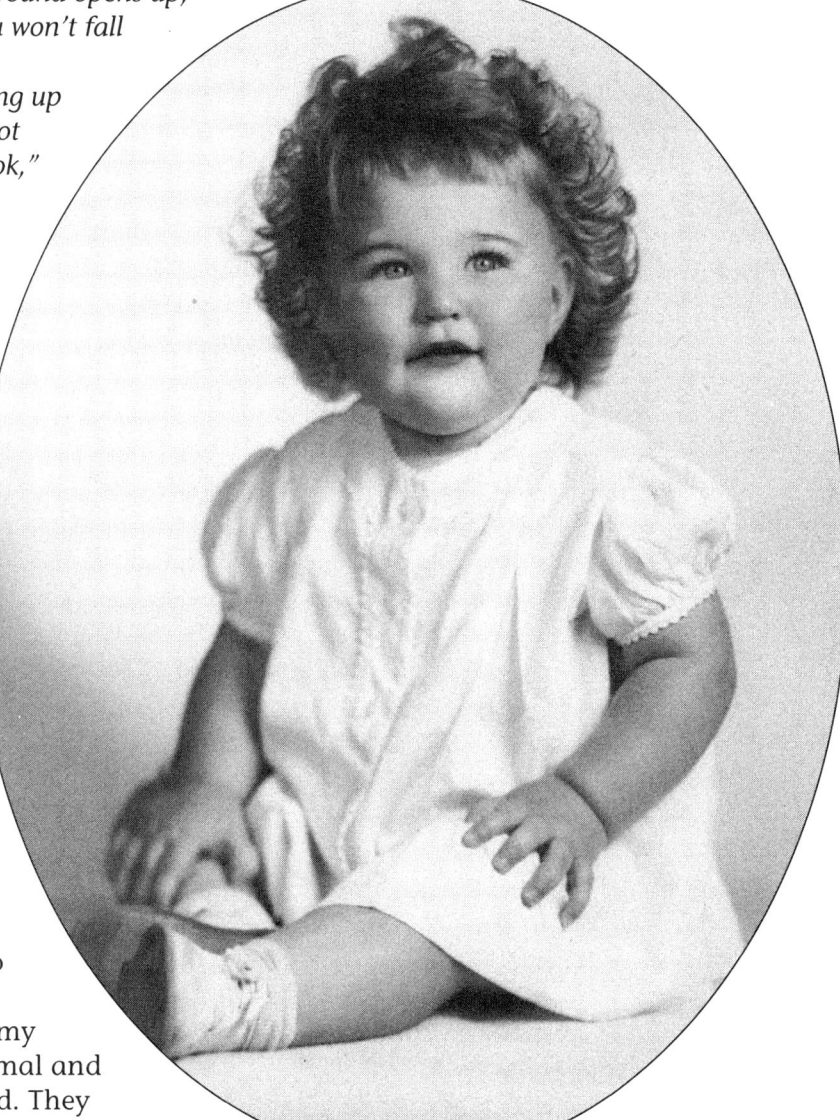

Darlene.

I went on playing with my marbles, but kept finding more dimes. I was on a treasure hunt. I started slinking around, searching for more. I must have found about a dollar's worth—an absolute strike. Dimes seemed to appear from nowhere.

Some time after that, my family was walking through the Ambassador Hotel, which my grandfather managed. I was talking with him, and we were walking ahead of my mother, father, Honey, and Darl.

My grandfather was telling me about the hotel business, and I was acting very interested because I was sure it was important to do that. Here I was, a youngster trying valiantly to hold up my end of the conversation with an older person for whom I knew my dad had tremendous respect. I was being very polite. I wanted to impress him.

When we stopped walking, he reached in his pocket, and he pulled out a nice, round, shiny dime.

"I want you to have this," he said.

"Thanks," I said. His simple act made me feel special. We walked on.

Maybe it was coincidence, but I believe that my grandfather was sending me an unspoken message. In spite of his reputation for frugality, I think he was saying, "You know all those dimes you found before? I put them there for you."

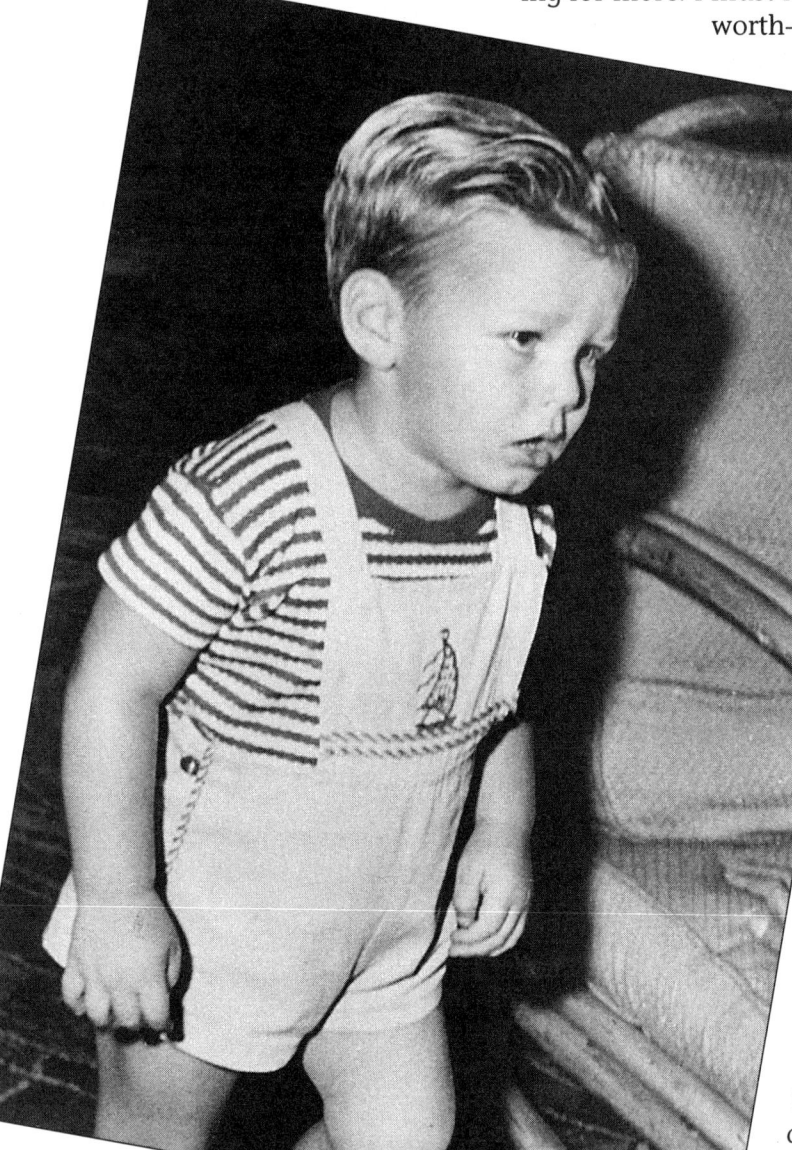

Me at age 2.

Some fifteen years later, when I landed my job on the television show, "Shindig," I had a similar experience. I was offered twenty-six shows and told my salary would be $750.

I said, "That's fine with me." I thought I was going to be paid a total of $750 for all twenty-six shows. Then it hit me—I was going to earn $750 *per show*.

In that moment it felt, again, like finding money that had fallen from the sky—I was a little kid finding those round, shiny dimes from my grandfather. This time it was a bigger strike! Once again, I received the unspoken message: I was on the right path. But I had to wait fifteen more years for success to happen.

 Don't Let the Milk Bottles Rattle

My family lived on La Brea Avenue in Los Angeles until 1951. During those early childhood years, I spent a great deal of my time daydreaming. There were two distinct sides to my personality. Part of the time, I enjoyed entertaining everyone around me. The rest of the time, I was a loner, daydreaming and creating things to do by myself.

Darlene

My mom was working at Tom Breneman's, a restaurant in Hollywood that had a daily radio show. She was a photographer there and took pictures of people at their tables. My dad would take us with him to pick her up.

Bobby was a little squirt then, but when people saw him, they just melted. They'd stand him up on a chair and he'd swing and sway to the music. It was just in him. He had those blue eyes and blond hair, and a very loving manner. Everybody just loved Bobby. He was a special kid, and he's always been that way.

Yet he's always been a loner, too.

At the age of about five, I created an imaginary friend named Frank. I talked to him but could only imagine his replies. I had been given a toy jeep for Christmas, but wasn't allowed to bring it inside. Frank's job was to watch the jeep for me. I pretty much left him in charge of things.

If we had breakdowns in the jeep, I would ask Frank, "What do you think it is?" He would answer whatever way I wanted him to. It's not as if I heard voices; I just assumed that he thought the same way I thought.

One time a crew was building an apartment complex down the street, and I wanted to be there in case they needed my help. Frank rode with me whenever I pedaled my jeep to watch the construction work. Occasionally, one of the workers would come over and give me a piece of wood to hammer. So Frank and I were having a good time.

Then one day, a little fox terrier came up to the site and sat and looked at me. I had my lunch and threw her a bite, which she caught. I discovered she was well trained and could do tricks.

"Can you sit up?" I asked her. She sat up.

"Lie down." She lay down. I was delighted. She was so sweet.

I had a kerchief of my mom's that I used as a bandanna, and I covered the dog with it to keep her warm. She stayed right by me the whole time. I petted her as the three of us watched the guys build the apartments.

After a while, I said, "Well, come on Frank. We have to go." I thought the dog belonged to one of the carpenters, but when I looked back, she was following us. I let her follow us home, and somehow she managed to get on my dad's good side. She must have liked Dad, too, because she stayed. We named her Suzie. She became my first dog—I have to say that Frank liked her, too.

Frank even helped me come to a child's understanding about death. I had become friendly with an older neighbor named Mary, who had a husband but no children. I suppose Mary regarded me as the son she never had. Mary's husband, an invalid, always sat in an overstuffed rocking chair, and I never missed a chance to talk to him.

When I was about six, Mary's husband died. I had some sort of concept of death, but I didn't really understand it. My mom told me, "He's no longer here. He's with God." What I knew of God, my mother had taught me. My family didn't attend church, nor did we belong to a specific religion because my dad always worked on Sundays. So, I tried to fathom what death meant just from what my mom had said.

From the time I was small, I've always had a belief in God. Even as a child, I felt some sort of connection to a higher power. Although I didn't understand the finality of death, I felt certain that if death meant being with God, then it must be all right.

The next time I visited Mary, I went over to her husband's empty chair. I felt sad that he wasn't sitting there, but I had a conversation with him anyway. I just told him I hoped he was feeling better now that he was with God. I turned around to find Mary smiling with tears running down her cheeks.

To me, her husband was real and still there because that's the way I thought of Frank. Just because I didn't see him, didn't mean he wasn't there. That was my philosophy at a very young age.

Frank played an important role in my life, but I realized he was gone some time before we moved to our new house in the San Fernando Valley in 1951.

It was a typical middle-class Van Nuys home of the time. My mom still lives there among the single-family, three-bedroom stucco homes that line the street. When we moved, I was in the third grade, and I started attending Gault Street Elementary School nearby.

Dena

Bobby took me to Gault Street Elementary School to show me where he used to swing from the rope on the flag-pole. In his own defense, he says, "I wasn't the only one."

Although the school was closed, he walked me around, pointing out various classroom areas. He had been genuinely touched, it seemed, by a visit he'd made there several years ago.

On that visit, he saw Mr. Fenton, one of his favorite teachers, who still taught there after all these years. Bobby proudly described how the school's office had hung a poster of himself as a way of saying, "This is one of our kids who made good!"

Age 11, at Gault Elementary School. That's me in the white shirt, front and center.

On Gault Street, there weren't many kids nearby. I had some friends, but they were basically sports-minded. For them, everything revolved around their games. They'd always say, "Okay, let's go play football. Let's go play baseball."

There was nothing wrong with what they wanted, but I was more interested in building things, experimenting with my ideas, and putting on shows.

Darlene

We always knew that this kid was going to be special in some way, because his imagination never quit. He was just sharp. He was bored with things that would have fascinated other kids.

Most kids would be happy with the fact that whatever it was worked. He wanted to know WHY it worked. He was so deep in thought into what he wanted to do. He had friends, but he really didn't have time to spend with them because he was so busy creating.

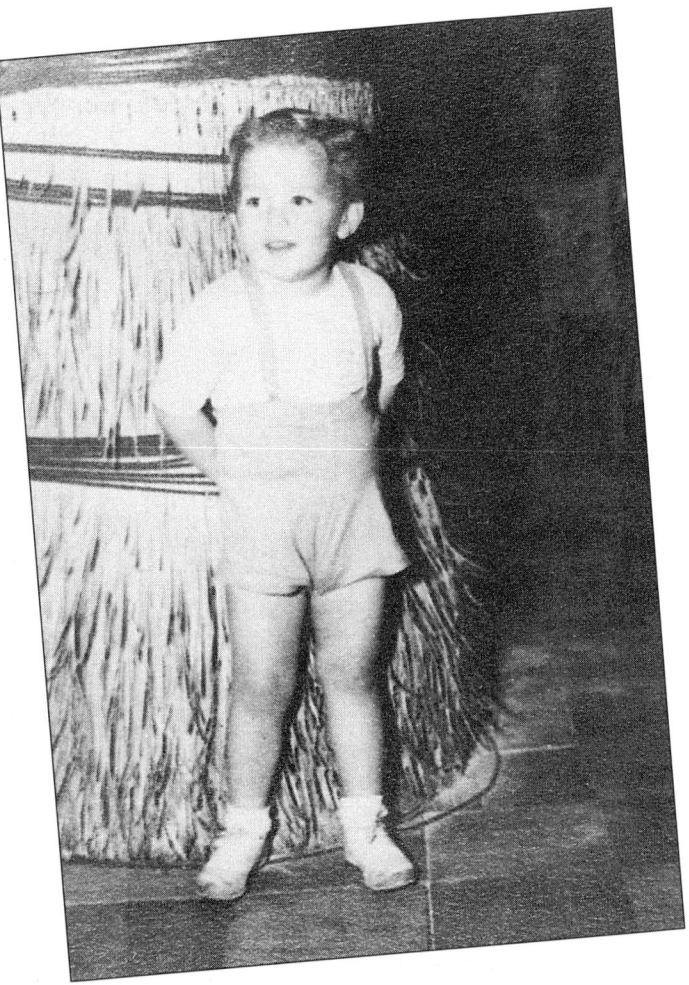

One of my friends, a kid named Johnny Marks, lived next door to me on Gault Street. We set up our own puppet shows, and we did magic shows to entertain anyone who would watch. I took on the role of the instigator or the producer for each show.

Both sets of parents would come over and be the audience. But in junior high, Johnny's family moved away, and I never saw him again. Nonetheless, my association with him was very influential to me during the age of nine to eleven. He helped me develop my creative side.

From the time I was eight until I was about twelve, I would take on major projects to entertain the other kids. Whatever I thought up, my friends would say, "Bobby will do it." And I did. It was certainly that way with the circus we put on for the neighborhood.

Like something out of a movie where kids say, "Let's put on a show," I decided to create my own circus. We put together a framework of sticks and sheets to create a circus tent. Inside, I set up a couple of benches for the kids to sit on and hung a single sheet as a curtain.

Kids came out from behind the curtain and performed their acts. I wanted to juggle, but I could manage only two balls instead of three. That's when I began to learn about showmanship. I made the act look complicated enough to seem as if I were actually juggling.

We featured clowns, blew up balloons, and did slapstick bits because I always loved to make 'em laugh. I assigned parts to some of the older kids. Once we perfected the show, of course we had to do it for the whole neighborhood. I probably had more fun than anybody else.

Then I came up with the idea of doing an episode of the TV show "Dragnet" in our garage. I had seen most of the episodes at least once, so when one was repeated I copied as much of the dialogue as I could. I wrote it in script form, but some of the kids were younger and couldn't read. So I had to teach them their lines. Our show went on without a hitch.

I loved "Dragnet." It appealed to the side of me that always wanted to be a soldier, a cop, or a fireman.

Darlene

Bobby was about ten or eleven and "Dragnet" was a very popular thing for us. We'd march around the coffee table doing the "Dragnet" theme. We would perform. He would write the scripts and everybody had a part. We'd have to recite the lines, and we would go through a whole show.

Dena

Bobby was telling me this story when we heard the accident. Two cars collided with ear-splitting clarity at the intersection near the park where we were working.

"I've got to go to work," he said when we heard the impact. I watched him racing toward the accident, his jacket flying behind him like a cape as he ran. For a moment, I wasn't sure what to do. I'd never had anyone run away from an interview before.

I hastily gathered my recorder and purse and trailed after him, sloshing through soggy grass. By the time I reached him, he already was administering aid to a woman in a badly crushed sports car. A man from the other car sat huddled on the sidewalk curb, complaining of pain in his leg. The two cars involved looked like battle-torn opponents left at perpendicular angles after a war. Shattered glass littered the street.

A crowd gathered around to watch. The young woman in the sports car looked disoriented and shaken. She complained of chest pains and said that she had a history of neck problems. Bobby told her to stay calm. He seemed to have switched into another gear, reacting without the slightest hesitation to a tense situation.

After calling for an ambulance, Bobby sat behind the woman, holding her head in place. No one was yet on the scene to direct the flow of traffic, but Bobby stayed in the car with the woman. It seemed to me he risked becoming an accident victim himself as cars maneuvered by in an awkward flow.

In the middle of all of this, he took time to chase me out of the street where I was trying to hear everything being said. "I didn't need another patient," he told me later.

Within minutes a fire engine and ambulance appeared on the scene and Bobby handed his patient over to people who were officially on duty.

"I can always tell a split second before a crash when two cars are going to collide," he said as we headed back toward our favorite bench in the park. "It's something I just know now."

Good deed done, we walked back to resume our interview.

Someone had taken our bench.

Producing shows was only one of my interests. I was also building things almost from the time I could walk. When I got my train set at about age eight or nine, I bought little plastic houses that were part of a series called Plasticville, U.S.A.

After I had everything all set up, with little shops and houses that snapped together, I realized that the train would just go around a few times and that was it. The thought struck me, "This is boring." I felt the need to go one step further.

So I made tiny newspapers and miniature bottles that looked like milk bottles. I started a milk route just like my dad's and a paper route to create some jobs and give me something more interesting to do with this model town.

Of course, I was in charge of the fire department and the police department. The train was always running over somebody or something, and the fire department had to respond. I always tried to make things move, make them work—especially when I had inspiration.

Not satisfied with toy towns, I once even tried to build a helicopter. My folks took me to an air show at Van Nuys Airport near our home when I was about nine. The moment I saw the helicopter, I wanted to make one myself. "That doesn't look so hard," I thought. I got together a bunch of lumber and put my own helicopter together in a box shape. I could even get inside it and close the door. For effect, I used one of my sister's old bikes which I put on its side on the top of the helicopter. To that, I strapped on a huge plank, which acted as the rotor blade.

From inside the "cockpit" I could turn the handle to make the blade go around. The weight of the blade would actually tip the box and give the sensation that I was starting to lift off. I swore it was going to fly.

I used to offer rides to the little kids. As soon as the box started tilting back they'd scream, "I don't want to go! I don't want to go!"

Nita

One day, Bobby came in the house. He was puffed up. Not only was he hot but he was red. I knew he was just about to spill it all and that even though he didn't want to cry, he was going to.

I said, "What's the matter?"

"I can't get it to fly."

I had to sit him down and say, "Look. You don't have a license. You'll get arrested. If that gets up in the air, they're going to see it and you'll go to jail."

"I will?"

"Uh-huh. You can't fly it until you get a license."

"Oh."

"But you know, if you do get just a little bit off the ground, it's okay. Just don't get up in the air."

"Okay." So with that, we had all the neighbors here because his helicopter would rock and we said, "It does look like it's going to fly."

When I was eleven, my parents started taking us to Las Vegas every summer. The problem for me was that in those days there

Bobby's Life History

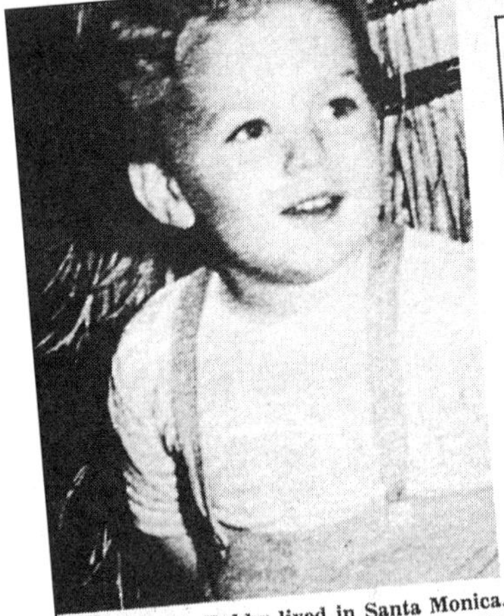

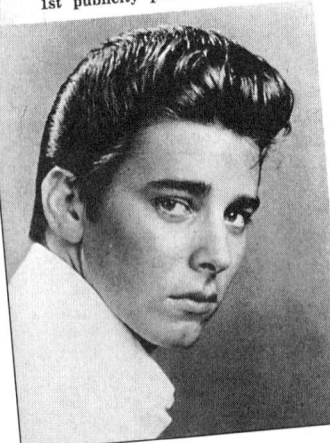

July, 1945: Bobby is born on a bright, summer day (July 22) to Juanita & Robert Sherman in Santa Monica, California.

September, 1950: He enters kindergarten and already makes lots of new friends!

June, 1952: Bobby moves with his family from their beach residence to a new home in the San Fernando Valley.

October, 1954: He begins showing an interest in music and starts trumpet lessons, later joining the school band.

July, 1962: He entertains at a Hollywood party where his singing talent is discovered for the first time. Such notable guests as Natalie Wood, Roddy McDowall and Sal Mineo like his style and encourage him to sing professionally!

September, 1964: Auditions are held to find a bright, young singer for a new television series in the works called "Shindig," and Bobby tries out and is selected!

January, 1965: Bobby's popularity soars as he begins weekend concerts around the country.

September, 1966: After two fun-filled years on TV, "Shindig" is cancelled, to the disappointment of many fans.

June, 1967: Bobby tries his hand at acting and proves himself capable in a episode of the "Monkees" where he portrays a teen movie idol, and later in the "F.B.I." in a straight dramatic role.

June, 1968: After months of taking personal inventory of his abilities, and readying himself for additional singing and acting, Bobby is discovered by Screen Gems representatives and is signed for "Here Come the Brides."

July, 1968: He meets with other ABC-TV stars and takes off on a promotional tour throughout Mexico.

September, 1968: "Here Come the Brides" debuts on television and becomes an instant hit!

CONTINUED ON PAGE 8

At 3½ Bobby lived in Santa Monica.

Bobby's playing bass in h.s. band.
1st publicity photo for "Shindig."

After "Shindig" Bobby tours the U.S.

"Here Come The Brides" debuts.
Bridget, Bobby & Sally tour Mexico.

Don't Let the Milk Bottles Rattle

BOBBY — CONTINUED

January, 1969: The series is going strong, and Bobby's recording career is becoming equally successful!
April, 1969: "Brides" goes on hiatus so Bobby and co-star Bridget Hanley do a promotional concert in Seattle.
July, 1969: He releases his first hit single, "Little Woman," and it sells faster than the speed of light!
August, 1969: At this stage a playful little puppy enters Bobby's life, which he takes home and names Dopey!
September, 1969: "Brides" makes its switch from Wednesday to Friday nights on television.
October, 1969: "Little Woman" is certified gold, and Bobby releases his first album titled "Bobby Sherman."
December, 1969: He does his first concert in California at the Anaheim Convention Center which launches a 15-day tour!
January, 1970: Bobby's second hit single, "La La La," becomes gold!
February, 1970: To the sorrow of many the cancellation of "Brides" is announced.
March, 1970: The "Here Comes Bobby" album is released, and becomes a million-seller in just a few short weeks!
April, 1970: It's almost beginning to sound "routine," but "Easy Come, Easy Go" has just become gold!
June, 1970: Bobby indulges in his long-time dream and purchases a beautiful green Targa-Porsche in addition to his Rolls Royce!
July, 1970: He does a TV commercial for Post cereal and offers a special cut-out record for his fans on the back of each cereal box!
September & October, 1970: time two in a row when "Julie Do Ya Love Me" and the album "With Love, Bobby" are certified gold for exceeding sales of a million.

Bobby & Bridget's Seattle concert.
Sadness as "Brides" is cancelled.
Bobby receives 1st gold record.
Darling "Dopey" enters his life.
Bobby buys a new Targa-Porsche. His parents give him "Wally."

BOBBY — CONTINUED

December, 1970: To the delight of his fans, Bobby does a special recording for the holiday season—the "Bobby Sherman Christmas Album."
Christmas, 1970: Bobby receives "Wally," a new pet dog from his parents as a special gift.
January, 1971: He films a pilot with Wes Stern about a new song-writing duo, which will spin-off from the popular "Partridge" series.
February, 1971: Tragedy strikes when Bobby loses pet dog Dopey following the California earthquake.
February, 1971: Bobby's spirits brighten when he gets a new dog named "Goofy!"
March, 1971: He packs up and moves from his long-time Hollywood apartment to a beautiful, spacious home in Encino.
March, 1971: For the first time in history two of the top faves were seen together on TV when Bobby's pilot debuted on "The Partridge Family." Indications are such that Bobby's new show will be a smash!
June, 1971: He has his own TV special and sings up a storm!
July, 1971: Bobby is presented with a Humanitarian Award from the Southern California Variety Club, for his unique ability to bridge the generation gap.
July, 1971: His birthday is celebrated in a special way, with none other than the Editors of TiGER BEAT, FaVE and TiGER BEAT SPECTACULAR!
August, 1971: He is made chairman of the "Bobby Sherman Cancer Research Fund of Concern Foundation."
September, 1971: "Getting Together" debuts, and promises to be one of the greatest television shows in history!

CONTINUED ON PAGE 11

Bobby guests on "Partridge Family."
A new home and a new dog, Goofy. "Getting Together" starts filming.
Bobby is "Humanitarian of Year."
Bobby celebrates his birthday! Bobby becomes Cancer chairman.

---

wasn't anything for kids to do in Las Vegas. By then I had started playing the trumpet so I took it with me on trips. Still, I couldn't spend the whole day doing that. I had to create some way to amuse myself. Then I spotted the television station across the way from our hotel—KLAS, Channel 8.

Without hesitating, I walked into the station and went up to the receptionist. She looked up at me.

"Can I help you?"

"Yeah, I want to apply for a job."

"Oh, really," she smiled. "What can you do?"

"You know. Pretty much anything. I can clean up and things like that."

Apparently she thought I was a cute kid, and she started asking about my Social Security number and other silly things. About then, one of the directors, Tom Cunningham, came in.

She said to him, "This young man wants a job."

"Really? Have you ever been a cable jockey?"

I racked my brain, trying to figure out what a cable jockey was. "Do I have to ride horses?" I thought.

It turned out he was looking for someone to keep the cable out of the way of the camera when it moved around.

"Do you think you can handle that?"

"Absolutely." Not knowing if I could or not.

"Okay. Come on in."

I went inside. It was one studio with one control booth. Tom demonstrated how films ran through the projector, then a mirror, and then the camera. It was fascinating. This was heaven. I was a cable jockey. My folks were happy about my job, too. This way, they always knew where I was.

One day, after I had worked there awhile, the great Satchmo, Louis Armstrong, came into the studio for an interview. I heard Tom say, "I sure wish we had a trumpet."

"I've got one," I said.

I ran over to the Stardust Hotel, got my trumpet, and ran back just in time. They opened the interview with a shot of my trumpet.

I jumped up and down yelling, "My trumpet is famous! My trumpet is famous!"

Then Satchmo picked up my trumpet and did a couple of licks on it.

HE PLAYED MY TRUMPET!

I couldn't believe it. I got chills. It was a moment I'll never forget.

From that time on, whenever my mom and dad went to Vegas for a few days, I would stop by the TV station and announce, "I'm back!" For days I was happy in Las Vegas while other kids were bored stiff. I suspect my wages came out of Tom's pocket, but they paid me a small amount for what was my first show-business experience.

After doing all that, I decided, "I can build a TV camera," and so I did. My camera didn't transmit, but it could project an image. I had to take apart my expensive telescope to build it, and I used my train transformer to put cue lights on it.

Nita

Everybody thought that camera was real. Of course his dad walked around for the next few weeks saying, "Do you know what Bobby did with this? Where is my . . . ?"

Bobby tore things apart in the garage. His dad could never find a hammer, could never find anything after Bobby had been in there. I said, "So what? We'll find the hammer someday. At least we know where he is and what he's doing."

My parents never had a dull moment. Between Darl and me, our house always seemed full of activity.

Darl loved horses as much as I loved to build things. Naturally, she wanted her own horse. And one day, she found one. Not just any horse, though. This one belonged to the Lone Ranger.

Darlene

I was about fourteen, and we lived on what was a dead-end street at that time. It's not anymore. We were the third house from the dead-end, and there was a big field at the end of the road. Past the field and right down the street was the house of the actor who played "The Lone Ranger," Clayton Moore.

One day one of his horses got loose and was out in the open field. Loving horses the way I do, I was ecstatic. I went and got a rope and said, "C'mon horsey. Let's go."

It was starting to rain, and I had no idea whether this horse had been broken or not. So I said, "Bobby, you want a ride?"

"Sure, Darl."

I gave him a lift up on the horse's back. I took him all over the place. The next thing I knew, I had all these kids following us. But it started to rain a little harder and I decided to get this horse in the house. I didn't want it to get wet.

Bobby was trying to push the back end and I was pulling from the front when Mom came in and screamed.

"WHAT ARE YOU DOING?"

"Mom, it's raining outside. I found this horse and it's mine."

"No, it's not."

I had to back him out of our living room. Then I had to go door to door to find out who this horse belonged to. Finally I found the owner. Clayton Moore was really kind. He said, "Look, any time you want to ride him, you just come on over." I never did go back for a ride. But it was fun to know the Lone Ranger's horse was always there for me.

Like any other brother and sister, Darl and I had our assigned household duties. She had to wash the dishes; I had to dry. Inevitably, for no reason at all, we would get into some sort of a stupid argument. She would hit me with the sponge and I would flick the towel at her.

Like most brothers and sisters, Darl and I had our disagreements, but there were times when we felt really close. Getting close to my dad, however—actually spending time with him—was another matter. Unlike my mom, my dad wasn't demonstrative to me. I knew he loved me, but he showed it by encouraging me to improve myself.

Dad worked long hours and our schedules were usually at odds. Then, when I was twelve, I started helping him with his milk route—an excruciatingly painful experience in my life.

I hated the early morning hours, the cold in winter and heat in summer, and the long ride of the route. More than that, though, I had become painfully shy upon hitting puberty, and working the route with my dad made every preteen problem I had much worse.

I had to wake up at three o'clock in the morning, which isn't my idea of morning at all. I was always freezing cold. Because there was no place to sit in the truck, I had to crouch on a milk crate, my teeth chattering. The doors to the delivery truck stayed open, and the numbing cold blew right on into the truck. Worse yet, I had to plunge my hands into the dairy freezer over and over to pull out the bottles. I felt like a human popsicle.

I never knew how my dad could do it every single day. Those cases filled with milk bottles weighed tons, it seemed to me. Yet he could easily move them in and out of the truck and had them loaded and ready to deliver along his route. At twelve, I was thin and wiry, but I did my best to help out and stack the cases properly—all the while dreading the coming workday.

After loading the truck we went to a doughnut shop on Balboa Boulevard called June Ellen's. We stopped there religiously, ordering a couple of fresh doughnuts and a hot cup of coffee each time. It should have been a break for me, a chance to warm up. But I hated coffee.

Robert, Sr., in his uniform.

Probably, because of that association, I still hate coffee, and I don't eat breakfast. Eating early in the day makes me feel lethargic and sleepy. But at that time, I was doing what was expected of me. I ate my doughnuts, sipped the coffee, and thought to myself, "It's dark. It's cold. I want this to be over." I was miserable.

Even during the summer, working with my dad wasn't pleasant. Once it would get hot during the day, I found myself constantly opening the freezer and sticking my head in to cool off.

Dad worked as a milkman for thirty-two years—a fact that still amazes me. Day after day, he got up at three o'clock in the morning and returned home at three o'clock in the afternoon. He immediately stretched out for a nap on the living room floor, and no one disturbed him. That was his spot, and his routine seemed natural to me. If friends came over, they just stepped over him. I'd say, "That's my dad. He's part of the furniture."

Because of his work schedule, my relationship with my dad was limited. Nonetheless, his steady example inspired in me a tremendous respect for the breadwinner. He was a terrific role model for sheer stick-to-itiveness.

I remember there were times when he was sick from asthma and smoking, and I used to say to myself, "My God. He gets out there in the cold and lugs those cases and the milk bottles." Being sick didn't stop him. For all those years, he went out in all kinds of weather and did his work each day.

I know he took me along because he wanted me to learn responsibility so I'd be prepared for the day I had to earn my own living. But it was hard for me when I had to deal with customers. Even though my friends were beginning to hit on girls, I didn't have that art down yet. People in general seemed mysterious and overwhelming to me.

Working with my dad compounded this problem by throwing me into situations I wasn't prepared for. Perhaps he thought he was helping me. Maybe he did. But terror struck my heart each time I heard Dad say, "Here's the order for this house." It meant I had to carry the milk up to the door. Each time it would be early, and people would be fast asleep. Holding the crate with both arms, I would walk up to the door so the bottles didn't rattle. Because of the way the racks were built, the bottles sometimes knocked against each other. If I walked and swung the rack, I'd hear, "click, clack," not enough to break the bottles, but enough to make a considerable racket.

If the bottles made too much noise, I might wake somebody up who would come out and say either, "Who are you?" or "Oh, are you the new milkman?" I was petrified of encountering customers.

I exchanged the fresh bottles of milk with the empties that were left on the doorstep, cradling them in my arms so they wouldn't make any noise. Sometimes there was a note asking us to leave something extra. That wasn't bad because it would usually be something like cottage cheese, which doesn't make noise.

Then Dad started throwing new stuff at me. He used to say, "All right, this is the Millers' order. I want you to take it in. Here's the door key. Go in and rotate the milk in their refrigerator."

Go inside someone's house? I was horrified, but I had to do it. If it was early enough, I wouldn't say anything as I entered the house. If it was late enough for people to be up, I was supposed to call out, "Milkman!" But I never knew what to do. I kept asking myself, "Is it time? Should I say it?" The uncertainty was agonizing.

Once inside, I opened the refrigerator. I felt like a cat burglar. I'd carefully put the new milk in, with the freshest toward the back. Then I closed the door and left, limp with relief. But every now and then I'd get caught.

A couple of times I encountered some ladies wearing some very "interesting" negligees. I don't know if they wore them on purpose. And I don't know if they were expecting my dad. But dealing with women in blue chiffon nightgowns used to petrify me. Undoubtedly, that's where Jeremy Bolt, the character I played on "Here Come the Brides," first learned to stutter.

The end of the day was a joy because the finished work became an accomplishment. I felt like I had done something. Best of all, my dad was always proud of me because I'd finished out the day with him.

I never confessed this to him, but working the route wreaked havoc with my metabolism. Dad could go home and take a nap, but I couldn't. I've never been able to nap. The effect of getting up so early acted like jet lag on me, and it would take me a while to get back to normal.

I helped him with the route until I was about sixteen. I was paid $3 a day to start, and that increased as I grew older. When I began dating, I went with him to earn extra money.

I liked being with my dad, but I never had fun doing the job. I think a lot of my problem stemmed from having to deal with other people when I was still trying to find myself.

Ironically, after all my years of meeting the public, I've become so comfortable being around new people that I think I would enjoy that work more now. Back then, though, I had other routes I wanted to follow.

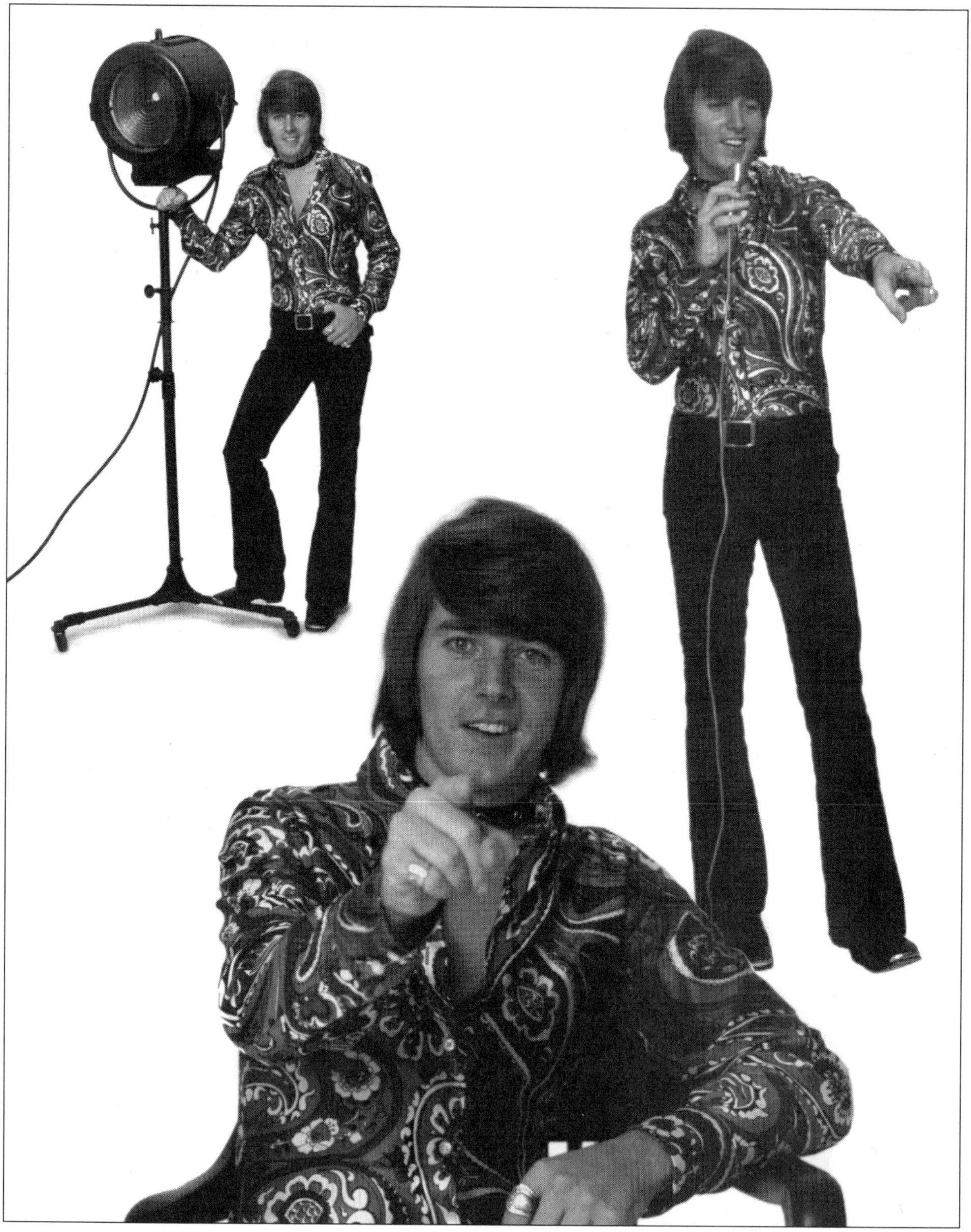

3 The World According to Disney

Gary Montgomery, a boyhood friend

Bobby was a lot more creative than most of the kids in the neighborhood. We'd put together model planes, and he was building Disneyland! When he would get into doing what he was doing, there was no dragging him out to do anything.

Watching construction at Disneyland always fascinated me. When they were first building the Matterhorn, a bobsled ride, I would stand there and watch. Decades later, after my divorce, I found myself going to Disneyland, watching maintenance work. I'd say to myself, "Oh, *that's* how they do that." From the first day I set foot there, the Disneyland Main Street captured my imagination.

The original Disneyland, which then covered sixty acres of park, opened on July 17, 1955. My parents took me there the first year it was open. I could walk from the 1890s into Adventureland, from the deepest part of the jungle to Frontierland. I just loved it.

The ambiance of the park intrigued me more than the rides. Once you went through those gates and walked onto Main Street, you were transported to another realm where the imagination ruled.

Right away I decided to build my own Disneyland. The souvenir program would serve as a kind of blueprint, giving me the layout of the park and all its attractions. The raw materials I procured from my friend, Bob Blank, whom I had met in junior high school. He later became my co-conspirator on a lot of projects.

Bob Blank

I used to build model airplanes, but I had outgrown that. One day Bobby came over and said, "You have all this balsa wood. Why don't you sell it to me?"

This was my chance to get in the dance band. Bobby had joined the band, a school-sponsored group that played for sock hops. Well, I wanted to be in the dance band, too.

I said, "I'll tell you what, I'll give you all my balsa wood if you quit dance band." I was next in line to get in.

That's how I got into the band, and that's how Bobby got the balsa wood to make the first miniature Disneyland in his backyard.

Balsa wood in hand, I started building my first Disney theme park. Over the years I've built three of them, two as a teenager and one much later when I had my own children. The first one, which I started at age thirteen, took me seven months to build and measured twenty-three feet by thirty-three feet. I constructed the entire park on a roughly 1/164th scale. I was going mostly by memory, just slapping it together. My model included Adventureland and the Rivers of America. I dug long ditches for rivers, used toilet-paper rolls for the castle spires of Adventureland, and planted vegetables for the jungle. The result looked crude, more like an abstract version of Disneyland, but the layout was accurate.

I became more and more obsessed with my model. Although it didn't have the structural integrity of the second one I would build, it was good enough to impress many people. Word about my park spread, and I ended up giving tours for ten cents a head to groups of Cub Scouts and Girl Scouts. I donated the money to charity, while enjoying the praise I received for my ideas.

Along the way some of my ideas nearly went up in smoke. Literally.

While I was painting some of the model buildings, I had pie plates full of paint thinner for cleaning my brushes. I had been putting together little streetlights hooked to a train transformer to make them light up. When I disconnected the wires, one of the lights accidentally hit the paint thinner and sparked, starting a small fire in the pie pan.

The fire was contained, but it panicked me. I grabbed a cloth to smother the flames. I had a moment of relief, but the paint thinner had saturated the cloth. All of a sudden, the fire ignited again, exploding in my face. I was frantic, grabbing more cloths to kill the blaze. When I finally put the fire out, I was shaking. I kept repeating to myself, "I'm okay. Everything's okay."

Trying to calm myself down more, I walked as nonchalantly as I could into the kitchen where Mom was working. I said something like, "How you doin', Mom?"

She took one look at me and screamed, "WHAT HAPPENED TO YOU?"

I said, "What's the matter? What's the matter?"

Both my eyebrows were singed. My eyelashes were partially gone. Part of my hair was gone, too, but I hadn't felt a thing.

Looking me over, in a state somewhere between anger and panic, my mom didn't quite know how to handle the situation. Once we determined I was okay, she took some eyebrow pencil and colored in my eyebrows so they didn't look so bad. All the while she was telling me, "Stay away from your father. Don't let him see you." She even used mascara to make my damaged eyelashes look like they were there.

I stayed away from Dad, shuddering to think what would have happened had he found out about my close call. I never got closer to him than about twenty-five yards for nearly two weeks. What if he noticed the mascara and asked, "What is this with Bobby?" My Disneyland might have been condemned.

Despite a few near catastrophes, I continued to invent things. Fortunately for me, I found a buddy who actually shared my creative nature.

Bob Blank

Bobby and I had a camaraderie right from the beginning. We liked to do the same kind of stuff. We didn't go home from school and go out in the sandlot and play ball, like our other friends did. Bobby and I would do some writing or make something electronic. We'd dream about the future and write down movie ideas.

Long before anybody invented answering machines, we built one out of parts from different electronics stores. We were using reel-to-reel recorders hooked up to our home phones.

We'd go home from school and practice our trumpets, do our homework, and then call each other. He'd spend a lot of time at my house. My mom was a very good German cook, and he liked that. She made him special dishes when he came over, and he was in seventh heaven.

Because Bobby liked her cooking so much, we worked out a system. My mother would make me a lunch every day, and she always gave me tons of food. Bobby never brought his lunch. Instead, his mother gave him lunch money.

The way we worked it out, I would sell all of my lunch to Bobby. I didn't get lunch money and only a very small allowance. So I would have his money, and he would have my lunch. And he would give me half of the lunch back.

That way, I had money for the weekend for the movies. Since Bobby also received an allowance, he had money for the movies, too, and we'd go together.

In spite of finding a kindred spirit in Bob, I still spent a good deal of time alone. In junior high, my free time became divided between work on the Disneyland model and practice on the trumpet and drums. I turned the radio or record player up and just played along, practicing until I sounded better and better.

Most of my friends, on the other hand, were out socializing. But I felt I was achieving something. As a result, by the time I was sixteen, not only was I popular with my peers because I was a capable football player, but I also had musical ability. All it boiled down to was that through the years, I had worked hard at it.

Darlene

For his ninth Christmas, Bobby wanted a bugle. My dad and mother stretched their money to buy it for him. We were going out to dinner that night, and we were all in the car. Dad said he had to go back in to get something from the house.

What Dad did was hide the bugle and attach it to some string. The string went up and under and over and through all around the house. He had attached a note: "At the end of this string you will find your dream."

When we came home from dinner, Bobby saw this note. He started following the string all over the place, finally finding his bugle. Everything was made more special by the unique touches our parents added to make things fun.

Bobby went on to learn the trumpet and then the drums—and that's when I moved out.

Darl married Reuben Mack on July 31, 1955, when I was twelve. Mac, as we called him, was working for Lockheed then, doing technical support for the Navy. I've always liked Mac. He taught me how to play chess—even if he did always beat me.

A few times he took me to a shooting range and taught me how to shoot at targets. I didn't have a brother and, in a way, he filled that place for a time. Come to think of it, I guess I did things with him to make sure he would stay in the family.

Darlene

Several months before Mac and I were married, we were on our way to take Bobby out for ice cream. He was driving us nuts. He wouldn't leave us alone, so we decided to drive him to an ice-cream shop.

He climbed in the back seat. We were in the front, and he came right in between us, looked at Mac and said, "When are you going to marry my sister?"

I wanted to kill him.

My third—and final—backyard "Disneyland."

I envied the independence my sister had gained. Married life looked attractive to me. However, my own freedom increased when Darl moved out. It was starting to dawn on my folks that they were losing their little family. They realized that I was growing, too, and would one day leave, and they began to treat me less like a child. So Darl's marriage was a benefit all the way around. I even inherited a bigger bedroom. That room went through another transition some years later, becoming the recording studio that my dad helped me build.

Dad was a skilled woodworker. He had his own projects around the house, for instance, lowering the living room ceiling and building shelves. He showed me how to use the tools for my Disneyland models. "This is a flat screwdriver that's used for wood screws," he'd say. Then he'd let me use it, and he'd judge what I'd done. When I finished a building, I'd bring it in and say, "What do you think?"

He'd either say, "Perfect. Now you've got it," or, "That's half-assed. Try again."

His approach was good for me because he didn't step in to make corrections. If he said, "That's not right," I would go back until I found out how to do it right. I learned a kind of self-reliant philosophy, as opposed to having somebody else fix my mistakes. That training helped me in a number of ways. I learned how to backtrack, analyze my mistakes, and then correct them. Otherwise, I wouldn't have ventured into building something as complex as Disneyland.

I started the second Disneyland when I was fourteen. There had been write-ups in the paper about my first model, and somehow Bob Gurr, one of Disney's original designers, had heard about it. Mr. Gurr came all the way to our house to take a look at what I'd done.

Nita

When Mr. Gurr came out, he absolutely had a fit. He couldn't believe the model Bobby had made. He told me what a genius of a son I had. I said, "Well, I wish my genius would clean up after himself."

Even though I was just a kid, what seemed to interest Mr. Gurr is that I showed some promise in construction and design skills. We spoke for a while, and then he retrieved five rolled-up blueprints from his car. What he handed me was the floor plan of the entire Disneyland park. I was thrilled! His interest inspired me.

Dad told me that if I wanted to build another model, the plans would help me do it accurately. Because of my dad's involvement, I regained an interest in working on the project.

For the second Disneyland, Dad helped me figure out the scale. I started building the train station and planned to work my way through the entire first block of Main Street. The buildings I made were accurate representations of the real thing. Because I was doing a lot of detail work, this Disneyland was taking me twice as long as the first one.

Maybe it was too much detail. As time went by, I got about halfway up Main Street and began to slow down. School-related activities started to become more important to me. Luckily, my dad didn't nag me to finish the second model, although he thought that I might become an architect. Gradually, as high school picked up, I lost interest in the model. There were other things—like girls—calling to me. And there was football.

As I grew older, much of my new social life centered around football. My folks got really involved in the football games. I had the cleanest uniform on the team, and, eventually, all the football team's parties were at our house.

My dad had built a powerful hi-fi system that we all enjoyed. At our parties, starting about my sophomore year, my folks let us play the music pretty loud. Ours was a house to be lived in. My mom and dad didn't put plastic covers on the furniture like some people. During high school, my friends all called my folks "Mom" and "Dad." It was that kind of home.

I had heard a couple of Ricky Nelson's records and bought one of his 45s. As it turned out, his vocal range was much like mine. I imitated his nasal quality and added that sound to my repertoire. When we had parties, girls kept saying, "Come on, Bobby, we want you to sing. Come on." So they'd put on a record and I'd sing along with it. I developed the ability to sing along to Ricky Nelson's records so well that almost no one could tell us apart. After that, not only could everybody play drums and loud music at our parties, but they also enjoyed live entertainment.

My progression from shyness to a sense of confidence came about slowly. I was able to use performing as both a safety net and a bridge. Playing the drums, for instance, put something between me and other people. It also made a connection.

The World According to Disney

To my great surprise, girls liked to see me play the drums or the trumpet—and they would come over to talk. I didn't have to approach them. This was a godsend! Girls even started asking me for dates.

Also, performing wasn't something that I had to improvise in front of people. I didn't have to come up with idle chatter. I could play along with what already was there, either on the drums or the trumpet or singing along with a record.

During my mid-teens, I didn't yet feel confident about having any particular identity. If I had to be just me, I had difficulty figuring out exactly who that was. But if somebody said, "Bobby, play the drums to this song," that was easy because the music already was there. I didn't have to think. I knew how to play along or sing along to a particular song. The words and melody already existed.

My shyness was worst when I had to be myself. When I was shagging milk for my dad out on the route and somebody said, "Hi. How are you today?" I'd have to come up with an answer. I had no answer, so that made the shyness worse.

I was about twelve or thirteen when I met my first girlfriend. A lot of the guys liked Vicki, a cute, petite strawberry blonde. She used to baby-sit for the people who lived directly behind us, and I could talk to her. When the kids were quiet, I'd meet her at the back fence. I used to stand on one side of the fence while she stood on the other. That's where I started my first make-out experiments. With Vicki, I learned a lot about kissing.

Then, at nearly fourteen, I was seduced by an "older" woman of sixteen, who seemed so much more mature than I was. She lived near my friends, Bob Blank and Tom Lupo. On Wednesday nights, I watched "Disneyland" at Tom's house. One night, she was there, too, and we went off together to her house.

She told me exactly what to do. I was fascinated with the new world she was teaching me about. Although I felt no particular guilt about my newfound sexual relationship, I did worry that my parents might find out about us. Fortunately, that never happened.

I never told a soul, but I certainly looked forward to Wednesday nights. Being with her gave me a sense of independence, because I knew more about the world and about myself. But it was a very compartmentalized relationship: because of the age difference, we didn't date or go steady. But I saw her for quite a while before things finally ended.

Even though my first sexual encounter was a big step to take, my partner didn't teach me social graces. My experience with her didn't help my shyness and didn't help me in courting other girls.

I still couldn't find the courage to approach a girl and say, "Would you like to go out?" The words just stuck in my throat. I asked my friends, "What should I say? I really like her. What should I do?"

They'd say, "Bobby, she really likes you. She'd go out with you in a second, man. Go up and ask her."

They came just short of standing behind me and pushing me. Then when we started having the parties at my house and I played the drums, a strange thing happened.

Invariably, the girl that I was interested in would come up to me. She would ask me if I would like to go out, although this was long before it was fashionable for girls to ask the boys. I discovered that performing could overcome the awkwardness of having to strike up a conversation, and it served me well through those awkward teen years.

Bob Blank

The guys were jealous that the girls found Bobby more of a challenge. He wasn't out there mingling with the girls. He was cute, and the girls wondered why he wasn't coming on to them. There was the challenge.

It was, "Let's see if we can get a date with Bobby Sherman," even before he was "Bobby Sherman."

I think his shy quality probably demanded that sort of female aggression—to perceive him as a challenge and then to take the first step.

I really started dating when I got my driver's license at about sixteen and could borrow my parents' car. My mom and dad encouraged me to date different girls. They didn't want me to be serious about anyone because I was so young, even though they had married so young themselves. I brought that up to my dad once and reminded him that he had fallen in love and made a serious commitment as a teenager.

With my dog Silly, July 3, 1962.

"That was a different time, and your mother and I fell in love instantly," he said.

"And that couldn't happen to me?"

He didn't think so. As it turned out, he was right. Relationships came and went. I would go steady for a while and then start seeing somebody else. No long-term commitments.

Going steady sometimes meant I gave a girl my letterman's sweater. I went steady a lot. It was a pecking order, especially with the football team. The most sought-after girl became the focus, so that's who we would pursue. It was silly, but that was high school. And, I admit, I was flirtatious.

Bob Blank

Bobby does have this special charisma he uses for soothing people, and he's a good listener. He's a good communicator. He's always had this shiny quality.

Unfortunately, many of my relationships took a serious turn very quickly. Whenever I went out on a date, girls immediately wanted a commitment. Often, they talked about marriage after we'd known each other only a short while. I remember one instance well. Not only was my girlfriend proposing to me, but her mother even came to my house, insisting that we were perfect for one another and that we should marry soon. Her mother had it all planned out. My parents were shocked, but explained that I was just seventeen! I really liked the girl, but there was no reason for marriage. I didn't feel that way. I was having too much fun.

From fifteen to eighteen, my life revolved around football—on the field and off. I tried out for the football team in my sophomore year, but at 134 pounds, I was a shade too light for the 135-pound requirement. My buddies told me to eat a lot of bananas and drink a lot of water before the weigh-in. That trick kicked me over the threshold to a hefty 136 pounds. I was sick of bananas for a long time, but it worked.

After that, Friday nights were the focus of my week. They were our game nights. I played "B"-ball because I wasn't big enough to be on the varsity team. Smaller and lighter players had their own league, which played before varsity. On game days, I would walk home from school, have a steak and a salad, and then walk back to school with my jersey stuffed into my football pants.

My dad would come home, take a nap, dress, and come to the game with my mom. The "B"-game would start about six in the evening. The varsity game started at eight. After the "B"-game, the marching band would come out and play the national anthem. Because the number of musicians was limited, the musical director pleaded with me to participate in the band for the anthem as well as at halftime.

I'd play football, run in, change into my band uniform, and get out on the field just in time to play the national anthem. Then I'd sit in the stands with the band and we'd play fight music for the varsity game. Next, at halftime, I'd go out and do the marching routines. It was chaotic, like something out of a Marx Brothers' movie. I managed the quick changes for about a year, but it was

BIRMINGHAM "B" ROSTER

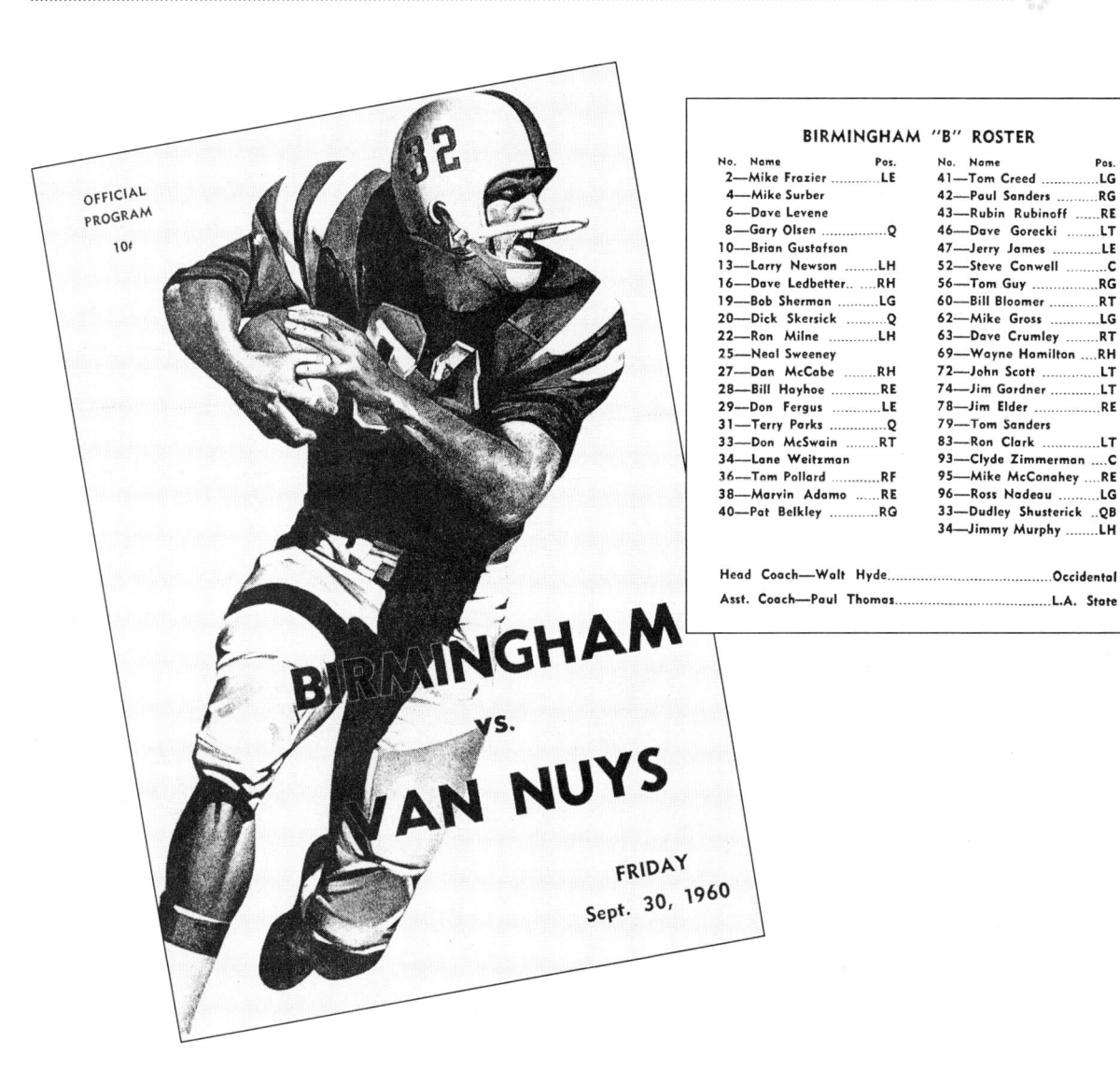

No.	Name	Pos.	No.	Name	Pos.
2	Mike Frazier	LE	41	Tom Creed	LG
4	Mike Surber		42	Paul Sanders	RG
6	Dave Levene		43	Rubin Rubinoff	RE
8	Gary Olsen	Q	46	Dave Gorecki	LT
10	Brian Gustafson		47	Jerry James	LE
13	Larry Newson	LH	52	Steve Conwell	C
16	Dave Ledbetter	RH	56	Tom Guy	RG
19	Bob Sherman	LG	60	Bill Bloomer	RT
20	Dick Skersick	Q	62	Mike Gross	LG
22	Ron Milne	LH	63	Dave Crumley	RT
25	Neal Sweeney		69	Wayne Hamilton	RH
27	Dan McCabe	RH	72	John Scott	LT
28	Bill Hayhoe	RE	74	Jim Gardner	LT
29	Don Fergus	LE	78	Jim Elder	RE
31	Terry Parks	Q	79	Tom Sanders	
33	Don McSwain	RT	83	Ron Clark	LT
34	Lane Weitzman		93	Clyde Zimmerman	C
36	Tom Pollard	RF	95	Mike McConahey	RE
38	Marvin Adamo	RE	96	Ross Nadeau	LG
40	Pat Belkley	RG	33	Dudley Shusterick	QB
			34	Jimmy Murphy	LH

Head Coach—Walt Hyde..Occidental
Asst. Coach—Paul Thomas......................................L.A. State

OFFICIAL PROGRAM
10¢

BIRMINGHAM vs. VAN NUYS

FRIDAY
Sept. 30, 1960

just too difficult. Also, I missed the camaraderie of my football buddies.

In the first year, I didn't play all that much. I made up for it, though. In my second and third years, I was ranked Most Valuable Player and All-City, a big honor. I played cornerback on defense, which is outside, and running guard for offense. I improved at laying out body blocks. I was able to read the offensive or defensive linemen as they came toward me. The result was they couldn't block me, and they couldn't slip by me.

Socially, I had worked out a successful system as well. We played a game, changed, and came back out while the varsity game was going on. Then my friends and I sat in the stands with all the girls. It worked out terrifically!

After watching the varsity game, we'd go to Bob's Big Boy, a carhop restaurant on Sherman Way, for hamburgers. After that, we might cruise Van Nuys Boulevard or have parties at my folks' house. That was Friday nights. Then Saturday nights would be "alone time" when everyone went off with his steady or his date. The whole era now seems like something out of *American Graffiti*.

Even after football season, the football squad still gathered at Bob's Big Boy for hamburgers. Sometimes, we'd go to a drive-in movie, but that was rarely a group activity. Usually, I would just take whomever I was seeing. After all, did anyone ever go to the drive-in to watch the movie?

During my last year or so of high school, some of us put together a musical combo. One of my friends from the dance band said, "Hey, I can get us a few bucks if we play at a party." So we played instrumentals for parties. We didn't make a lot of money, but we had fun doing it. I don't even think we had a name for the band—we just called it a combo.

When we played parties, I occasionally sang because I was the only one who had enough guts to attempt "Happy Birthday." I played the drums in the combo because I had my own drum set, and I was fairly up on the current tunes.

Aside from Top 40 rock 'n' roll hits, the records I bought were often instrumentals that I could play along with on the trumpet or the drums. I loved Dave Brubeck's "Take Five" and "Green Onions" by Booker T. and the MGs, because I could play the drums with them. I played the trumpet to Perez Prado's "Cherry Pink and Apple Blossom White." I was sharpening my skills by doing what I enjoyed.

Just before graduation we disbanded the combo because the guys were more interested in planning what they were going to do next. The only problem was, I didn't know what that meant for me. I had my dreams of doing something as a performer, but nothing substantial on which to base them.

Two confusing years passed before I found my professional footing. It all started with a date for a party that changed my life forever.

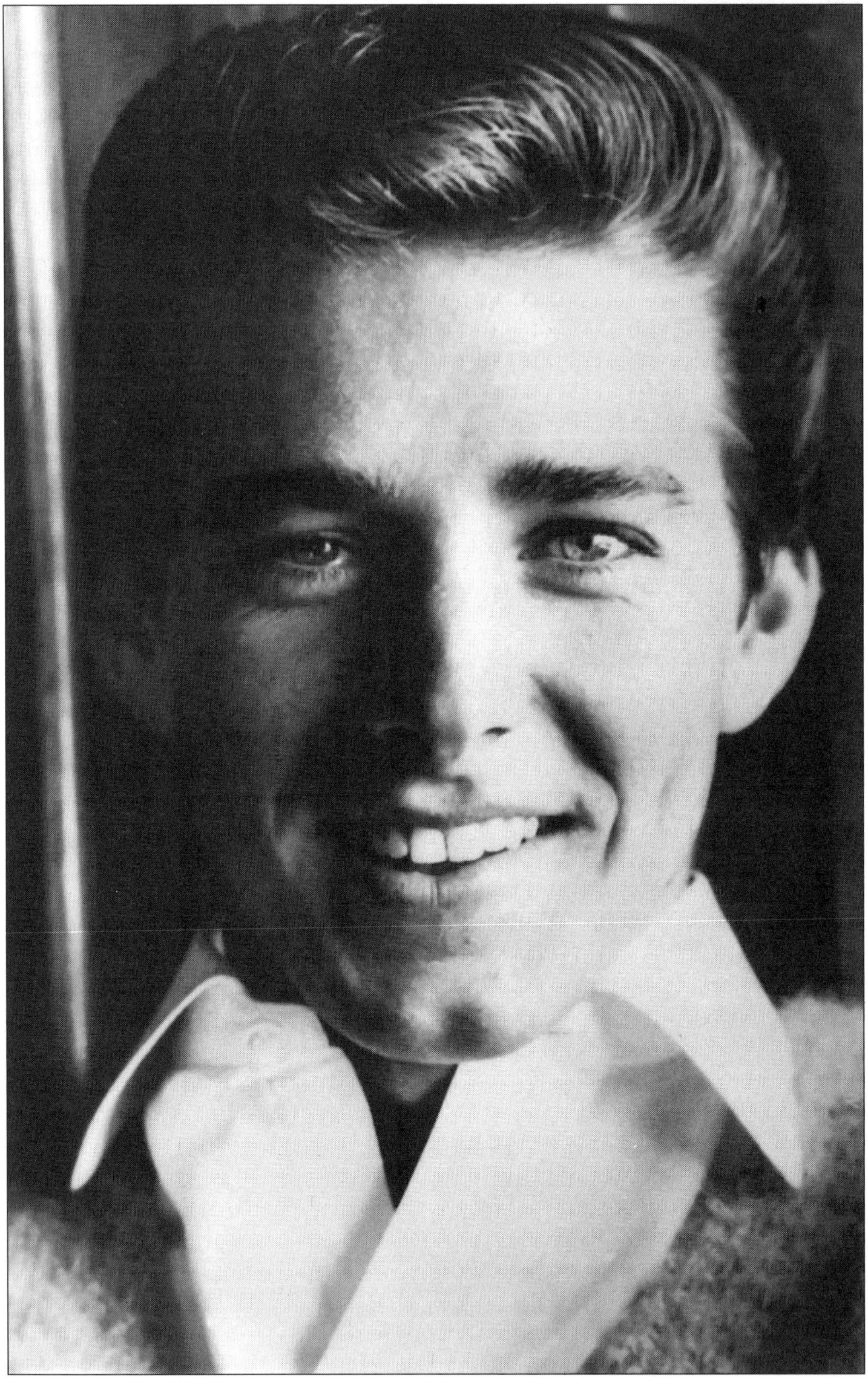

4 Discovery

At the beginning of 1964, I was twenty years old. In the two and a half years since high school, I had made a few recordings and local television appearances. Nothing seemed to come of them. Despite my best efforts, I seemed no closer to my dream of performing.

I wanted to be in show business, but I also wanted more independence. My dad had told me when I graduated from high school that if I didn't go to college, I would need a job. I had decided to cover my bases, and went to work at Litton Industries, a government supplier doing projects for the Navy.

On this job, I discovered something new was happening to me. I talked to everyone. I made friends with everyone. My shyness was finally evaporating. The supervisor put me in charge of the tool crib on the swing shift, working from four until midnight. By all standards, I was successful at earning my own way.

The problem? My dream and reality weren't fusing. Since graduation I had been searching for a foothold. I wanted to be in front of an audience holding a microphone. Instead, I was handing out tools at the beginning of the shift.

After a time, the supervisor put me on the day shift, where I worked as an expediter. In that position, I purchased the tools that were needed for the tool crib. The job had some advantages. Suppliers took me to lunch to make their pitches, the work was easy, and my salary was $60 a week. Not bad for 1962.

Then my supervisors started sending me out if they needed something. I suddenly had more freedom. Being out on the road made it easier to go to auditions for show business jobs. The tug toward performing kept getting stronger. I wanted a different life than I could find at Litton.

All the while, I was trying to make decisions about my future. During my first year at Litton, I lived at home, paid room and board to my folks, and took classes at Pierce Community College.

At Pierce, human behavior was a required class. To my surprise, I not only enjoyed the subject, but I also found that I had some aptitude for it. A professor suggested that I consider going into the field of psychology. He thought I might work well with kids. He was right. I moved into advanced psychology and found myself working with "exceptional children," bright kids who had learning disabilities or other challenges.

Suddenly, in college, I had discovered a subject that interested me. In grade school and high school, I hadn't been that fond of English or history or math. I did well enough to pass, but I had no love of anything except music and sports. In college, after switching my focus to child psychology, I found myself receiving praise for my academic work for the first time.

I began to be intrigued by the problems unique to children. More than anyone, children are especially vulnerable and have the most trouble communicating their problems. Because of my own experiences and my struggle to overcome shyness, I felt I might be able to help them.

Although psychology interested me, and I liked the idea of working with kids, I wasn't stimulated by the other required subjects. Finally, after about a year and a half, I got tired of juggling school and work. Even though I enjoyed psychology, show business was still the main dream in my life. I found it easier to work at Litton and go to auditions when I could.

I gave up on academics altogether and quit college. Soon afterward, I nearly quit show business before I had even started.

I had been taking acting and singing lessons and performing wherever I could to gain experience. It wasn't long before I had a succession of managers and my disillusionment began.

Discovery

My first manager was an older woman who turned out to have more than just a professional interest in me. When I didn't reciprocate, she threatened to sue me.

My second manager cost my parents money. He bought me some clothes for performances and signed for them but didn't pay for any of the items. My dad took me to the stores, where we paid for the clothes. Dad's integrity always set an example for me. He told the store owners, "I know you won't take the merchandise back, but we want to make it right."

I really thought the last manager of the three was legitimate. He filled my head with dreams. "Any second, you're going to hit," he'd say. I was sitting at his house one evening watching "The Andy Williams Show" on television, and he was telling me, "You can do that. You could carry your own show."

Just as I was reveling in that fantasy, the doorbell rang. I was astonished to see a sheriff's deputy standing in the doorway with a warrant for my manager's arrest for passing bad checks.

As the deputy led him away, he pleaded with me, "Hey Bobby, can you call your folks and see if they can bail me out?"

I went home completely devastated. For the third time in a row, I had been burned by a bad experience with a manager.

It was all one big lie—again. I was only nineteen, and I had been taken in again. I sat down and cried.

"Maybe I should stay at my day job," I thought to myself. I started to wonder if I should just chuck it all and do something else.

But my parents wouldn't let me give up. They said they would support me in any way they could. They wanted me to have the opportunity to "do it right," as Dad said.

"Give it one hundred percent of your effort," they both urged me. They showed their faith in me by paying for voice lessons and acting classes. I didn't want to let them down. I began to work harder.

By then it was 1963. My vocal coach found me a job singing at the USO, an organization that entertained military personnel in

Hollywood. I had a piano player, and I sang a couple of songs. Nothing memorable, I thought. To my surprise, the performance led to my first recording contract.

Jerry Wallace, who recorded "Primrose Lane" many years ago, owned an independent label called Starcrest Records. One of Wallace's staff happened to be in the audience that night and asked if I would be interested in working with them. I was ecstatic. I thought, "This is it! I'm on my way."

I made some decisions based on what I thought was happening. Although I liked a number of the people I met and worked with at Litton, I knew it wasn't for me. I quit my job.

Starcrest put out my recordings of "Judy You'll Never Know" and "Telegram."

Nothing happened.

I don't remember even signing a contract with Starcrest. If the records had done any business, maybe I would have. Then again, I didn't get paid. Get paid for singing? It didn't seem to work that way.

For promotion, I sang the two Starcrest songs on local dance-party television shows. Still, I wasn't making any money. The television station had to pay me union scale, but I had to endorse the check back to them in order to be on the show. So I was on and off and that was it. On and off. Hot and cold. I started to feel a bit numbed by the highs and lows.

I needed to do something creative.

For fun, I began to dabble in making films. I had been interested in filmmaking since about age seventeen. I remember going to Lloyd's Camera in Hollywood and finding out the dimensions of a movie camera. Then I went to a metal shop in Van Nuys and had them make a shell that looked exactly like one. It didn't work, but I was really into facades. Bob Blank and I would go around and pretend we were shooting a film.

Then I struck on the idea of really making a movie. I borrowed my folks' little eight-millimeter Bell & Howell camera and started shooting. I had a tape recorder, but the sound wouldn't synchronize with the movie frames. Trying to get them to match was like pulling teeth.

My first movie was called *Thumbelina*. Of course, Bob Blank was in it. The premise was that Bob makes a startling discovery when he walks out to discard some trash in a desolate place. On the way back to his car, he hears a tiny voice yelling, "Hey mister, hey mister, I'm down here."

I had painted a little plastic figurine to represent a man who supposedly didn't know how he had become so small. I was off camera doing the dialogue, as well as shooting and appearing in the film. In the story, Bob decides to exploit the tiny fellow as the eighth Wonder of the World. The film ends tragically when a dog (our poodle, Silly) eats the little guy by mistake.

Could stardom be far behind?

The signs of success seemed to keep appearing—and then dropping out of sight. After the false start I'd had with Starcrest, I had another chance to cut a record. I was dating a girl whose father was a record producer. With his help, I cut "You're Nobody's Sweetheart Now." "Surely this time people will notice," I thought. The song wasn't released.

Again, I had tried everything. I kept auditioning—and waiting. I felt my turn was just around the corner.

It was 1964, and the girl I was dating at the time invited me to a party. Because of her parents' show business connections, she was going to the cast party for the film *The Greatest Story Ever Told*. This was no regular sock hop. This party was true Hollywood glamour.

The film, a religious epic that was released the next year, contained numerous cameo roles. Because most of Hollywood was in the movie, everybody who was anybody was at this party.

Sal Mineo, one of the film's stars, was hosting the party at his beach house. Sal was riding high, having won acclaim for his work with James Dean in *Rebel Without a Cause* and *Exodus* with Paul Newman.

I was totally in awe of the number of stars who were there. Natalie Wood, who was beautiful and sweet; Jane Fonda, a wonderful person who encouraged me; and Roddy McDowall, a very witty man, who always had a camera in his hands.

I looked around and saw Angela Lansbury, Shelley Winters, Ed Wynn, Hope Lange, and Lee Remick. Charles Bronson was there, too, stealing Jill Ireland from David McCallum. The list of stars went on and on.

I was still trying to adjust to the company I found myself in when I heard some familiar voices.

"Hey, Bobby. What are you doing here?"

As fate would have it, three guys from my high school combo had reunited after graduation and were playing parties. This was about the time when the Beatles were hitting it big, so bands were now expected to be vocal groups rather than just instrumental groups.

One of the band members said, "Bobby, everybody's been bugging us to sing. Can you help us out?"

I didn't want to take that on. First of all, I didn't think it was my place to walk in and start entertaining in a room full of entertainers. Second, I had nothing prepared. Then my date started pushing me.

"Why don't you sing?" she asked.

I had sung to her one day, following along with a record, and I suppose she wanted to see me perform with a band. I thought, "What the heck?" Besides, I hoped it might impress her, so I agreed.

This was it. I had been preparing for this moment all my life. All my creative projects. The shyness. Ricky Nelson. The drums . . . voice lessons . . . failed records . . . They all fused into this moment.

I sang one number, the Ray Charles song "What'd I Say?" I could lead the audience to participate, working half the room against the other half in the refrain. I had seen it done before, so it wasn't even a question of making something up. I just had to perform; I didn't have to create it cold.

The whole scene was like a beach-party movie. The band started playing, and the fact that someone was singing caught everybody's attention. People began coming over to where we were.

While I was singing, I could see everyone looking at each other. It was that kind of half-surprised, half-nodding, "Hey, this is good" look.

I kept catching Natalie Wood's and Jane Fonda's eyes. I saw a flash in each of their gazes. Big smiles filled their faces. They were having a good time. I couldn't believe what was going on. Once I started performing, I just let go. The fuse was lit. It was natural. Some sort of internal spark ignited.

When I finished my song, everybody applauded. The astonished looks had been replaced with something more solid: respect.

Afterward, many people came up to shake my hand.

"Hey, great!"

"Good job!"

I'm sure I glowed. I suddenly felt special. Needless to say, I had achieved my mission. The girl I was with was impressed, especially when Sal, Natalie Wood, and Jane Fonda came up to congratulate me.

I heard either Natalie or Jane say, "Oh, he's so adorable." I thought, "Oh, Lord, help me." But then someone said, "You're very good. Who's handling you?" I had no idea what that meant. I didn't have a manager. I didn't have an agent. Even when they asked for my number, I didn't think that much about it.

I didn't know it then, but that performance was a turning point. Nothing else I had tried had worked. I guess I had to stand up and sing in front of an audience. Or, in this case, the right audience.

For more than two years, my work had gone virtually unnoticed. Suddenly, people—famous people—thought I was good.

It wasn't until late that night, when I was lying in bed, that I reflected on what had happened to me. "Just what on earth did I do?" I asked myself.

Not long after Sal's party, I received a call from an agent who had not even been there that night. I never knew who told him, but I believe it was either Sal, Natalie, or Jane.

His first words were, "You don't know me, but . . ."

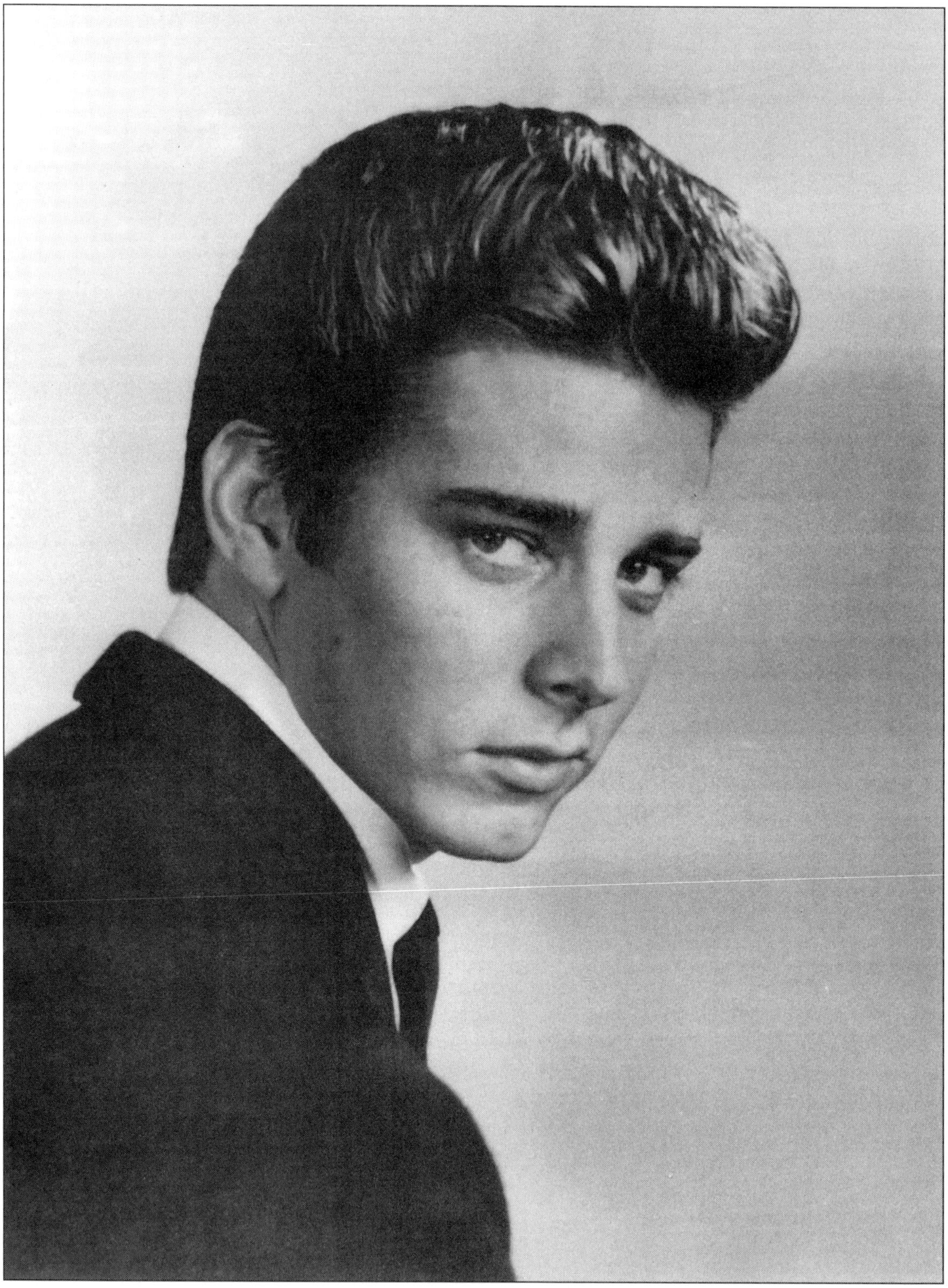

5 "Shindig"

I hung up the phone. The agent, whose name was Dick Clayton, had managed to track down my phone number. He offered to set up some auditions. Was this the break I'd been waiting for?

I began the rounds.

During that period, Sal Mineo and I became friends. I often stayed at the beach house that Sal had rented. It was a huge place, and there were about eight other people who stayed there as well. It was a good place to hang out.

When the sun went down, we all sat around and played party games or rented movies. This was long before video rentals. We just rented films and put up a movie screen.

Sal was generous and had a marvelous sense of humor. I met a number of people at his place, several of whom were helpful to me in the business. "This is a good person for you to meet," Sal would whisper to me, pointing out someone among the influential people who came over to his house.

I ended up going to New York and doing some recording for Cameo Parkway Records. Sal happened to be in New York at the same time. I think he was proud of the fact that I had made some connections there because of him.

I recorded "Goody Galum-shus" for Cameo Parkway Records. To my great disappointment, it didn't sell. After the excitement of

Sal's party and all the contacts I'd made, I felt a complete letdown. "What's it going to take to make it in this business?" I wondered.

Because I was on the East Coast, I took the opportunity to visit Darl. She and Mac had moved from California to Maryland in 1959 because of his work at Lockheed. Since then, their family had grown to include three children, Debra, Michael, and Mary-Ann. My godson, another Bobby, was on the way. Sal and I went to see them. It turned out to be a strange visit.

Darlene

Bobby and Sal came, and we tried to keep their visit a secret because Sal was popular then. Well, everywhere we went, everybody knew right off he was Sal Mineo. We had dinner at a restaurant nearby. Fans were bringing napkins, toilet paper, anything they could lay their hands on for these two boys to sign. Even though Bobby wasn't known yet, he was with Sal. I guess they figured that since Bobby was good-looking, and he was sitting with a famous movie star, he must be "somebody," too.

We had to leave the restaurant because there was so much commotion. The next place we went, though, was even worse—someone had set up a professional camera to record Sal's arrival. How anyone knew where we were going, we don't know.

Bobby and Sal were staying at my house. Sal was a smoker, and he had left cigarette butts in an ashtray on the table. While we were out, some kids had sneaked into my house, looking for souvenirs of Sal Mineo. They took the cigarette butts and ashes out of the ashtray. Then they took the used glasses that were in the kitchen sink and walked out the door with them.

My baby-sitter said, "Your glasses are gone."

I didn't mind that they'd emptied the ashtray, but when they took my glasses, the poor baby-sitter didn't know what to do.

I looked at Bobby and said, "Is this what we're in for?"

In spite of my association with Sal, I was still unschooled in show business matters when, a couple of months later, I auditioned for "Shindig," a musical television show. "Shindig" was something completely new, offering current rock 'n' roll hits by original artists on a weekly basis.

Dick Clayton had arranged the audition. When the big day came, I met him on the street corner outside the audition hall, and he went in with me. It was an unusual gesture of support from an agent, and I gratefully welcomed it.

I auditioned for Selig Seligman, who owned the production company; Jack Good, the show's producer; and a couple of other people in a big room. I had no idea what they wanted me to do.

I was so naive that when they asked me what I did, meaning what kind of performing, I told them I was a college student. I went into an explanation about how I was studying psychology. They nodded politely. An uncomfortable silence fell.

"Can you play the piano?" one of them asked.

"Yes, but I'm a bit rusty."

I didn't have an accompanist. I didn't have a guitar with me. I could see this group of executives starting to fidget.

I knew they were thinking, "Why is this kid here?"

Finally, just as I was sure they were about to kick me out, Jack Good came to my rescue. I guess he saw something in me.

"All right," Jack said. "There's a stack of records. Why don't you look and see if there's anything there you can sing along with."

Bingo! That was most of my training, after all. Now, this was something I knew I was good at. No problem.

I hurriedly went through the stack of 45s and finally found one song I knew I could do. It was Freddy Cannon's "Palisades Park."

"I know this one," I said with relief.

"Okay."

I put the record on and did exactly what I had done in my parents' living room for friends so many times. I sang along with the record. When I finished, they asked me to wait outside—alone. After fifteen or twenty minutes, which seemed to drag like hours, Dick came out.

"How would you like to do twenty-six of their shows?"

"What shows?" At age twenty, I had no idea what this was all about.

He explained the concept of the show and my job in it. Then he announced what I'd earn.

"Your salary is $750."

"That's fine," I said, feeling grateful for being paid at all.

The real amount of money I was about to make didn't hit me until the drive home. Dick had meant $750 *per show*!

I tried to add up how much money twenty-six shows was worth to me in dollars. I kept losing numbers trying to calculate it all. It

BOBBY SINGS!

Now you're invited to Bobby's super-secret recording session! It's an exciting time you won't want to miss!

EVEN WHEN BOBBY'S busy recording his super-groovy first album, he can still make time to sign autographs. PEACE TO YOU TOO, Bobby and here's hoping your album is the biggest seller ever!

MORE EXCITED THAN EVER about his first album, Bobby spent long hours in studio making things perfect.

WORKING WITH HIS producer and recording engineer, Bobby makes sure the sound is just right. Below, he listens intently to a playback of the song he's just recorded. Look for the album on Metromedia Records.

was more money than I had ever imagined I'd earn. Again, money from the sky—like so many dimes from my grandfather.

To do what I wanted to do, I was about to be paid $19,500—more than six times what my salary had been at Litton! I couldn't comprehend it. Everything had happened so fast.

Darlene

My son Bobby (my brother's namesake) was born on July 20, 1964. Bobby called and said, "That's my godson. He brought me luck."

Bobby was disappointed that his godson wasn't born on the 22nd, his birthday. But my son was born on the very day Bobby signed his contract for "Shindig."

After I knew my job on the show was definite, I called Sal to tell him. He was going over to Natalie Wood's place for a barbecue and asked me to meet them at her house. There were only a few of us: Natalie and her mother, a couple of other people, and Sal and his girlfriend, the actress Jill Haworth. They congratulated me on my new role as the house singer on "Shindig." The day marked an understated passage for me. As I settled into the greetings and conversation, I wasn't even aware of how comfortable I felt among this group of celebrities.

I had overcome my shyness so much that I even spoke a few phrases of Russian to Natalie. Although she was born in the United States, her family had roots in Russia. At first, I suspected she might have thought I had learned it because of her. Then I explained that I'd taken Russian in high school, and she realized I wasn't putting it on. She became more relaxed, so I was more at ease.

In a few short years, I had not only developed the ability to talk to girls, but I was speaking Russian to Natalie Wood! In many ways, that experience provided excellent preparation for the metamorphosis my world was about to undergo.

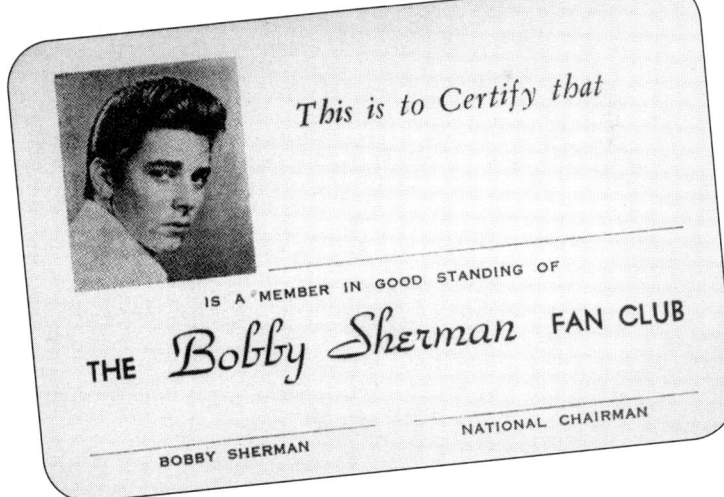

Sadly, somewhere during the middle of working on "Shindig," I became so busy that I didn't have time for socializing, and I lost touch with Sal.

He was always a kind, generous, forthright friend to me. I would have trusted him with my life. His brutal murder in 1976 came as a terrible shock. It was tragic to have lost him so young. I certainly feel grateful to him for the role he played in my career.

One of my first fan club cards.

The first telecast of "Shindig" appeared September 16, 1964, on ABC. From the start, "Shindig" had been produced piecemeal. ABC had ordered a contemporary music show, but I don't think anyone knew exactly how to go about it.

Jack Good wanted me to do two songs for the pilot, or sample show. One song was "Back Home Again in Indiana." Although in retrospect this might seem like a strange choice, Jack Good wanted to broaden the musical lineup. He was afraid that if they did only rock 'n' roll, parents and the older audience would turn it off.

In the 1960s, rock 'n' roll was considered by the older generation to be, at worst, immoral and, at best, a bad influence on the younger generation. Before this time, entertainment was basically family oriented. Rock 'n' roll became a symbol of youthful rebellion, so the show's executives wanted to add music that was a little more mainstream.

"Indiana" was a corny song, but I was elbow to elbow with some of the biggest performers in the record industry. I thought, "They're paying me to do this." I got into the act real quick.

The night the pilot aired, a reviewer called Lucille Ball's children, Lucie and Desi Arnaz, Jr., to ask what they thought of the show. Fortunately, their responses were positive. The important thing for me was that Lucie, as a representative of the youth of America, said that "Bobby Sherman was really cute."

After that, Jack promised he'd move me out of the "Back Home in Indiana" genre, and that's when I started doing other artists' current hits.

My role, basically, was to stand in for anybody who had a hit record. If the original group couldn't do the show because they were on tour or something, I performed the song. Hearing Bobby Sherman sing "I Can't Get No Satisfaction" was not quite like hearing Mick Jagger sing it, but somebody had to do it. I remained the male house singer for the two and a half years "Shindig" was on the air.

New artists came on the show each week, and Jack Good always made the whole thing enjoyable. "If we are actually having fun," he would say, "it's going to show on the screen."

We worked, but we had a great time in the process. The "Shindig" era was the fastest two and a half years I ever spent—everything happened at a nonstop pace. Here's how a typical week went:

On Monday I'd go into the studio, learn which songs I'd be performing, and find the right keys in which to sing the songs. Later that day, the musicians would cut the instrumental track. Then we'd do some rehearsing. On Tuesday, I'd go back into the studio and put down the vocal track. On Wednesday, we'd rehearse on the stage and work out the choreography. Thursdays would be a run-through that included the opening and the finale. Thursday was also the day the big acts would arrive. I'd be standing there next to Ray Charles saying, "Wow! This is unbelievable." And I was being paid for it!

So from Monday through Thursday, we rehearsed. I was surrounded by recording stars and dancers. The music was played louder than you'd ever want it to be. During those four days, all we did was party. But that was our job.

We filmed the show on Friday nights so teenagers could be in the audience. Those times were too chaotic for me to feel nervous about performing in front of a live audience. On Fridays, it was just work.

In fact, all through the first few months, I didn't feel nervous or overexcited. I seemed to fall right into the show's work rhythms. I was so busy making sure I was doing the right things that I had no time to consider the impact the show would have on my career. Also, too much reflection could have caused me to worry myself sick over my performances. I couldn't risk the doubts that create failures. I had to believe I could do it.

For most of my time on "Shindig," I was singing other people's songs. It was the best on-the-job training I could have hoped for. I absorbed everything while I learned my way around.

It took my family a few weeks to realize what was happening. Certainly they thought the show was cute and entertaining, but they were surprised by the power of television. So was I. But if at the start of "Shindig," I didn't understand how powerful the medium was, I was about to get a crash course.

After the first couple of weeks, kids started to recognize me. Fan mail started coming in and write-ups about me appeared in the press. Fan magazines began asking me for interviews. I was amazed. I thought, "What's going on here?"

The shift from being "unknown" to being "sought out" occurred abruptly—almost overnight. There wasn't time for me to assimilate the sudden surge of attention I was receiving, and I was working too hard to take it all in. At the outset, my parents had to deal with my sudden fame more than I did. Fans started driving by our house after the second or third week the show was on the air.

Nita

During "Shindig," mothers would bring their children and leave them on the front lawn all day. There could be 100 kids on the lawn. It happened every day. They'd rap on the windows, pounding and screaming.

If I went out to go to the store, they were all over me. Then at the end of the day, we had to go out and clean up the lawn. It was a mess. There were even times that we had to get Bobby out the back and over the fence so he could leave the house.

I saw large numbers of fans in the studio audience for the taping. When they announced, "Here's Bobby Sherman . . ." the screaming started. At first, I wondered why it was happening. What was all the screaming about? But I didn't dwell on it—instead I concentrated on knowing where to stand, figuring out which cameras were which, and remembering my words.

We sometimes prerecorded the vocals, but I sang most of the songs live. If I blew it, we wouldn't go back and do it again unless something was really bad. At "Shindig," if someone messed up, he just had to live with that for the whole week.

I was learning to be a professional. I'd go home and rehearse each day. We had cue cards, but I still wanted to make sure I had everything down. I believe that's one of the reasons I remained on the show for its full term. I didn't cause any trouble, and I came into work knowing what I had to do. Thanks to my folks, I had learned about discipline, respect, and hard work while growing up. That's what kept me in line.

To my surprise, Dad seemed more excited about my success than I was. He felt that my efforts were paying off because of his encouragement, his telling me I should go after a show business career if it was what I wanted. I do credit him. He didn't push me, but he handed me the opportunity to believe that I could succeed if I wanted to. When I did, he couldn't have been more proud of me. That's when my dad and I became close friends.

When I was growing up, Dad and I hadn't been able to communicate that much. We didn't have the kind of father-son relationship where we'd go out and play catch every day. He had been a lot closer to my sister than he was to me. My mom, on the other hand, was much closer to me than she was to my sister. That's just how it panned out in the family.

Of course, Dad had been proud of me when I'd become an All-City football player, and we grew close during that time. But the fact that I was becoming successful in a very difficult business was something in which he could take a great deal of pride. He also received a lot of comments and praise from his customers out on the route. He was eating it up. He truly enjoyed my growing success. He got a kick out of helping me hone what he perceived as my "image."

First of all, he wanted me to dress well. Greene's Men's Store was where we bought a lot of my clothes. They had a lot of the "in" clothes and were attempting new looks. During "Shindig," the store came up with wardrobe ideas because they knew their merchandise was going to be on television. They let me experiment, and the velour shirts I wore on the show became a fad. Everybody from the show, including the singing group, the Shindogs, wore the same velour shirts.

The next part of my "image" was my car. My first car was a white 1954 two-door Mercury with green upholstery and green color insets. I bought it for $400 from a kid going in the service.

Once "Shindig" came along, I traded my Mercury in for a 1962 Cadillac. My dad was so proud of me that day. I hated letting go of that Mercury, but having two cars was out of the question. Dad loved that beige Cadillac. He noticed it before I did, and he talked me into buying it. And I liked it. The Cadillac was sharp. I remember Dad saying, "This would be a good car for you to be in." It was.

I wanted to do everything right. As time went along, I noticed that some people on the show developed negative attitudes. I watched what happened and realized those people didn't last long. I decided negativity wasn't a good philosophy. I always kept my mouth shut. Sometimes on the show they gave me songs I didn't particularly care for, and I probably could have complained. Instead I figured, "How bad can it be? This is a great job." So I did whatever they asked me to do.

After all, how many young performers had the Righteous Brothers' dressing room right next door to theirs as I did? They used to bring in teeny cans of Coors beer. They would sit and sip them, and sometimes I'd join in. We never drank to get drunk, though.

I think they invited me in because I was one of their best audiences. They were hilarious. I loved them. We were great friends during that whole period of "Shindig." Then they started hitting it with a couple of records that were big. They became so famous that they were gone all the time. I missed my buddies.

When they first started to make a name for themselves, I felt a little jealous. They scored a hit record, and I thought, "I can't get a hit record." Then I realized that it didn't make any difference. I wasn't the Righteous Brothers, and I didn't have the same material. I had to stop myself from becoming envious by deliberately walk-

"Shindig"

ing away from that kind of feeling.

After that, I could genuinely feel happy for them. They deserved their success. Through the years, our paths would cross occasionally. Sad to say, we've never had a chance to get together and sit back with a Coors beer again.

My own recording career still wasn't taking off. During the "Shindig" era, 1964 to 1966, I recorded "Hey Little Girl" and "It Hurts Me" on Decca. "Hey Little Girl" had a Beach Boys sound since Gary Usher, who produced the Beach Boys, worked on the recording. Glen Campbell, who was working as a studio musician then, played guitar on "It Hurts Me."

In 1965, "It Hurts Me" won some recognition because Jack Good was kind enough to let me perform it on "Shindig." That year I met Casey Kasem, a disc jockey with KRLA radio in Los Angeles. Back then, disc jockeys could choose their own play lists. Casey played the song, and it was on the air frequently in L.A. "It Hurts Me" did all right, but it wasn't a big smash. For a week I was number one on the charts in L.A., but then the Temptations knocked me off with "My Girl."

Even though "It Hurts Me" generated some attention, it wasn't enough to launch my recording career. Worse yet, after "It Hurts Me" came out, "You're Nobody's Sweetheart Now," which had not previously been released, appeared without my knowledge on Dot Records. It was an apparent effort to capitalize on my surge of success. That really annoyed me, but there was little I could do.

I decided to concentrate on what I could control. While working on "Shindig," I began to develop my own style. Even though I was singing other people's songs, I was adding my own spin. I was happy that "It Hurts Me" represented my own style. Earlier, "Judy

You'll Never Know," had been my style, too, but it hadn't yet matured.

I worked and gathered experience. I met virtually everyone in the recording industry during the time I was on "Shindig." One day, Ray Charles told me, "I really like your voice and I think you're a terrific singer." That vote of confidence went straight to my heart.

Among the people I met, I particularly remember the Rolling Stones, the Beach Boys, and Sam Cooke. Sam was very polite, very much a gentleman. He was a real professional and knew how to work.

I also thought Glen Campbell was very good. He provided a country-western flavor on the show. Then there were the Turtles, the Yardbirds, and Gerry and the Pacemakers. It was a constant flow of new records. Herman's Hermits also made an appearance. In 1993, I reunited with Peter Noone on an episode of his TV show "My Generation" for VH-1.

I dated a couple of the dancers as time went along. One of them was Brenda Benet, who later married Bill Bixby. She was a marvelous dancer and a great-looking lady. Tragically, they lost their son, and she ended up committing suicide. It was very sad.

In spite of the celebrities connected with the show, the environment remained somewhat insulated. Everyone hears about wild parties in Hollywood, but as far as I knew, there weren't any surrounding "Shindig." This was before the drug culture took shape, years before cocaine and hard drugs surfaced.

I knew grass was around. I would look the other way, or, I found, it was never offered to me because people knew I wouldn't be interested. I said, "I can't even smoke cigarettes. I'm not going to put something like that in my system."

About the wildest thing that happened was that girls used to try to attack us after a show, just to touch us. At first, the guards weren't prepared for it; eventually, we all got used to it. I could tell how many Bobby Sherman fans I had or how many Shindog fans there were by the screams in the audience.

I sometimes dated women who came up after the show. The "Shindig" fans were mostly close to my age. They probably figured that I was approachable, and I was.

In addition to our regular schedule, I did a "Shindig" personal-appearance summer bus tour put together by Dick Clark. Gerry and the Pacemakers ("Ferry 'Cross the Mersey") were the headliners, and Donna Loren and the Shindogs were on the bill. Since I didn't have a hit yet, I'd come out first and sing a couple of songs, including Herman's Hermits' "Mrs. Brown, You've Got a Lovely

Daughter." We started in New York and worked our way across the country until we finally wound up in California.

"Shindig" taught me a lot. I learned how the camera operates and how to perform with an audience. I began to understand how to work with a variety of people, as I had at Litton. This time, though, I was in my element.

Perhaps most important, I learned that I couldn't count on things lasting forever. I learned how to roll with the punches. When we found out that the show was going to be canceled, some people were just devastated.

I had profited from the show in every way I could. "Shindig" gave me a lot of opportunities, but I was ready to take my next step. The last "Shindig" telecast was on January 8, 1966.

I had a feeling something else would happen and, eventually, it did. Everything happens for a reason, I suppose. Ultimately, I don't think I would have had a shot at "Here Come the Brides" if it hadn't been for "Shindig." It was time to move on.

★ ★ **NEW FRID SECRETS** ★ ★

APRIL Ind 35¢

TiGER beat

Davy:

IS HE STILL KING?

SAJID ON "BIG VALLEY" EXCLUSIVE PICS

SPECIAL PICS OF THE NEW MONKEES!

MICHAEL COLE: "I Want a Wife & 50 Kids!"

WHAT'S AHEAD FOR MARK AND THE RAIDERS?

BOBBY'S NEAR DISASTER
Chapter 2 of his complete life story PLUS: Secret photos of his special girl

INTERVIEW YOUR FAVE
FIND OUT HOW INSIDE

NEW SURPRISES FROM THE BEATLES!

PLUS: Mary Conroy, Tom Jones, Peggy Lipton, Cowsills, Nivie, Steppenwolf, Deel

6 The Monkees

In 1966, I still hadn't made a big hit record, but, because of "Shindig," I was a television star. For a year or so, I went on the road performing current hits by other artists.

I sang at a dinner theater in Canada, went on a singing tour in South America, and appeared in bars all across the United States. The bars were similar to classier discos later on; they brought in famous names and packed in a lot of people.

It was a peculiar time in my life. I was a long way from home, but my singing was well received. My tour of South America included a singing spot on a television show in Buenos Aires. To my delight, the show went over well, even though I was singing in English!

While I was on tour, my dad was working on a surprise for me. He knew I'd wanted a recording studio of my own. I returned home to find that he'd renovated Darl's old room and had started building my studio there.

I was deeply touched by his gift and overwhelmed by the amount of work he had invested. The joy of having my own studio was made even more special because he had built it for me. I would later add my own work to it, but at that time I wasn't home enough to enjoy it.

I was traveling a lot and learning even more. When I performed in a dinner theater in Windsor, Canada, just across the border from Detroit, I faced a challenge with my act. Normally, I

49 THINGS THAT TURN BOBBY ON AND OFF ABOUT GIRLS!

ON – She has long, shiny hair OR short, shiny hair. Clean hair is a definite turn on—it feels so neat!

OFF – She accuses me of liking someone else—being overly insecure or sensitive, just so I'll tell her how much I really DO like her. I want to tell her when I get that certain feeling, not because she's made me feel guilty.

ON – She says "please" and "thank you"—she never forgets all the little courteous things a person is never too old to do.

OFF – She wears long, dangly earrings. She'll never get a kiss on the ear from me.

ON – She tells me she thinks of me when we're apart, and I can tell she's being honest from the look in her beautiful eyes.

OFF – Every time I call her she wants to go on "chatting" about nothing hour after hour. I dig talking to her, but I've got other things to do.

ON – She sits and stands like a lady. She never forgets to be feminine, and it's never "too much trouble."

OFF – She giggles at everything I say, usually because she can't think of anything to say herself.

ON – She digs spur-of-the-moment dates as much as I do, and sometimes she comes up with some wild ideas of things for us to do.

OFF – She raps about her newest diet and how much weight she's going to lose.

ON – She blushes when I compliment her. She may know she looks great, but she doesn't let everyone else know!

OFF – She smokes! I don't smoke and having smoke drift into my eyes is a bummer!

ON – She respects her parents and other family members.

OFF – She wears six, clunky bracelets—you can hear her coming a mile away.

ON – She really *cares* about other people and their feelings. She looks for the good in everyone she meets.

OFF – She tries every new make-up on the market, so she never looks the same twice.

ON – She's not the greatest cook in the world, but she does have one special dish that is fantastic and she

DO YOU HAVE SHINY HAIR? A bright smile? A voice that says Happy? Then you may be the girl for Bobby!

makes it just for me!

OFF – She knows nothing outside of her own little world. I like a girl who's interested in people, places and things!

ON – She doesn't gossip and she catches me if I do. Groovy!

OFF – She bites her nails and doesn't even try to stop.

ON – She makes some of her own clothes and she's proud of them.

OFF – She copies her girlfriend's expressions, hair styles, and ways of dress. In other words, she's not being herself.

ON – She always gives original and imaginative gifts. Many times she makes her own gifts and cards, even though she's not a great artist.

OFF – She tells me lies.

ON – She never quizzes me about my dates with other girls.

THE MOST IMPORTANT quality in a girl to Bobby is that she's honest and cares about the people around her!

OFF – She touches up her make-up at the dinner table.

ON – She sends me notes in the mail just to say "Hi!"

OFF – She's too moody. I never know what to expect when I call.

ON – She tells me she wants to get married someday, but has lots of things to do and see first. We agree!

OFF – She always demands reassurance of my love. That can really take the fun out of dating. If I want to get serious, she'll know without asking!

ON – She likes to daydream with me.

OFF – She buys me expensive gifts and lets me know the price.

ON – She enjoys sports as much as I do.

OFF – She's prejudiced against people she's never met.

ON – Children turn her on—and me too!

OFF – She *never* wants to do simple things that can be so much fun—like driving to the beach just to watch the surf roll in.

ON – She likes high-style clothes, but doesn't go overboard.

OFF – She's always fixing her nylons, combing her hair or pulling up her slip.

ON – She shows her affection in many little ways—like squeezing my hand, kissing me on the cheek and whispering in my ear.

OFF – She's jealous of my fans.

ON – She's on time. She cares enough about me to be punctual.

OFF – She tries to be "hip" by using the latest hippie sayings. I can't dig it.

ON – She's a good listener and doesn't interrupt me when I'm talking. When I'm finished she has her say. I like that.

OFF – She talks about all the other "stars" she knows.

ON – She smiles when I look at her; and that makes me smile too.

OFF – She drives like a maniac. She's got the idea she's on a dragstrip or something.

ON – She loves to snuggle up in my arms while we watch TV

OFF – She forgets things I've told her. It makes me think she wasn't listening to me the first time I told her.

ON – She's always happy and that makes me happy.

18

---

performed twenty-minute sets when I was in a bar. Right off the bat, the owner of the theater took me aside and said, "You have to stretch your act out to fifty minutes." I thought, "Now what do I do?"

At a dinner theater, the audience wanted to sit down and see a show. They didn't want somebody who was going to take a break and come back. I was booked for two weeks, and the theater was paying me $1,500 a week. I was scared to death because I was out of my element.

Miraculously, help was on the way. Neil Bogart from Cameo Parkway Records happened to be in Detroit, and he came to Windsor to see me. He said, "You might want to do this . . ." and he helped me write a passable act. I ended up with enough material for a forty-five-minute show. Thank heaven, the audience loved it. The owner asked me to come back. I was so relieved.

Soon afterward, I was asked to be a contestant on "The Dating Game." The format was simple. Bachelors and bachelorettes appeared on the show. It was the contestants' job to choose a date from three potential candidates by asking silly questions. I appeared on the show three times. Once I was being chosen, and twice I was doing the choosing for the dates.

The first time I was on the show, the contestant chose me. As our prize, we went in a chauffeur-driven Oldsmobile to a restaurant in Hollywood called Edna Earl's Fogcutter and afterward to a jazz club called Shelly's Mann Hole. It was a fun, lighthearted evening, and I had a great time. I had no idea that my future manager and partner was sitting across the street at dinner that night.

Ward Sylvester, Bobby's manager and partner

I was having dinner with a friend at a place called Small World Emporium in Hollywood. As we went out, there was a commotion across the street, with a television camera and lights. We walked over to see what was going on.

There was a lot of "Who's that?" "What's happening?" from people around us.

Somebody said, "Oh, it's Bobby Sherman, and he's on a date from 'The Dating Game.'" None of this made a real impression on me at the time, but somehow, later, I knew to ask my casting director about Bobby when I was producing "The Monkees."

In my next "Dating Game" episode, a couple of years later, I was the one who chose the date. We won a trip to Athens, Greece, and our chaperons were Chuck Barris, the producer of "The Dating Game," and his wife.

Both flying there and back, Chuck tried to convince me that I should host an upcoming show he had just created called "The Newlywed Game." I didn't consider myself a game-show host, so I just let it go in one ear and out the other.

The rigorous itinerary left me no chance to acclimate from jet lag. The trip felt like a whirlwind. We flew sixteen hours to Athens, went sightseeing for two days, and returned to Los Angeles. I couldn't enjoy any of it because I was too exhausted.

The last time I appeared on "The Dating Game," the lady I chose and I were supposed to be sent to Russia. We were to attend a ceremony for a giant, simultaneous wedding of a thousand couples. By then, however, I was so busy that I wasn't able to go. To tell the truth, I didn't mind. I didn't relish the idea of another exhausting trip, even if my date was a cutie.

Between the end of "Shindig" in 1966 and the audition for "Here Come the Brides" in 1967, I cut another record, "Think of Rain," for Epic Records. Although it didn't sell, I loved the song. I still wish I had used it for a later album.

For a while after "Shindig," I worried about how well I was doing, but then other things kept happening.

I became one of the "I Came Back" pitch men for the Vitalis hairdressing television commercials. In the commercial, I was on a date with a girl who sat on a merry-go-round in a park. I was spinning her around, and at a particular cue I looked at the camera and said, "I came back." I did guest appearances on "The FBI" and "Honey West" and had a small part in the film *Wild in the Streets*. For the film, I played a reporter, but I'm seen only from weird angles.

Then, just before "The Monkees" came on the air in 1966, I was chosen for a part on the show. The character I played was a kind of Frankie Avalon put-on. Frankie Catalina was the character's name. I mean, how close can you get?

That's when I met Ward.

Ward

When I asked to meet Bobby, I was producing "The Monkees," and we had a script that was a parody of beach-party movies. In the episode, the Monkees were hired to be extras in a beach-party movie, and the story made fun of that manufactured image. It contrasted the real California beach scene, which we liked to think the Monkees were part of, with the kind of sanitized world of "Gidget."

The writers came in with a character called Frankie Catalina, who was clearly a parody of Frankie Avalon. He was a sort of vain, hair-sprayed star who had a double for the water scene, a double for the fight scene, and a double for the love scene. Frankie Avalon was a friend of mine. I was a little embarrassed because I thought he might not appreciate the humor of it.

The writers' first idea was that we would ask Frankie to play himself. We had done that a couple of times. Liberace, for instance, had played himself. The times we had done that before, though, it was more of a contrast of legitimate styles. Clearly, Liberace wouldn't care for the Monkees' music, and the Monkees wouldn't care for Liberace's music. It wasn't quite so much a personal attack. I thought, "I can't ask Frankie to do this." So we started thinking that we wanted a performer who could project something a little more old-fashioned, like a Pat Boone image to contrast with the Monkees. I remembered Bobby from "Shindig," and I asked our casting director, Eddie Foy, if we could get him.

Bobby came in, I met him for the first time, and he read for the part. He was terrific and saw the humor of the part right away. I was very impressed. Without looking any further, we cast him for the role.

....

The part I played on "The Monkees" was fun, except for one small problem. During the shoot, I had to do a concert at Disneyland, which meant I was on a tight schedule. The Disney people had asked me to do a show in front of a display of *20,000 Leagues Under the Sea* in Tomorrowland.

I was worried. My parents were coming to pick me up to drive me to Disneyland, but the shooting was running late. My hair had been sprayed blond for the "Monkees" part to make me look more artificial, and the paint wouldn't come out. I finally managed to wash my hair, but then I looked like a punk rocker because I couldn't make my wet hair stay down. It was terrible. We were running so late I had to change clothes inside the car on the way to the park.

In spite of all our efforts, I reached Disneyland late, and the Disney people were really miffed. This was the Disney organization—for which I have tremendous love and respect—and I had blown it. I was terribly upset.

I did the second show, and, fortunately, the audience was receptive enough to make the Disney people forgive me. Of course, I wasn't asked back again until I hit fairly big with "Here Come the Brides." The whole experience was like another "Monkees" episode!

As a group, the Monkees were very spontaneous. That's what made the show successful. You had the feeling they used spur-of-the-moment dialogue and ideas, and it was fresh. Although the production was a bit chaotic, I really enjoyed my work on "The Monkees."

Ward

Bob Rafelson and Bert Schneider were the ones who created the show. The idea of "The Monkees" was to find four real young musicians and actors in Hollywood and let them portray characters much like themselves. That had advantages and disadvantages.

Once you make that type of creative decision, it's counterproductive to try and school the guys into becoming professional actors playing roles. That's why we encouraged them to improvise.

We even had an improvisation coach. We used the scripts as a springboard, and the boys basically said whatever came into their minds. They did whatever they felt like doing, and the camera followed them.

The show was hailed for innovative jump-cut techniques. The reason was really that we couldn't put the show together any other way. By the end of the second season, at least two of the four Monkees still did not understand why a master and a close-up have to match. So I'd try and edit it, and nothing would go together. I'd have these jump-cuts, and everyone would say, "My, how innovative and fresh and imaginative it all is!"

I don't mean this in any way as a criticism of the Monkees. We went out of our way to keep them fresh and unschooled. But it had its difficulties. The set was chaos. You could never find all four of them at any one time.

Then Bobby appeared as sort of the antithesis of the disorder around me. The first thing that I noticed was that, without calling attention to it, Bobby not only knew his own lines, he knew everybody else's lines as well.

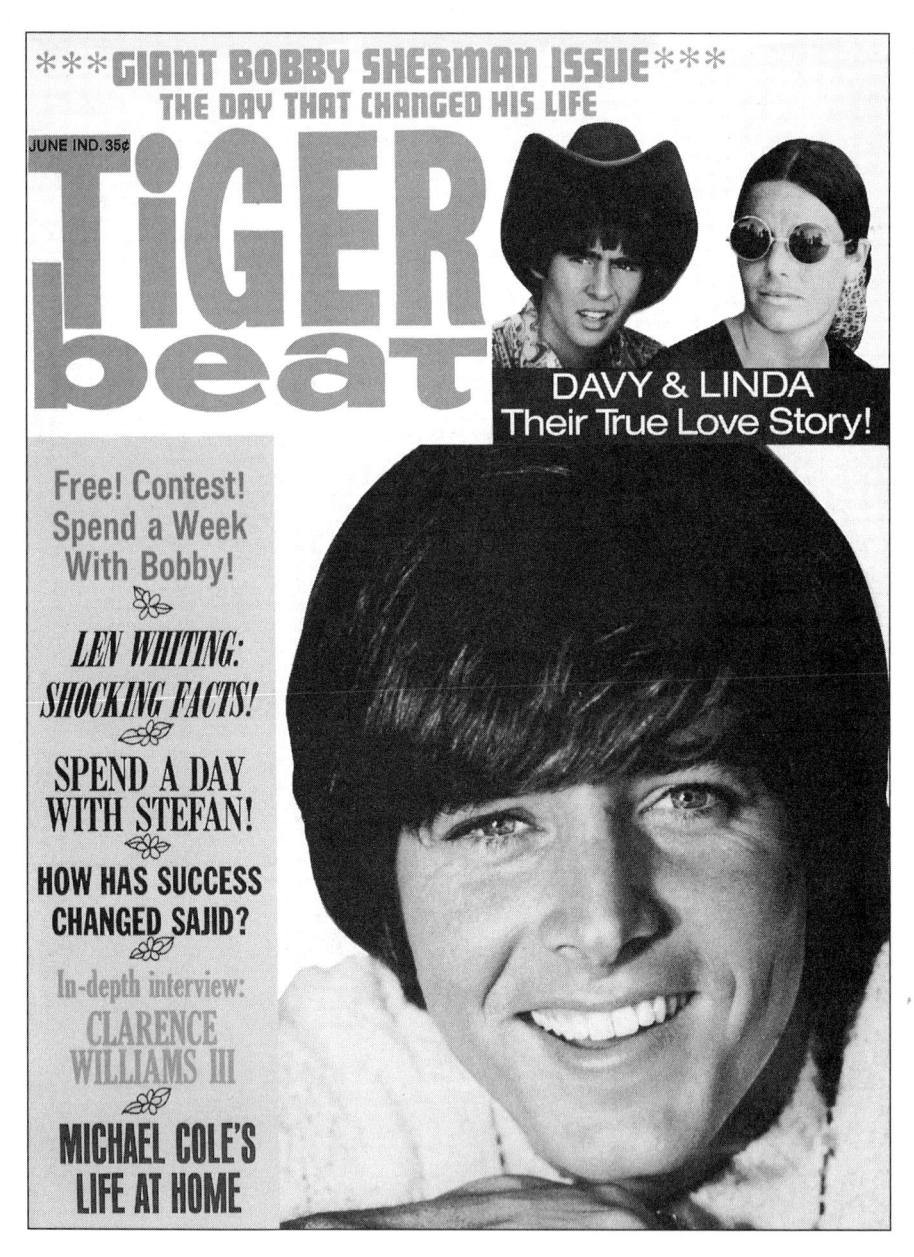

The second day Bobby was on the set, I overheard him asking the cameraman, Irving Lipman, about his two children. Now, the cameraman is *very important to how an actor will look in a scene. Not only was it a nice gesture, but I thought, "This is somebody who knows what he's doing."*

We all got along fine during my stint on "The Monkees" and I became good friends with Mickey Dolenz. I helped put together a sound system for him at his house on Lookout Mountain in Laurel Canyon, California.

Mickey Dolenz

I already knew Bobby, and, to be honest, I don't even remember from where. So when he came on the show, it was more like a friend joining the show.

Later, he built my recording studio for me. He's really into recording studios and recording equipment and so was I. I was working real hard, and I couldn't take the time to figure it out. He said, "Hey, I'll do it for you. I just put one in my house. Just let me know what you want."

We discussed it and sure enough, there was Bobby Sherman every day in my house, up to his elbows in wires and soldering equipment doing my recording studio. He was there for at least a couple of weeks on and off. It was a real studio, proper equipment and everything.

I recorded some great stuff there. I have some great basement tapes from that studio with Harry Nilsson and John Lennon and Paul McCartney and Brian Wilson—I mean, all kinds of good stuff.

At the end of filming the "Monkees" episode, as a joke, Ward gave me a can of paint for my hair and the awful paisley Cabana outfit that I wore in the show. The best thing that working on "The Monkees" gave me was my association with Ward.

Even though the show had not yet gone on the air, I could see how smart Ward was. A graduate of both Princeton and the Harvard Business School, Ward's idea of a weekend getaway is a graduate seminar in theoretical physics at UCLA. If there's one right choice I've made in my life, it was asking Ward to be my manager. Back then I couldn't have imagined that thirty years later, he'd still be my manager, business partner, and best friend.

Ward

Bobby struck me as a real pro. He certainly wanted to be in all aspects of the business. He seemed to me to be someone like Bob

Hope in that, no matter how much money he makes, he's still going to do it because he enjoys doing it.

On the last day of shooting, Bobby and I were at the beach walking along Santa Monica pier. He said to me, "Would you like to be involved in some of the things I want to do?"

I told him, "I have my hands full with 'The Monkees,' but I really enjoy working with you, and I think we'd make a good team. Let's give it a try." That's as much of a contract as we've had between us in thirty years.

Between the end of "Shindig" and the start of work on "Here Come the Brides," my professional life was pretty uncertain. My personal life, in contrast, had never seemed better. Through the years, I had dated a number of wonderful girls, but I'd never truly lost my heart. Just at the end of "Shindig," however, I had fallen in love.

Her name was Lynn. I wrote "July Seventeen" because that's the day I met her. I had dropped by a drive-in restaurant at the corner of La Brea and Sunset for a root beer freeze and the chance to flirt with the carhops.

Lynn was having car trouble and had been dropped off by one of her friends on the street nearby. She caught my eye right away. She had an animal look about her. She had long, wild dishwater-blond hair, sort of a Farrah Fawcett style. Guys were driving by and honking their horns. Then she saw me and knew that I saw her. When I pulled around, she stuck out her thumb, as if she were hitchhiking. In fact, she recognized me from "Shindig."

I offered her a ride, and we hit it off. She was a hairdresser and very earthy. She wore washed or faded jeans when the style wasn't yet fashionable. She was hip and worldly in a way that was good for me.

I can't say that she was really beautiful, but she was striking. Lynn had an energy that came from within. Barbra Streisand is like that. I don't consider her a classically beautiful lady, but when she sings, something happens and she becomes extremely attractive. I understand that that's what a lot of women feel about Mick Jagger.

Often, the women that I dated were "starstruck" or demure because I was a television personality. But Lynn was different. She wanted to be a singer, and she actually had a style. I brought her into my studio to record a couple of times.

She was a few years older than I was, and already had been married and divorced. She had two young kids, Kelly and Jody. That appealed to me because it was a ready-made family. I was such a kid myself, I could make them laugh all the time. They were healthy, they were fed, and they were clothed, but their dad didn't give them a lot of time. I joked around with them and bought them presents. I hadn't really started making big money yet, but I had enough from the tours that I wasn't poor.

I was able to give the kids Christmas presents and take them out for ice cream, something they didn't have in their lives. I could tell how much they loved the attention.

I was so young, I think that's what made me susceptible to the relationship. I was suddenly playing an adult role as the man of the family. I often entertained the kids while Lynn made dinner—and she was a wonderful cook. Things fell into place right away.

I don't know if the relationship would have been fulfilling enough for me or if it would have blossomed into something deeper, but it was doing the job then. I started staying with Lynn about two weeks after we met. I was either at my parents' house or hers—but mostly at hers.

Maybe the reason our relationship ended was my decision to focus on my career. We had been going together for more than a year when I auditioned for "Here Come the Brides" in 1967. I was trying to make up my mind. Did I want to be married with a family—or did I want to throw myself into my career?

I think now that Lynn helped me make that choice by breaking up with me. Maybe she knew that I was having difficulty making a decision, and she probably thought it best that I continue my career. Maybe she thought that I would come back to her if I hit it big. At the time, I didn't interpret her actions that way, however. The night we broke up I felt like I had been hit by a truck.

We were standing in front of her duplex, talking, when she suggested that we should see other people. That wasn't something I wanted to hear. It wasn't as if she was giving me a green light to date other women because I hadn't been thinking in those terms. Her declaration just went immediately to my jealous streak. I thought, "That means YOU want to see other people." I felt devastated. She had to leave for an appointment, and I stood there, alone. I was simply stunned.

For the next year I avoided all potential romantic relationships. It was a very hard time in my life. I was lonely and I couldn't stop thinking about Lynn. I did a lot of growing in the next year. Still, I didn't know if I'd ever want to risk feeling that way again.

In 1968, I started work on "Here Come the Brides." I'd go to work and come home. I'd eat something. Watch television. Work on my lines. Go to sleep. Get up the next morning. Go to work. That was it.

I talked to David Soul, one of my costars on the show, about my breakup with Lynn. I was desperate. I was trying to connect with anybody else that might have had those feelings. It's similar to when somebody who's close to you dies. I wondered if that lost, empty aching would go away, that feeling nobody likes. I don't remember what David said. He might actually have given me good advice. If he did, I don't think I was hearing it then.

To get away from my feelings, I immersed myself in my work. I should have been at the top of the world. Here I was, finally beginning to make it, to become well known. I received all kinds of proposals from girls. It didn't matter. I just wasn't interested.

Soon after my breakup with Lynn, I moved out of my parents' house. I leased the fourth-floor penthouse at James Terrace Apartments with a private balcony on Hollywood Boulevard. Unfortunately, my balcony looked straight down La Brea. That's where Lynn lived.

That fact didn't even dawn on me when I first leased the penthouse. Every time I looked out that window, I would go into a blue funk. For that year, I didn't date, I didn't do anything. I was absolutely beside myself.

I had actually considered marriage with Lynn. After all, I was twenty-three, and she was twenty-six. Then when "Here Come the Brides" started up, I realized that my work would have conflicted with the marriage.

I'd have to be on the set for long hours and not be able to have a family life. As time went along, the idea of marriage seemed less and less pressing, and I became stronger and stronger emotionally.

I didn't talk myself out of saying that I loved Lynn, because I knew I did. But eventually I was able to encapsulate the whole incident, put it somewhere in my heart, and let it be, knowing a future was never going to happen with her.

Lynn came back about a year later. I hadn't called her; she found me. We had been apart just long enough, however, that I'd gone through that period of adjustment. I had lost that special feeling for her.

I also had met Patti Carnel, my future wife.

In hindsight, regarding Lynn, I think I probably made the better choice to consider my career rather than focus on a family at that point.

As "Here Come the Brides" started, my career was about to consume my life, day and night, for the next four years.

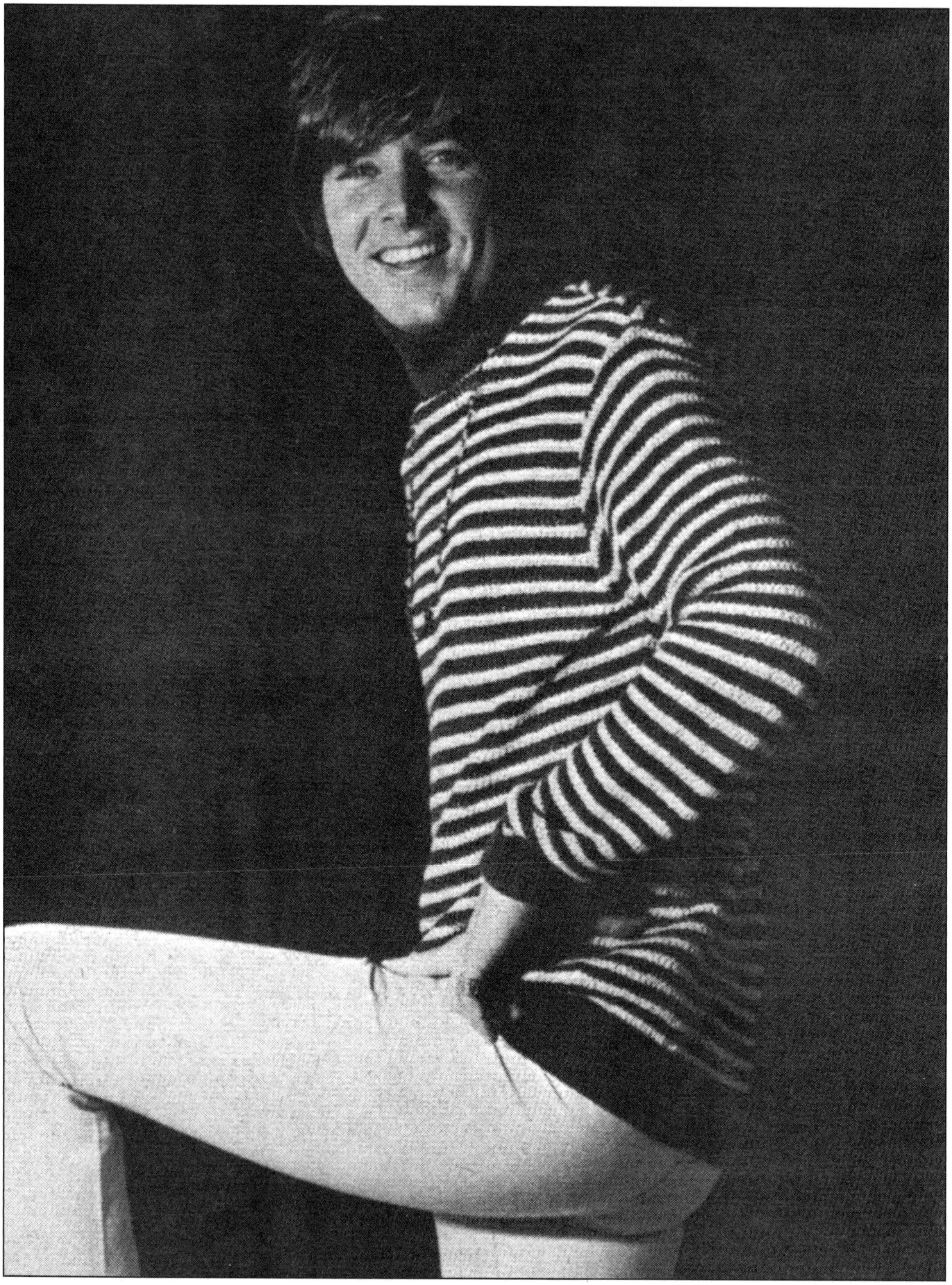

7 "Here Come the Brides"

Soon after I appeared on "The Monkees," I met Steve Blauner, the head of development for Screen Gems. Something about my style apparently reminded him of Bobby Darin, whom he used to manage, so we hit it off immediately.

Steve, in turn, introduced me to Bob Claver as we were walking down a corridor at Screen Gems one day.

"Hi, Bob. I want you to meet your Jeremy."

Steve's introduction to the soon-to-be-executive producer of "Here Come the Brides" caught me off guard.

I was flattered by his support. Ward had told me about the forthcoming show, set in the early days of Seattle, but I didn't believe anything would come of such a casual meeting.

However, in the summer of 1967, I was surprised to be called in to audition for the part of Jeremy, the youngest brother. I met with studio executives, including Steve, Bob Claver, and Jackie Cooper, who was then head of Screen Gems.

On reading the script, I felt a kinship with Jeremy Bolt. He was shy and awkward. I knew him. The character fit instantly. I left the audition feeling buoyant, but I had one more hurdle to jump.

I was flown to New York for a screen test directed by E. W. Swackhamer, the show's director, known to everyone as "Swack." To my relief, the test went extremely well. I knew I was right for the part—and I wanted it.

BOBBY'S PRIDE AND JOY

It's not hard to spot Bobby Sherman driving around town. While you may see a lot of XKE's and Stingrays and little sports cars you can't even identify, you can't miss Bobby's beautiful midnight blue Silver Cloud Rolls Royce. And one very nice thing you might like to know about Bobby—he loves to share. So, don't be surprised when you see him if he asks you to join him for a spin around the block!

KEEPING A CRYSTAL clear shine on the outside is something Bobby is very particular about. He makes it clear that he didn't buy a car to show off, but just to be as comfortable as possible on long drives he loves taking.

COULD THIS BE A letter to you? Quite possibly. When the "Here Come The Brides" cast is on location, Bobby's free moments are spent answering fan mail at his compact little desk which folds down in the back seat.

"LIKE RIDING ON A CLOUD" Bobby says about driving this car. Sometimes to relax or to unwind from a long day's work, he loves to drive down the California coast feeling the cool breeze and stopping to watch the stars. Below, there's a back view of the car. Bobby has lined the shelf behind the back seat with thick white angora. For him, the car is a dream come true.

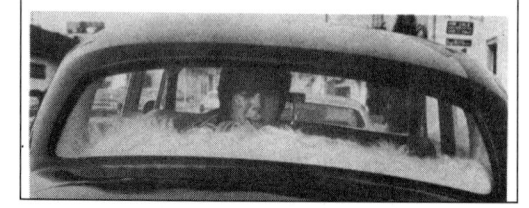

I heard they had considered a couple of other potential Jeremys, but I was hopeful about my chances. My hopes were confirmed when I stepped off the plane in California. Ward and Steve Blauner were there to meet me.

My heart leapt upon hearing Steve's two simple words: "Hello, Jeremy."

Looking back on that day now, I still feel happy. This was better than the day I found all those dimes. It was better than the day I signed my contract for "Shindig." My salary for "Here Come the Brides" marked a transition in my life both financially and professionally.

To celebrate this new high point, I did something I had always wanted to do. I walked into a Rolls-Royce dealership, found a classic, midnight-blue 1962 Rolls sitting on the showroom floor, and went over to the manager. I pointed to the Rolls and said, "I want that car." I still have it.

I now know how much freedom Jeremy Bolt gave me. My work on "Here Come the Brides" gave me the exposure necessary to succeed at the singing career I had long sought—and the riches that accompany that success. It also made me the actor I had always hoped to be.

While growing up, I had spent hour after hour experimenting in front of the mirror. I felt extremely curious about what lets you be someone else, what lets you overcome fear or shyness to be able to portray another person. Finding that ability in myself validated all the struggles and the failures I had experienced up to that point.

I didn't know I actually had the talent until I used it on a daily basis. The more acting I did, the more confident I became.

Like everyone else I worked with on "Here Come the Brides," I believed in the show. I liked the values the story lines espoused and the sweet quality of the stories' presentation.

The premise for "Here Come the Brides" centered on two opposing logging operations in early Seattle. The Bolt brothers, Jason (Robert Brown), Joshua (David Soul), and Jeremy, ran the local logging camp. The brothers owned Bridal Veil mountain, the base for their logging operation. The lumber mill was run by Aaron Stempel (Mark Lenard), the proverbial wealthy businessman and stick-in-the-mud villain.

In the pilot, the Bolt brothers faced a crisis. They were about to lose loggers due to a lack of available women in the primitive town. In order to keep peace among their workforce, Jason made a pact with Aaron to find and bring 100 respectable women to the town. The potential brides would live under chaperoned conditions for one year. If any of them left during that time, however, the Bolt brothers lost their mountain to Aaron, who financed the expedition.

To fulfill their contract, Jason, Joshua, and Jeremy find 100 eligible women in New Bedford, Massachusetts. The brothers endure an uncomfortable, six-month ocean voyage in Captain Clancey's mule boat, finally returning to Seattle with the "brides."

Taunted and teased by some of the girls on board, Jeremy finds no one attractive until he talks to beautiful, red-headed Candy Pruitt as she hangs out her laundry. That scene on the ship set the foundation for the special relationship between Jeremy and Candy. It was used for Candy's screen test.

"I stttutter," Jeremy reveals to Candy.

"I bite my nails," she responds.

"Well, you better quit that. You bite too hard, you'll bleed to death," Jeremy replies.

With Candy, Jeremy figuratively and literally finds his voice. She's the first woman he relates to at all. Saying, "I can talk to her," takes on a whole new meaning for Jeremy.

I already was cast as Jeremy, so testing began for the other roles. The show's producers were searching for the right chemistry between me and the actress who would play Candy. They found it when I tested with Bridget Hanley.

Together, Bridget and I found a special resonance. Like the David and Lisa characters from the 1963 film of the same name, Jeremy and Candy connected on a real level. There was truth between them. Locked into his own private world by stuttering, Jeremy suffered from his shyness. Candy, beautiful and independent, was willing to gamble all her hopes on a voyage to an unknown territory. They complemented one another.

The relationship between Candy and Jeremy was integral to the ongoing plot of the show. Because of that, casting our roles was particularly important.

Bridget Hanley

The first time I met Bobby was when "Here Come the Brides" was going to be done. He had already been cast, and they were trying to find a Candy. I was under contract to Screen Gems (the television arm of Columbia Pictures). They were bringing people in from both coasts to screentest, and several of the young women under contract were being tested.

I couldn't figure out why I wasn't getting my chance since I was a young woman, I was from Seattle, and I bit my nails. I couldn't figure out why they weren't going to give me a shot.

So I went pounding on all the executives' doors, went begging to Bob Claver's office, and drove everybody crazy until finally they decided to "go ahead and give her a shot."

I had been, at that time, already dating my future husband, E. W. Swackhamer, who was to direct the pilot. Once all the powers that be finally said, "Okay, okay. Let's just test her and get it over with," he backed away from my test. He wanted to make sure there was no conflict of interest.

So wonderful Bob Claver directed my test with Bobby. It was on Stage 7 at the old Gower lot. Bobby could not have been more generous. I, of course, was nervous because I wanted that part. I thought it was the part of a lifetime, and, as it turned out, it was.

I wasn't big on rock music, but I certainly knew who he was. I thought he'd be so damn hip I wouldn't be able to communicate, but he was just darling and dear and gentle and intelligent and caring—and a spectacular actor.

So that's how we met. I was fortunate enough to win the part, and we were able to play opposite each other for a couple of years. Lucky me. [Lucky him!]

Bridget didn't have to make a great transformation to be Candy. She brought Candy from within her. The one thing that Bridget didn't really have an opportunity to do was reveal her own sense of humor as Candy. Bridget has a terrific sense of humor, and a lot of that couldn't be brought out in the show because of the character. She's quite a nutsy person. I think she had to keep that down, but every now and then some of it would sneak out in a giggle or a glance.

Once I started doing concerts, people always asked about Bridget, but the audience had a sixth sense. They could tell certain things, and they seemed to recognize that in real life Bridget and I were not in a romantic relationship. I don't think anyone ever asked if Bridget and I were going together. Perhaps because of the way the fan magazines portrayed our relationship, the fans seemed to know we were just close friends.

We both took our jobs seriously. I never considered a romance with her because, first of all, she was involved with Swack. Second, it could have made the work difficult. We were able to create together. If we had been lovers at that particular point, we might have become too emotionally connected and that could have somehow tainted the special relationship between Candy and Jeremy.

Just before one of my first scenes on the first day of shooting, several cast members had been talking about the development of the romance between Jeremy and Candy. As I was about to start my scene, an extra leaned over and teasingly said, "You know Bridget Hanley's going with the director!" I was supposed to stride into that scene. Instead, I was thinking, "Oh my God. Swack's going to kill off Jeremy in the third episode!"

Swack liked me, though, and we became great friends. He and Bridget enjoyed a happy marriage, raising two wonderful daughters. His death in 1994 was a tremendous loss for all of us.

A lot of thought went into the development—or lack of it—of Jeremy and Candy's romance on "Brides." When the second season started and Candy's little sister and brother came to live with her, the inevitable question of Jeremy and Candy marrying went on the back burner. It was feared that if they married, some fans would take it literally and think that Bobby Sherman was married. I was single, and that's the way the fans liked it.

Bridget Tells All on Bobby! Part II

Bridget Hanley probably knows Bobby Sherman better than any other girl in his life. She's worked with him for a whole year and off the set they're good friends. Here is her exclusive story:

HAVE THERE EVER BEEN ANY REALLY FUNNY INCIDENTS THAT HAVE HAPPENED TO YOU ON THE SET OF "BRIDES?"

It's just terrible! Every time we have scenes where we have to run to each other or turn around quickly to each other or grab each other or hug each other, I always miss. If we're supposed to run together and hug, I'll run right by Bobby, and I don't mean to! Once, I fell right through a wagon! I was in a wagon, one of those big wooden ones that are drawn by horses, and instead of getting out like a lady, I always jump out. Well, this one time I started to jump out and I threw my body forward, but my leg went right down through the floorboard. Luckily, the hole was big enough so that my leg came right out. But I always have skinned knees and ripped dresses. The wardrobe lady has to have doubles on most everything I wear because I fall down all the time and rip things!

CAN YOU THINK OF ANY OTHER TIMES THAT WERE FUNNY ON THE SET?

We have started laughing on some of the kissing scenes. We all get that mantic scene and there are always so many people around and we'll just start giggling and when Susan Tolsky gets going I can't stop laughing.

You know, Bobby's very dear with her. They go to lunch and talk. She has a boyfriend, but sometimes you can't talk to your boyfriend like you can talk to a very good friend. And Bobby's like that with her.

Another thing Bobby and I will do is during rehearsal we'll do a scene totally the wrong way, just to crack everybody up and make them think that that's the way we're going to do it. Bobby and I get hysterical sometimes, but when it comes time to do the scene, we have to pay attention to that. I can remember doing one scene and it was very serious and my line was, "Well, Jeremy, you just better go out there and get them!" and he said, "Well, okay, come on." Then we were supposed to walk out the door. So I turned around and there was one of those old pot-bellied stoves and I knocked the stove over and the side of the wall out and then Bobby and I went right on with the scene and we had to turn our backs to the camera because we were just shaking we were laughing so hard. But there's always something like that, Bobby sometimes will run and he'll slip on the stairs.

HAVE YOU EVER DONE ANYTHING OFF THE SET TOGETHER, LIKE DOUBLE-DATING OR GOING OUT SOCIALLY TOGETHER?

No. And I think that's maybe one of the reasons for our success as friends. Bobby's a very private person and so am I and he has his group of friends and I have mine. I mean, we've been at many social functions together and we don't hang on each other, we kind of go our own ways. But I know he would always be there if I needed him.

WHAT DO YOU THINK IS BOBBY'S BEST TRAIT?

Oh, dear! He has so many. Honesty, his talent and the talent goes in the musical area, the acting area, the business area, the technical area as far as films are concerned. I would say his best trait is his totality. I think that word kind of sums it all up without leaving out anything. I don't think I've ever met anyone, a friend, that has as many things going for him as Bobby.

YOU WERE IN SEATTLE WITH BOBBY FOR APPEARANCES THERE, HOW IS HE WITH HIS FANS?

Bobby is absolutely incredible. When we were in Seattle, I had never seen him perform live, he is so full of electricity! My mother and dad and my younger sister came in to see the last show and they were flipped out about him. They were! My mother was a musician a long time ago and she said he is not only a very talented, good musician, he's a fantastic performer. He is, and it just comes out like he's wide open and he's all there and he loves it. With the fans, he's fantastic. He gives them what they need and what they want. He sees as many and talks to as many and signs as many autographs as he can. He's really great.

WHAT DO YOU THINK BOBBY WILL DO IN THE FUTURE?

I've wondered, because Bobby, even when he gets older is going to look very young. He's going to look like a young leading man for a long time. I wonder, and I wonder if he wonders. I think that his singing career could go on for a long time. I know now that he's pushing that and his acting career will go on for a long time. I think that every actor wonders at some time "How long am I going to last?" It's hard for me to say what will happen to Bobby. I don't know what's going to happen to me, or David or Robert. I just hope for a very long, golden, fantastic, beautiful career for them and for Bobby. And I think he has the talent and the will power to do whatever he sets his mind to.

There has been a big debate over whether Candy and Jeremy would have married if there had been a third season. That's one thing we'll never know. Over the two years "Brides" aired, I experimented constantly, creating different facets for Jeremy's character. After performing a role once or twice, you become comfortable enough with it to add new dimensions and to experiment with the part. That was certainly true for Jeremy. By the time we actually started filming the pilot, the character no longer seemed new to me.

Born in Seattle, Jeremy had never had a girlfriend. He was green. I was able to extend Jeremy's range without losing sight of his essence, which was honesty and sensitivity. I could never do something as out of character as make him walk in with a limp or speak with a brogue.

I worked hard to make sure his stutter wasn't awkward; that it didn't seem unreal or overly sympathetic. When Jeremy did speak, the things he said were basically honest and forthright. The fact that he had the stutter made it much more difficult for him to voice his opinions. However, when he finally uttered the words, he generally had a winning point!

Bridget Hanley

I think Bobby was so willing to be vulnerable. I think that is a wonderful trait in a man, and I'm not so sure how many men feel sure enough of themselves to be able to show that side. I think it's much more prevalent now than it was then. He was just so vulnerable—and attractive.

I think the vulnerability was one of the key things to him being so wonderful as Jeremy.

They were lucky. It wasn't just him being in the right place at the right time; it was the producers and the network being in the right place at the right time.

The fans, both girls and boys, adopted Jeremy because he was the young one, and they related to him in various ways. For a long while, many people believed I really stuttered. Parents wrote in to say that their children stuttered and watching Jeremy helped them. I found that very rewarding.

Nonetheless, the show's producers decided that Jeremy had to lose his stutter. For one thing, I was chewing up the scenery. A line could be as simple as, "What time is it?"

I could expand it to, "Whhhhaaat ttttime issss ittt???"

"C'mon Bobby, cut it out."

I wanted the stutter to eventually slip away anyway. Jeremy needed to overcome it for the character to grow. I accomplished that through an episode called "A Man and His Magic," with Jack Albertson.

Jack played Merlin, a snake-oil salesman, who gave Jeremy a "magical" stone to cure his stutter. That episode worked well, and we received a terrific response to the show.

Until then, the lines were written for normal speech, and I decided where I wanted to stutter. Bill Blinn, our head writer, shaped much of Jeremy's dialogue. The words just flowed. The right words made slipping into character dramatically easier. Our writers gave Jeremy story lines that allowed him to show different colors.

"A Man's Errand," for example, allowed Jeremy to prove himself as a businessman. In his first attempt at winning a bid for a logging contract, Jeremy made a successful sales pitch to an influential San Francisco contractor.

Throughout the course of the series, Jeremy and I both developed confidence. Jeremy learned about romance, gained emotional strength, displayed his unfailing integrity, defended honor, instilled courage, and taught others about commitment.

I developed the ability to display those qualities for him. The work I do now as an Emergency Medical Technician demands many of the same qualities Jeremy exhibited. He and I helped each other grow personally and professionally. From the first days of shooting, I faced a number of challenges with Jeremy—not the least of which was seasickness.

We had a full day of shooting out on an unseaworthy schooner for the pilot scenes aboard Clancey's ship. Everybody became seasick.

Susan Tolsky, Biddie on "Here Come the Brides"

The boat was built in 1800-something. It was a very old wooden boat, truly authentic, not a Hollywood boat. We left San Pedro harbor with the crew retching over the side. Not a good sign.

They said, "Don't go on that side of the boat." We were afraid to ask why, only to find out that there was a large hole in that side of the boat. So we could only film from one side—the side without the hole in it, of course.

That was in December of 1967, the coldest winter in the history of California in 9,000 years. Out in the water, it was in the low thirties, and that's without the wind chill factor. We had box lunches, but I don't remember anyone eating. We filmed most of the day.

The women had about 970 pounds of clothes on. We had to dress down in the hold. We started out with tights. Next, we had thermal underwear and three to four layers of petticoats with the clothes on top of that. In addition, we had the muffs and the hats and eight pounds of hair. Then we had those dumb little purses that don't carry anything.

We shot all day, then we went back to the harbor and docked "Das Boot." They never took that boat out again. About a month later there was an article in the paper that the boat sank in San Pedro harbor. Nobody touched it. No one grieved.

Is there a God or what? We all could have drowned. The women surely would have sunk to the bottom. The guys would have had a chance, but we had so much poundage of clothes on, we would have sunk right to the bottom with our petticoats fluttering over our heads.

"Here Come the Brides"

We started the pilot knowing that we were going to be picked up for twenty-six shows; however, a major cast change occurred immediately. Lottie originally was supposed to be younger and serve as an ongoing love interest for the oldest brother, Jason, played by Robert Brown. However, that would have prevented us from bringing in guest stars as romantic possibilities for Jason. So, instead of Gail Kobe, the original Lottie, the more mature Joan Blondell stepped into the role and became the surrogate mom for all of us. As a result, we had to redo many of Lottie's scenes from the pilot.

"Here Come the Brides" was first telecast September 25, 1968, on ABC. We had finished about three shows when we went on the air. By then, I had learned that life on the "Brides" set was going to be different from life on the "Shindig" set. Instead of rehearsing all week as on "Shindig," and then shooting on Friday, we filmed "Brides" every day, Monday through Friday.

We had tough schedules. Mine became tougher during the second season because I began doing concert tours on the weekends. Between "Brides," "Getting Together" (a short-lived situation comedy I did in 1971), recording, and concerts, I basically worked seven days a week for three years straight.

During weekends, when I traveled, I had my people to point me where I needed to go. I even had nightlights in hotels to keep me from waking up and being disoriented in the dark. During the week, however, I depended on a scheduled routine.

If I had an early call, I woke up at 4:40 or 5:00 A.M. In the happy event of a late call, I could sleep in until 7:00 A.M. Typically, I showered, dressed, and drove my Rolls to the Columbia Ranch in Burbank where we had the Seattle set. There, we shot all the Seattle town scenes: Lottie's bar, the church, the town square, Clancey's boat, the brides' dormitory, and the Bolt brothers' cabin.

The lot contained sets for shows such as "Bewitched," "The Flying Nun," and "I Dream of Jeannie," which were shot there at the same time. Because of the other sets, we had to be careful of camera angles. Clancey's boat, for instance, backed up to some building facade from the nearby "New York" street, which was used to film movies.

I saw Sally Field at the studio quite often, but I rarely had time to visit with her. The lack of a commissary kept us from having a common area in which to spend time with cast members from other shows. Larry Hagman was the exception. He loved champagne, which he kept on hand, and he shared a glass with me from time to time. Usually, though, there was little time to socialize.

Once I arrived at the studio, I went to my trailer, put on my red-and-brown plaid shirt, corduroy jeans, and boots, and strolled over to makeup. I was in and out of the chair faster than anybody else because I had a tan most of the time. The makeup lady just powdered me down . . .

Susan Tolsky

For the women, the call was 6:00 A.M. because we needed two hours for hair and makeup. I had three hairpieces, totaling about eight pounds of hair, and I would get hideous headaches. Bobby would jump into his Jeremy clothes, and makeup would slap a little powder on him, and he was out. I hated him!

Bridget Hanley

I still get letters saying, "Oh, how I tried to get that Candy look!"

We started out with a three-quarter fall for the longer back section and used all my own hair for the curls that were hanging down the back. We then used, of course, my bangs and part of my hair to go up over. But then we added some of the curls up on top, and then I think we ended up with two or three of those little numbers [hairpieces] by the end of the second year.

Bobby Writes To You..... EXCLUSIVE!

Hi Babe!

This morning when I was sitting in my dressing room on the "Brides" set, I was kind of worried about what I'd write to you this month. Even during filming, when my mind should have been on the scene, I found myself thinking about you.

Anyway, after I finished for the day, I scrubbed off my make-up and I was heading towards my car, still thinking about this column, when a girl walked up to me and introduced herself and said she was a fan of mine.

I thought she wanted an autograph but she looked up into my eyes, then quickly looked down, and asked in a voice that was barely a whisper if she could talk to me for a few minutes. I parted her long hair out of her face and raised her chin with my hand and I could see she'd been crying.

TERRIBLY CONCERNED

Well, I was flattered that the thought of me as a big brother but I was also worried that maybe she had a problem I wouldn't be qualified to help her with and I was terribly concerned for her. I took her hand in mine and led her over to a quiet corner of the lot where there's some grass and trees and we sat down. Jan, that's her name, started telling me her problem.

"Bobby, have you ever been tempted to do something that you knew was wrong and that would get you into trouble and still you went ahead and did it anyway?" she asked me, blotting away her tears.

Jan and her girlfriend had gone to school that morning and on the way to their first class, they'd passed some boys in a car who said they were cutting for the day and invited them along. Jan said she didn't want to go but her girlfriend agreed and then they all called Jan a "chicken."

IT WAS WRONG

Rather than lose face, Jan got into the boys' car and left with them though she knew it was wrong. Now she was terrified that her parents would find out or that her teacher would catch her and she just didn't know where to turn.

I promised Jan I wouldn't tell you any more about what she'd done so I can't break my promise... but I can tell you (like I told Jan) what I did when I got caught in a similar situation.

I don't know what it is with some people... they don't look into their own heads very well... but they think it's funny to stick others in the position of having to do something wrong or be put down for being a "chicken."

A GAME ON PEOPLE

When I was in school, it was a game to do that to people. If you didn't do something like cheat on a test or cut a class or pass a note or something, you weren't one of the popular people for very long.

I used to like to have parties. My parents were very cool about not intruding but they did have one rule: no liquor.

One week I invited the most popular people in the class to my party and they said they'd come! Before I knew what was happening, they were planning to bring liquor and I knew it but I didn't tell them not to because I was afraid they'd stay away.

STARTED DRINKING

That Saturday night, two of the guys showed up with a couple of bottles of liquor and they started drinking. Immediately I knew it was wrong to allow them there. But I didn't say anything because I was afraid. Then I started thinking about what could happen if I didn't tell them to stop and you know what? By the time I finished adding up all the consequences, I discovered I'd lose a lot more than my pride.

I gathered all my nerve and I walked over to where they were sitting on the couch and I said, "John and Frank, I know I didn't say anything to you earlier but now I've thought about it and I have to ask you to either throw away the liquor or you'll have to leave."

John and Frank really started putting me down. "What do you mean? You knew we were bringing stuff with us!" they kept shouting. "What are you? A chicken?"

GETTING SCARED

I didn't know what to say and they didn't leave and I was getting scared and I thought about letting them stay anyway. But I realized that would be wrong so I asked them again and still they didn't do anything. Finally I got really furious. I mean FURIOUS. I ordered them out and they left. So did most of my other guests.

But before I could clear out the liquor bottles, my parents came in to see what was wrong. I told them how first had happened and I explained how first I didn't say anything but finally I thrown John and Frank out though I knew I'd lost face with the entire crowd. My parents were pretty upset with me but they were very cool about it and from then on, they trusted me even more.

So I told Jan that she should go home, explain what she'd done and why she'd done it and tell her parents that she now understood all the consequences and that she wanted to tell them before they found out from someone else.

DO WHAT'S RIGHT

And I want to tell you, Babe, that when you find yourself in the same situation, whether at school or at a party or on a date or whenever you are tempted to do something wrong, you should be yourself and do what you know is right, no matter how much pride you think you might lose. In the long run, I know it's worth it. Don't you agree?

Until we're together,
Love,
Bobby

... but they never did anything to my hair.

During "Shindig," the show's producers wanted me to look clean-cut. During the pilot for "Brides," my hair had grown a little longer, but was combed back. In the first few episodes, some of the scenes I played were in bed, so my hair wasn't supposed to be combed. I remember a lot of reaction from people saying, "That looks good. You ought to keep it that way." So I let it grow longer and looser. Actually, Lynn had been an influence. She thought my hair looked a lot better down in a bell shape.

By the end of "Brides," my hair had grown and did the flip at the end. It still flips when I let it grow too long. Back then, fans liked that style, and I didn't have much time to have my hair cut.

The teen magazines wrote articles about the length of my hair. One magazine compared "long" or "short" hairstyle photos, side by side, and printed letters from fans to determine which length was most popular! I just let it fall where it went naturally. I washed my hair in the shower and took a hair dryer to it. Period.

After makeup, I walked over to the set, said hello to the crew and a general good morning to everybody—and waited. And waited. When I was called into a particular scene, I went to work. When I finished the scene, I sat down—and waited some more. Working on the set was nothing glamorous, far from it, with lots of lag time between scenes. Time between my scenes never went fast.

Some days, when the lunch truck came, I ate a cup of cottage cheese with little bits of chives in it. Again, nothing glamorous. Then I finished out the day on the set, changed into my street clothes, climbed into my car, and drove home, usually after 7:00 P.M.

As my popularity grew, leaving for home took longer. Groups of fans waited at the front gate. When I could, I tried to stop and meet them. If they were going to take their time to wait outside for me, the least I could do was take the time to visit with them.

When I was living at the penthouse, I'd arrive home after dark, decide on something to eat, and make dinner. I liked to cook and was usually too tired to go out to a restaurant, so I developed my cooking ability. I'm a good cook now. My culinary skills fall somewhere between backyard barbecues and gourmet candlelight suppers. Even then, I had developed my own repertoire of dishes. I'm fondest of my version of beef stroganoff, "Shermanoff," made with ground beef instead of beef strips.

After dinner, I watched a little television, worked on my lines, and fell asleep.

The routine was dull, but necessary. As my confidence grew, I realized my strict routine kept me on track. It enabled me to have

"Here Come the Brides"

all my lines memorized when I walked on the set each day, which made me feel comfortable. Knowing my lines at least freed me to concentrate on the scene, rather than on the words themselves.

Not to say I didn't experience some insecurities. I often had bad dreams about messing up. In one dream I showed up on the set without a clue about what anybody else was doing. I didn't know what I was supposed to do or say—a terribly empty feeling. Nightmares like that made me work harder.

Even after I started doing concerts on the weekends, I always knew my lines for "Brides" when I walked in on Monday morning. I didn't want to look like some sort of rock star who didn't care. I wanted to come in there as a professional. Nothing for me was worse than dropping a line. It happened every once in a while, but I never wanted to cause delays for anyone else.

My costar, Robert Brown, could start to work on his lines while he was getting made up in the morning. He did pretty well, but memorizing that way would have scared me to death. I chose to take the script for the next week's show with me to concerts on the weekends. Learning my lines on an airplane never seemed too

Bob Claver, "Here Come the Brides" executive producer

I think Bobby worked very hard, or if he didn't work hard, he certainly prepared himself. He never came onto the set saying, "I don't know my lines." He was a professional.

The most difficult moment during filming came at the end of the day when everyone got the giggles and everything was funny. Concentration became impossible, especially in a serious scene. Once I saw a quiver in the corner of Bridget's mouth or saw Robert begin to grin, I would break up.

"Don't do that," I'd say, and then I'd lose it. We worked such long hours on the set, we began to slip into exhaustion. Then the production crew and others on the set became angry because we were holding everything up.

"Come on," they'd plead. "We have to get this shot!"

I'd try to get serious again. "I'm sorry. I'm sorry."

I even tried digging my nails into the palms of my hands. Catching the giggles was fun, but it was a nightmare if you didn't come out of it quickly enough. Time literally meant money. The show was expensive to shoot, and every wasted moment cost more money. We always had a large number of extras as townspeople. In the pilot, for example, we shot a huge party sequence in the town square. We had our regular extras and regular bit players. The show's writers ended up creating parts for the characters they liked. Corky (Robert Biheller), one of the loggers, for instance, became a regular character.

Several of the regular cast members made a point of interacting with extras on camera to get them "bump" pay from the production. The way it worked, extras received more money if they could respond in some way to a cast member. For example, if I walked through the town square and said, "Hello, Sonny," all my friend Sonny Jones had to do was say, "Hello, Jeremy," back to me. Susan, Bridget, and I were especially good at creating "bumps."

I still miss the family atmosphere on the set. At the outset, David Soul (Joshua Bolt) and I became friends. We had a lot in common through music and our work. Because we were close in age, I felt comfortable asking him about relationships after my breakup with Lynn. I couldn't understand all the emotions I kept dealing with.

"Is feeling so lonely usual? Is not being sure I want to be in love again normal?" I asked him.

Not that David knew the answers, but the fact that he listened helped me. During breaks, David and I often went out to Stage 29. There, we tossed a football back and forth or sat around and strummed guitars. As the show progressed, the cast became tighter and tighter, and we grew together as a family.

"Here Come the Brides" generated a tremendous amount of fan interest, especially from the kids who sent in thousands of letters. Most of the letters were for me. Perhaps because of that attention, Robert Brown started to warm up to me. As the show progressed, I noticed that he talked to me more frequently, and I felt I began to gain his respect.

I thought of Robert as a big brother. In fact, I ended up becoming Jeremy, in a sense, and sometimes related to everybody else as the characters they portrayed. I got just as used to answering to the name Jeremy as I did to Bobby. He was a part of me then and still is.

Bob Claver

Bobby's just a very good soul. There are not a lot of people like Bobby in the entertainment business—or any other business. I don't think that Jeremy was so different from Bobby as a person. They were decent, nice people. They're the same.

The other cast members were somewhat the same. David played Joshua and was Joshua. Henry Beckman was Clancey in real life—a charming, irascible character. Of course, Joan Blondell was Lottie—a total sweetheart. Joan mothered us all and told great Hollywood stories as well.

It was the same with Susan. Whether it was on or off the screen, Susan, who played Biddie, and I related as who we truly were. Occasionally, we would have a short scene together. On camera, I was always asking her something or she was responding to me.

Susan and I never caught each other acting. The relationship remained the same if I went up to her off camera and said, "Susan, where is . . . ?" And she would say, "Well, I don't know, Bobby, it would be . . . " and it was as natural as could be.

I never found any difference between Susan and Biddie and I'm sure she found no difference between Bobby and Jeremy.

That's why we connected.

Susan Tolsky

Bobby is special.

I was upset about something in my personal life one day, and I had pulled my chair away from where the set was. I remember Bobby coming over to me, squatting on the ground, taking my hand, and saying nothing. I just squeezed his hand, and we stayed however long until we both had to go. He did the perfect thing. He said nothing.

If we were all who we seemed to be on screen, then the only exception was Mark Lenard. He, of course, played Aaron as the "fly in the ointment." I genuinely liked and admired him. I knew him to be much different from the character he portrayed. I always thought it interesting to watch him do his shift from Mark to Aaron.

When I first started out, I found it much harder to hit those emotional buttons, but that ability came in time. Doing scenes in which you're angry or happy is something anybody can do, but making them believable is hard to do well. The audience can sense whether your emotion is a facade. If you can take the feeling all the way within you, not only is it believable to the audience, but it's believable to you. And if you believe it, they're going to believe it.

I probably was able to access my own feelings because I was such a loner while I was growing up. I entertained myself and Frank, my imaginary childhood friend. I was able to stay within myself rather than having to go outside. I drew all my information from the inside.

Working with the guest stars on "Brides" taught me a great deal about myself. I liked the qualities of concentration and curiosity they brought out in me. I especially enjoyed working with Ed Asner and Jack Albertson. I picked up a lot of good techniques, which I applied to my own skills.

JOIN THE
BOBBY SHERMAN FAN CLUB
THE MOST EXCITING THE MOST COLORFUL
FAN CLUB KIT *EVER!*
ONLY $1.50 EACH (U.S.)

My need for believability led me to insist on doing my own stunts. Though the show's executives didn't always approve, they usually let me have my way because I insisted. Most of the horse riding and the falls and the climbing were really me.

I didn't worry about horses because I had learned to ride as a kid, thanks to Darl. When I was small, traveling pony rides came around the neighborhood. Darl would groom and feed the ponies, so I had free rides. Learning to ride is basically overcoming fear. As long as the fear has been overcome, you can pretty much do anything.

During "Brides," I had one horse I particularly loved. Brownie was an absolute sweetheart. He just loved me and could pick me out of a crowd. What a team we were! He was such a camera horse. Each time I rode him, I simply took him to the location of the camera shot.

"That's your mark there," I'd tell him.

Then we'd go back to the starting point. I wouldn't have to do anything else. Brownie was such a smart horse that he knew his mark. He knew if he was too far back or too far forward, so he would invariably inch his way to his mark. He was remarkable! I wanted so much to buy him, but they wouldn't let him go because he was so extraordinary. In my heart, though, Brownie belonged to me.

Handling my own stunts kept me busy, and I enjoyed doing them. In the episode "The Soldier" about a bear Jeremy shot, I did all the falls and rolling down the hill because that way camera shots could be kept tight. Only one or two stunts required Joey Hooker, my stunt double. We looked enough alike that he was believable in a long shot.

Joey also did a lot of the fight scenes because of the choreography involved. When a big fight scene was filmed, there was a chance of stumbling into someone's elbow or fist. An injury to my face could have caused delays in shooting.

The only episode that caused real concern about my safety was the show about an imprisoned Indian boy. In "Hosanna's Way," I had to break in to free him, and I had to climb up a latticework vine on the outside of a building.

No producers were around, so I took the opportunity to say to the director, "I can do that."

So I started climbing. In the scene, I crashed through a skylight and landed on the floor. The cameras didn't have to pull way back trying to fake it. I didn't want my fans to think that a double had to be used for a lot of things that I actually could do. Jeremy could do it.

One of the fight scenes I did do was special because of my opponent. Jeremy and Candy's continuing relationship provided few openings to bring in other love interests for me. In the "Marriage Chinese Style" episode, however, we created a funny-but-awkward situation in which I saved the life of a Chinese girl named Toy. Consequently, she insisted she belonged to me by the custom of her culture.

In that episode, I ended up in a fight with Toy's boyfriend, Lin, and I won. I didn't know who the actor was at the time, but now that's one feat I can claim. I beat up Bruce Lee on camera.

Actually, I could pick up the choreography for fight scenes pretty easily. My musical ability helped me to understand timing. When anyone took a swing at me, I could react right at the point the blow would have made contact. That helped sell the scene because the camera could stay in close.

Most of the filming required only one camera. Two or three cameras were sometimes used for special stunts or scenes that would be difficult to duplicate. Once, we felled a large tree at Angeles National Forest. The tree was diseased, so the authorities gave us permission to cut it down. We had three or four cameras rolling so all the angles could be covered when it went down.

Oddly enough, we never shot anything in Seattle. We filmed many of the exterior shots, including the camp scenes, at Franklin Canyon Reservoir in Los Angeles because it looked like a lake.

We also shot many scenic views at Angeles National Forest, two hours away by car, a trek I came to dread. After the first trip, there was nothing new to look at. I couldn't read during the drive because it threw my equilibrium off. I can't sleep in a plane or a car even today. So I had to just sit there and do nothing. That drive wore me out.

Regardless of location, I usually shot a scene just once, or at most, two or three times. Sometimes, though, I didn't mind doing extra takes. In fact, I had fun during the extra scenes in Lottie's bar.

Beer can't be faked, so we had real beer at Lottie's. The first thing David and I always did was head for the bar. We'd say, "Do two takes on that one, will you?" We'd start laughing, and the crew would say, "No more for you guys."

We didn't need beer to have a little good-natured fun, though, and poor Susan was the one with whom we had the most fun.

Susan Tolsky

I was the one they played jokes on a lot. I had worn contact lenses until we started filming ninety-seven hours a day, and then I decked them. So I had glasses on in between scenes. I am legally blind without my glasses and have no idea who I'm talking to. They thought of the most heinous jokes to play on me, and Bobby was frequently an instigator.

We would block a scene, in Lottie's bar for instance. Then we'd start to rehearse, and I would write the blocking out, such as "cross to the chair and exit the door." Then, inevitably, they would come up with something to lure me off the set.

"Touch-up. Girls, go for your touch-up," or "Susan, your hair is crooked," or whatever, and so out I went like an idiot—every time.

Then they would move the furniture. They moved the tables. They moved the doorway. They have outtakes of me trying to exit the door and hitting a wall.

Worse yet, those damn Bolt brothers exchanged their shirts one day. David had Bobby's shirt on, and Bobby had David's shirt on. Of course, I was talking to the wrong one. I was saying, "Jeremy..." and they were saying, "No, that's not Jeremy, that's Joshua." I was talking to his shirt because I would use color and wardrobe as marks. They did hideous things to me, and I have Bobby and his red-and-brown plaid shirt to thank.

I rarely did any singing for "Brides." I did one voice-over song in a montage for the "Absalom" episode which featured Mitch Vogel from *The Reivers*. I also sang a duet with David for the Christmas show in the first season.

After "Brides" had been on the air a year, Metromedia Records released what became my first huge hit record in September 1969. "Little Woman" spent nine weeks on the charts in the Top 20 and went gold. At the time, the gold singles (45 RPMs) represented a million records.

When I started doing "Brides," I didn't think I was ever going to sell records. Len Levy, the CEO for Metromedia Records, wanted to offer me a recording contract. I said, "Hey guys, don't waste your time. I tried for two and a half years on 'Shindig' and nothing happened. I'd hate for you to waste your time and money." They said, "Oh, we'll be the judge of that."

I have to give him credit. Len stuck with it. "This is going to happen," he said. So, we did a session that included "Little Woman," "La, La, La," and "Easy Come, Easy Go." I wanted to release "Easy Come, Easy Go" first because I liked it, but they elected "Little Woman." They were right.

I was in Buffalo, New York, for an appearance, and Ward called.

"The record is snowballing," he told me.

I had no idea what he meant by that.

"What happened. What's the matter?" I asked him, panicked.

"NO. NO. NO," Ward said. "It's happening!"

WKBW in Buffalo had started playing the record. At night their power picked up, and they could be heard up and down the eastern seaboard. We were getting airplay from Buffalo, but it was all over the East Coast. Record sales spread like wildfire across the country.

At that point, I said "Wow! I guess we're in." Nobody was more surprised than I was.

Len said, "Told you so."

Years before, I had been thrilled the first time I heard "It Hurts Me," as I drove along the street in my Cadillac one day. After that, I had waited so long that when the success of "Little Woman" finally came, I was too busy to revel in it.

Then all of a sudden, the fan magazines appeared again. I enjoyed a second, much more pronounced wave of popularity than with "Shindig." BOOM. Everything hit at once: "Brides," my records, the concerts, and the fan mail.

The audience that had followed "Shindig" was an older crowd. When "Brides" happened and I had that boy-next-door look, the show hit a whole different age bracket. Because of their youthfulness, these fans were highly demonstrative.

They vocalized their feelings. They wrote. They came to the concerts. They dragged their parents along. They couldn't get enough.

In December 1969, "La, La, La (If I Had You)" was released, spent six weeks on the charts, continued into 1970, and went gold. Just three months later, "Easy Come, Easy Go," hit the charts, also went gold, and spent eight weeks in the Top 20. Because of the airplay and exposure, my career began to heat up dramatically during the second season of "Brides."

My status on the set changed during the second season. For the first season, Robert Brown occupied a bungalow, and David and I shared one long trailer. David had one end and I had the other. It was bleak: four walls, with electricity, a heater, and an air conditioner. I brought in a bookshelf, television, refrigerator, and couch.

Then, for the second season, I was given my own trailer. I felt awkward about it because David didn't get one. My new trailer

THE DAY THE BRIDES DIED

AS TOLD TO TIGER BEAT

It was going to be a beautiful day. The clouds that dropped buckets of rain over Los Angeles had melted like ice cream on a hot day, giving way to a bright and warm sun that made no hint of the approaching doom that would soon affect the lives of so many people!

The sun rose high in the heavens and spread it's golden rays over Columbia Ranch in Burbank. It shone with a smile upon the Midnight Blue Rolls Royce parked by Bobby Sherman's dressing room and upon the streets of Seattle!

LAST DAY OF SEASON

Inside on Stage 29, there was a touch of excitement in the air. Today was the last day of shooting on "Here Come the Brides" for the season! Everyone looked forward to the big cast party to be held later that week and then to a couple of months vacation until filming resumed in the fall.

Susan Tolsky was thinking about flying to Hawaii for some extra sunshine—Bridget thought about doing some decorating on her home and Bobby was eager to be off on another tour!

Although there had been some talk about the cancellation of "Brides" before, it had died any idea that "Brides" would really be cancelled!

The shooting was completed by late afternoon and a cheer went up in Stage 29 that must have been heard all over the city! The exhausted cast and crew were indeed ready for a long vacation!

Columbia Ranch saw few people in the next few days but on Friday night the cast party was in full swing! Everyone had agreed to wear their "Brides" costumes for the celebration—which was taking place right in the streets of "Brides" Seattle!

BARBECUING THE STEAKS

The weather was just right and a big bonfire burned hot and bright to warm any traces of chill. Henry Beckman was barbecuing the steaks and Susan Tolsky had made so much lemonade punch, hot cocoa and coffee that one would think an army had gathered together!

Bridget sat by the side of her husband "Swack" who had come along. He had directed the season's last "Brides" show and Bridget was so very proud of him!

Robert Brown and his wife Anna helped themselves to all kinds of Hors d'oeuvres everyone had brought while Joan Blondell and Mark Leonard danced through town square and round the Seattle Totem with all the other people who had helped make "Brides" a success! Everyone was there—laughing, joking and having a wonderful time! But someone was missing! Where was Bobby?

In Stage 29, one solitary light burned among all the props! Bobby alone among all the first and only Sherman had been the one to know. Just that afternoon he had gone to see Bob Claver, the "Brides" producer, to find out for himself if the millions of letters fans all over the country had sent to Mr. Elton Rule in New York had saved the show!

BOBBY WAS THE FIRST to learn the tragic news about the cancellation.

WHEN BRIDGET FIRST CAME OVER to talk with Bobby about the party, she sensed something was strange, then Bobby told her the sad news.

CALLING HIS NAME

Suddenly Bobby heard light footsteps coming closer and then he heard Bridget calling his name! He remembered with a rush of warmth the first day he met her and how he knew that she and Jeremy would be beautiful together. Bridget was almost like a sister to him and he loved her in a very special way!

Now as he watched Bridget walk slowly towards him Bobby recalled the episode where Candy got lost and fell down a steep cliff, hurting herself and tearing her dress! Even all messed up she was beautiful. Candy and Jeremy had come so far—from the magic of discovering each other through little lover's quarrels and spats—through trust and distrust to their engagement and marriage plans that would never be now!

Then Bridget's hand was on Bobby's shoulder and she looked into his eyes reading there the overwhelming sadness he was feeling! "It's over isn't it," she said softly, knowing the way a woman sometimes does exactly what a man's thinking! "Yes," Bobby whispered gazing into Bridget's blue eyes where a small tear was beginning to grow larger. "That's it, but it's been wonderful."

DEFINITELY CANCELLED

It hadn't worked. "Brides" was definitely cancelled! How could Bobby go to the party and face everyone else when they didn't even know yet that there really wasn't much to be celebrating?

So suddenly it would be over. There would be no more Jeremy, no more Candy and even Seattle would cease to exist at Columbia Ranch! Somehow it felt as though he was losing his whole family. Robert and brothers to him! Together they had come to Seattle and made their lumber camp a success. Together they had brought the "Brides" to Seattle and built the dormitory, standing side by side through the first year's trial when they might have lost Bridleveil Mountain!

And the "Brides"—silly wonderful Biddie always looking for a man, Clancy, Lottie, Aaron—they were all a part of his daily life and now would they too only become memories?

Quietly Bobby got up and walked among the props. Here was the gambling wheel that had won Jeremy and Joshua a bankrupt saloon. And the gypsy wagon the Greeks had come in to Seattle. The manger where two little girls had substituted a real baby in place of a statue of Jesus!

Over by the wall were the buckets the "Brides" picked berries in and an old beer barrel from Lottie's Saloon. And there in a large box gathering dust were all the scripts from the past two years! Scripts that told the entire story!

ARM IN ARM

There weren't any words to be said then. Together Bobby and Bridget walked out of Sound Stage

BOBBY AND BRIDGET, dressed as Jeremy and Candy, tried to hide their true feelings of disappointment, but it was no use.

CONTINUED ON PAGE 60

had a couch, a stove, a refrigerator, and a bedroom. It was all mine—with my name on the door.

In response, I did everything I possibly could to downplay my fame. I was proud of my accomplishments, but I didn't want to step on anyone's toes. Fortunately, I was surrounded by support instead of envy.

One morning in makeup, for example, Mark Lenard turned to me and said, "God, I turn on the radio, and I can't get away from you anywhere." Thank heaven he had a sense of humor about it. In fact, he was quite proud of me.

I knew that David wanted to be a recording artist, so I tried to help. In fact, he came to my recording studio, and we tried a couple of songs, but nothing came of our work. There was no reason he shouldn't have had a record career while "Brides" was on. Later on, when he starred in "Starsky and Hutch," he finally had a hit record of his own.

During the second season, to our dismay, we learned the show had been canceled. The "Mod Squad" era in television had begun. A new trend in car chases and hippie street scenes pushed aside hour-long costume comedy-dramas. "Brides" took its place among the last of the quality period shows such as "Bonanza" and "Gunsmoke."

The final episode of "Brides" aired on September 18, 1970. It was a sad time for all of us. We were a family, and I missed that community for a long time after the show ended. I didn't miss the hours and the drudgery, but I did miss the people.

We all went our separate ways because our careers took us in different directions. But even today we still manage to keep in touch.

Worst of all, Jeremy missed out on those ninety-nine other girls!

INSIDE: GIANT BOBBY COLOR POSTER!!!

JULY IND. 35¢

TiGER beat

DAVY'S NEW RELIGION

PETER TORK'S NEW GROUP!

WIN A DATE WITH BOBBY! FLY FREE TO HOLLYWOOD!

BRIDGET'S SADDEST DAY!

MIKE COLE SAD FACTS

VISIT ELVIS AT HOME!

SCOOP INTERVIEWS: LEN, ROBERT BROWN, DAVID SELBY, MARK, CLARENCE W. III

8 A Dream Date with Bobby

"Win a phone call from Bobby!"

"Fly to Hollywood to meet Bobby!"

"Imagine a Day with Your Dream Date!"

"Enter Now! Now! NOW!"

Teenagers in the late sixties wanted to know my favorite color (blue), my favorite food (steak), my favorite song ("Easy Come, Easy Go"). They wondered about where I lived, whom I dated, where I hung out, what attracted me to a girl. Most of all, they speculated about what it would be like to be my "steady" girl.

I tried to be as honest as possible in my answers to reporters. During the concert years, the fans were my charges, and I took the responsibility very seriously.

The teen magazines conveyed a specific message to their youthful readership, but it was also a true message: I was who I seemed to be. I loved my family. I didn't take drugs. I believed in honesty and treating other people with respect.

I was never going to say to the fans, "Okay, now you're older, and we can tell you the truth." What I said I believed was, in fact, what I did believe. There were no hidden agendas.

Giving interviews to the teen magazines started after two or three episodes of "Brides." I saw Ann Moses from *Tiger Beat,* for instance, almost every week. I went to the *Tiger Beat* offices for photo sessions and Ann frequently came to the set of "Brides."

Bobby Writes To You
AN EXCLUSIVE NEW TiGER BEAT COLUMN

Hi Babe,

Each month here in Tiger Beat, I'll be writing just to you & sharing, with you, some of my most private thoughts & feelings.

I hope you'll read my messages when you are alone, so that you will fully understand that these feelings I'm expressing are direct from my heart to yours.

Until we're together.....
all my love
Bobby

I worked most with Ann and Gloria Stavers from *16 Magazine*. Because I talked to them all the time, they gained a sense of who I was and what I was all about.

In some cases, Ann would come to the set with an article already typed that she asked me to write out by hand. That way, my note appeared on the magazine page in my own handwriting for the authentic look of "A Message from Bobby," which was a feature in the magazine.

I cooperated, since some of the articles were supposed to be by me, and I had no time to sit and write them myself. Besides, I felt that Ann knew me well enough to write things in my name.

Generally, after an interview, the editors wrote an article and asked me to add some closing remarks to authenticate it. The magazines competed for the honor of claiming, "We're closer to Bobby than anybody else." Teen magazines are a big business.

For four years, the articles appeared nonstop. Even my mom and Darlene gave interviews. In fact, Darlene had her own column in *Tiger Beat*.

Darlene

When I returned home for Bobby's first concert in Anaheim, I met Ann Moses, and we really hit it off. She asked me if I would start writing articles. I said, "Sure," and I started sending in a column every month. To my surprise, she never changed a word I wrote.

Photos accompanied every article, and I spent hours in photo shoots. Some of the shoots had a theme, such as being out by a pool, which required me to take off my shirt. Later, the magazines wanted photos that made me take my shirt off for no reason other than just beefcake shots. I know the photos sold magazines, but I began to feel it was cheap, and I didn't like it.

Photo sessions were never easy, especially when the photographers were going for a cover. To achieve the perfect shot, they put me through many poses. They took pictures of me standing, sitting, leaning, doing handstands, bike riding, flashing the peace sign, pointing, and most of all, SMILING.

Many of the clothes I wore for photo shoots were my own because I felt comfortable in them. I particularly like leather and suede, and I still have the brown suede jacket used for a lot of photos. In fact, I loaned it to Jeremy Bolt for some of the "Brides" episodes.

In addition to photographing me in my wardrobe, the magazines wanted me to try on different outfits like Nehru jackets, turtlenecks, bell-bottoms, and buttoned-down shirts with fringed vests. I cooperated, but I dreaded the feel of certain materials. It stemmed from having to try on new clothes when I was a kid.

My dad's mom, Honey, used to take me shopping for Easter clothes. I loathed it, even though the items she bought were sharp. The clothes were expensive and they looked good, but I remember some of them being itchy. They were tweeds or something. They scratched me, and I felt like I was walking funny. I hated the whole experience.

Years later, some of the photo sessions evoked the same sensations.

"Okay, let's try one with that green shirt."

"Let's not," I thought.

Tiger Beat, especially, knew my sizes and often had me try on different colors, such as purples, blues, and greens, for the color art they wanted.

To be fair, the variety did add appeal to the photos. And I sometimes ended up with the hottest new clothes.

"It's yours," they said, if I commented on something I liked. I appreciated their generosity, but I didn't abuse the privilege. I was always relieved when we finished. Maybe some men like having their pictures taken, but for me it was something of an ordeal. I never could have been a male model, that's for sure.

The photos appeared in the teen magazines for centerfolds, montage pages, special photo booklets, poster pullouts, and accompanying shots for articles—and contests.

The magazines created contests for every imaginable item related to me. They held drawings to win "Jeremy's" shirts, "Bobby's" peace rings, Bobby Sherman albums, and even locks of my own hair! The magazines gave me the clothes and rings to wear, took the pictures, and then sent the items to the winners.

Bigger and better contests followed. Next up the scale, they gave away phone calls and "handwritten notes from Bobby." When magazines started running "Bobby's Dream Girl" and similar contests for a "Dream Date," they generated enough interest for ten contests over four years. Winners and their parents were flown to Hollywood. The magazines could afford it. Their business was booming.

At the time, preteens and girls from twelve to fourteen didn't have a lot to do for entertainment. Television choices were limited, they couldn't yet date, and there were no computer or video games. Few shopping malls had been built yet, so there was nowhere for girls to congregate. Girls that age didn't have a lot of spending money, but they had enough for single 45 RPM records and fan magazines—a lethal combination.

Charles Laufer, founder of Laufer Publishing (*Tiger Beat* and *Fave* magazines)

The average age (for readers of fan magazines) is still about thirteen and a half. I used to read the mail very carefully, and his (Bobby's) name started popping up. This was when "Here Come the Brides" had just started. I said, "Put Sherman on the cover." We put Bobby on, and we received a good response.

He was the most sympathetic, good-looking young guy who stammered. He was perfect!

In addition to *Tiger Beat* and *16 Magazine*, I gave interviews almost every week to magazines like *Fave*, *16 Spec*, *Flip*, *Teen* magazine, and *Teen World*.

At first, I worried because I found myself repeating the same information over and over. The reporters didn't know the difference, but I did. I prided myself on being original and spontaneous. I finally realized I didn't have to search for new and different ways to present the same facts about my life. My parents were always going to be the same parents. I would always have grown up in the same neighborhood. The date I was born would never change (except for the occasional slip by some writer). I learned to relax and try to stay spontaneous, regardless of the repetition.

I never took classes in media relations. My best teacher was common sense. The studio simply thought I should know better than to say stupid things, and I realized the main element was to be polite. I learned that on my own.

Susan Tolsky

Reporters waited around to talk with Bobby, and I never saw him be rude. I never saw him be ungracious. People waited for him between takes, for lunches, and by the dressing rooms.

> *If the director called Bobby back on the set, he used to pull back, saying, "Excuse me, I have got to go do this scene, but just hang on, I'll be back with you."*

Articles about me ran continuously in all sorts of magazines from 1968 to 1970, the "Brides" years. Much to my displeasure, I often found that my words had been twisted to fabricate stories. One day in a store I happened to look down and saw my name on a magazine, but it wasn't *Tiger Beat* or one of the teen publications I was accustomed to appearing on. The headline read: "Bobby's Secret Son," with a picture of me.

"Now what?" I wondered. I picked up the magazine and started leafing through it. I hoped no one in the store would notice me reading about myself. The article turned out to be about my sister's son, Bobby. I'm his godfather, so he's my godson. I thought that article was a cheap shot.

Several of the teen fan magazines, as well, took liberties with the truth. They started with a shred of the real story and fabricated articles to fit their purposes. Article after article discussed my first date, or a girl's alleged first date with me; the first girl I supposedly ever loved; the next girl I thought I could love; lists of things I professed to love; and why I chose not to love just one girl at any point in my life.

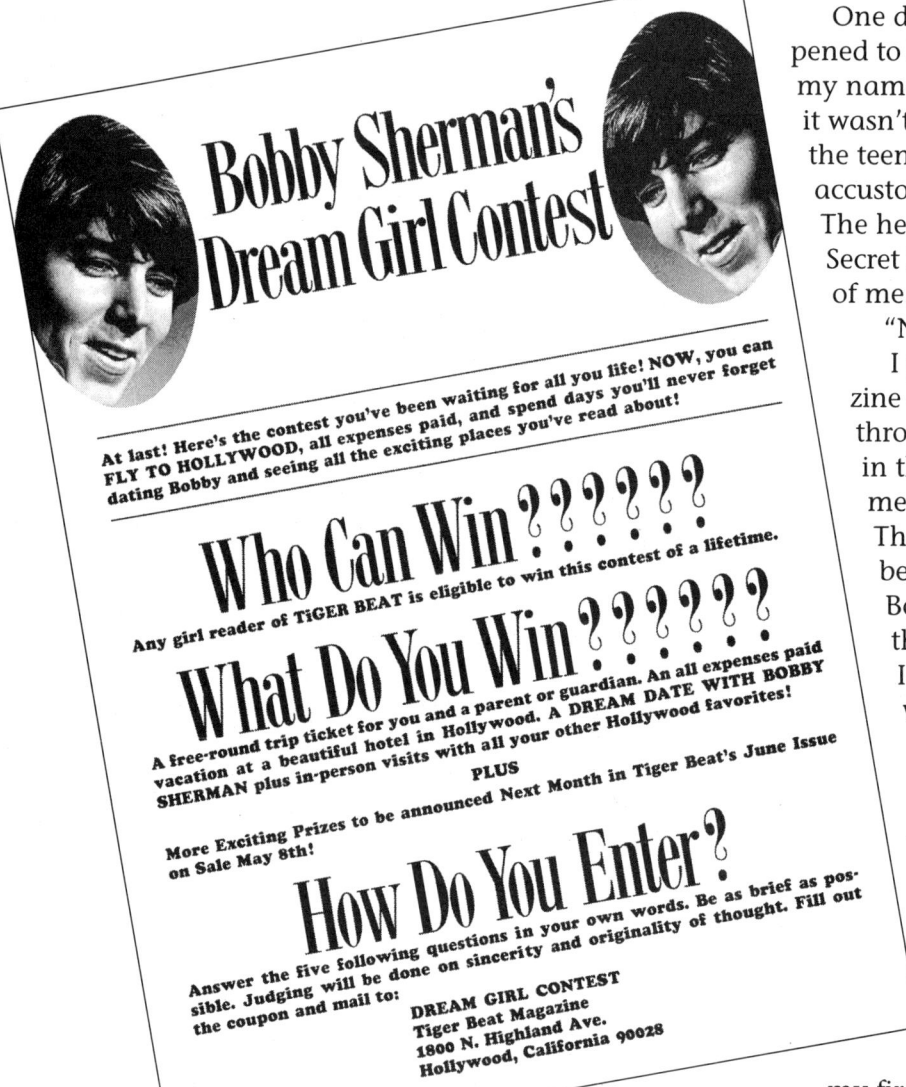

Dena

Fans often made scrapbooks for Bobby filled with articles and photos of him. His mom kept quite a number of them. Several scrapbooks I looked at were constructed over a long period of time, serving as a chronicle of Bobby's career. They also act as a representation of the articles printed by the fan magazines.

One day, Bobby and I flipped through one of the scrapbooks together, and I pointed out various photos and articles. He seemed shocked by the abundance of misinformation.

He never bought a house in Beverly Hills; he wasn't in love with the girl next door; and he doesn't like to go dancing or out to clubs.

But "Bobby facts" sold magazines.

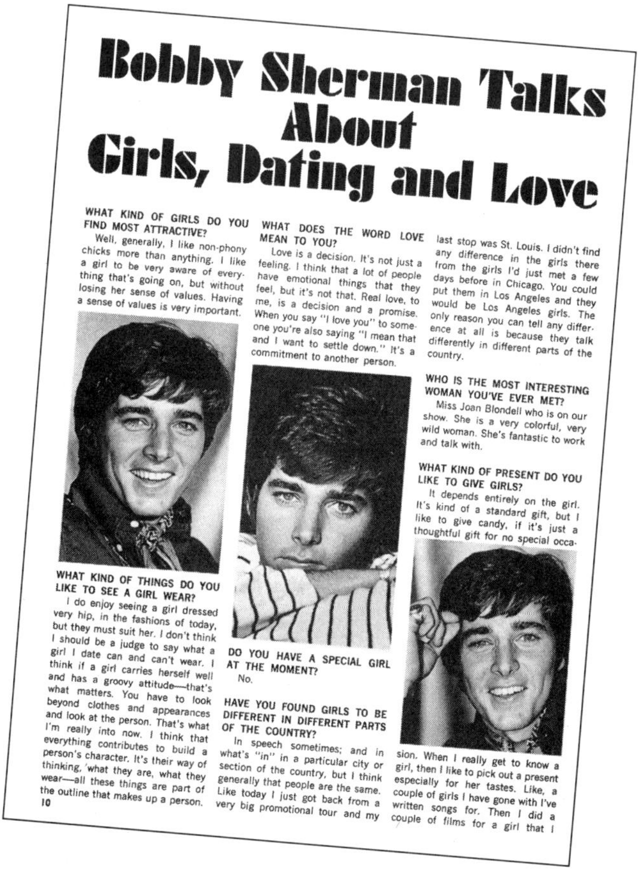

Bobby Sherman Talks About Girls, Dating and Love

WHAT KIND OF GIRLS DO YOU FIND MOST ATTRACTIVE?

Well, generally, I like non-phony chicks more than anything. I like a girl to be very aware of everything that's going on, but without losing her sense of values. Having a sense of values is very important.

WHAT KIND OF THINGS DO YOU LIKE TO SEE A GIRL WEAR?

I do enjoy seeing a girl dressed very hip, in the fashions of today, but they must suit her. I don't think I should be a judge to say what a girl I date can and can't wear. I think if a girl carries herself well and has a groovy attitude—that's what matters. You have to look beyond clothes and appearances and look at the person. That's what I'm really into now. I think that everything contributes to build a person's character. It's their way of thinking, what they are, what they wear—all these things are part of the outline that makes up a person.

WHAT DOES THE WORD LOVE MEAN TO YOU?

Love is a decision. It's not just a feeling. I think that a lot of people have emotional things that they feel, but it's not that. Real love, to me, is a decision and a promise. When you say "I love you" to someone you're also saying "I mean that and I want to settle down." It's a commitment to another person.

DO YOU HAVE A SPECIAL GIRL AT THE MOMENT?

No.

HAVE YOU FOUND GIRLS TO BE DIFFERENT IN DIFFERENT PARTS OF THE COUNTRY?

In speech sometimes; and in what's "in" in a particular city or section of the country, but I think generally that people are the same. Like today I just got back from a very big promotional tour and my last stop was St. Louis. I didn't find any difference in the girls there from the girls I'd just met a few days before in Chicago. You could put them in Los Angeles and they would be Los Angeles girls. The only reason you can tell any difference at all is because they talk differently in different parts of the country.

WHO IS THE MOST INTERESTING WOMAN YOU'VE EVER MET?

Miss Joan Blondell who is on our show. She is a very colorful, very wild woman. She's fantastic to work and talk with.

WHAT KIND OF PRESENT DO YOU LIKE TO GIVE GIRLS?

It depends entirely on the girl. It's kind of a standard gift, but I like to give candy, if it's just a thoughtful gift for no special occasion. When I really get to know a girl, then I like to pick out a present especially for her tastes. Like, a couple of girls I have gone with I've written songs for. Then I did a couple of films for a girl that I thought was very groovy. Original gifts are the most fun to look for and to give.

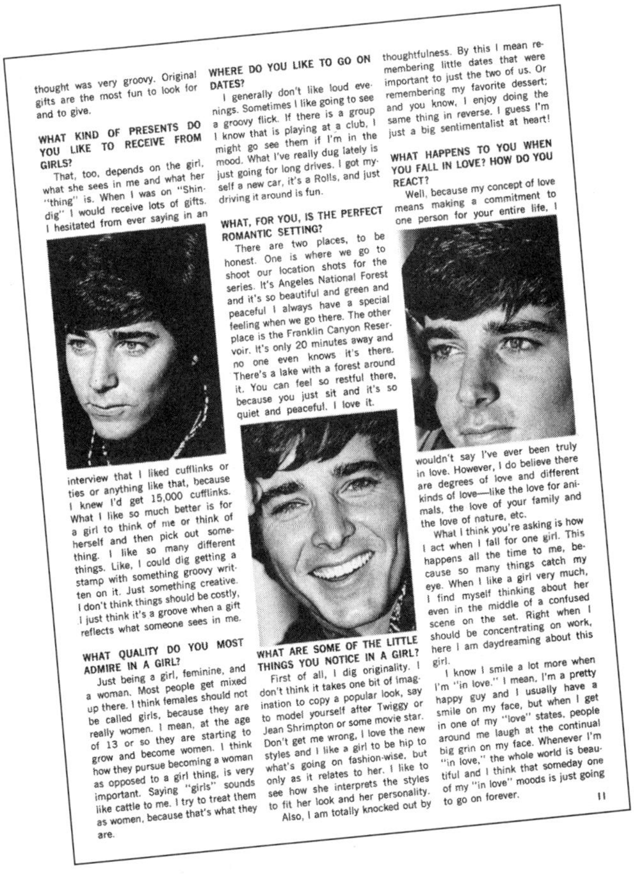

WHAT KIND OF PRESENTS DO YOU LIKE TO RECEIVE FROM GIRLS?

That, too, depends on the girl, what she sees in me and what her "thing" is. When I was on "Shindig" I would receive lots of gifts. I hesitated from ever saying in an interview that I liked cufflinks or ties or anything like that, because I knew I'd get 15,000 cufflinks. What I like so much better is for a girl to think of me or think of herself and then pick out something. I like so many different things. Like, I could dig getting a stamp with something groovy written on it. Just something creative. I don't think things should be costly, I just think it's a groove when a gift reflects what someone sees in me.

WHAT QUALITY DO YOU MOST ADMIRE IN A GIRL?

Just being a girl, feminine, and a woman. Most people get mixed up there. I think females should not be called girls, because they are really women. I mean, at the age of 13 or so they are starting to grow and become women. I think how they pursue becoming a woman as opposed to a girl thing, is very important. Saying "girls" sounds like cattle to me. I try to treat them as women, because that's what they are.

WHERE DO YOU LIKE TO GO ON DATES?

I generally don't like loud evenings. Sometimes I like going to see a groovy flick. If there is a group I know that is playing at a club, I might go see them if I'm in the mood. What I've really dug lately is just going for long drives. I got myself a new car, it's a Rolls, and just driving it around is fun.

WHAT, FOR YOU, IS THE PERFECT ROMANTIC SETTING?

There are two places, to be honest. One is where we go to shoot our location shots for the series. It's Angeles National Forest and it's so beautiful and green and peaceful I always have a special feeling when we go there. The other place is the Franklin Canyon Reservoir. It's only 20 minutes away and no one even knows it's there. There's a lake with a forest around it. You can feel so restful there, because you just sit and it's so quiet and peaceful. I love it.

WHAT ARE SOME OF THE LITTLE THINGS YOU NOTICE IN A GIRL?

First of all, I dig originality. I don't think it takes one bit of imagination to copy a popular look, say to model yourself after Twiggy or Jean Shrimpton or some movie star. Don't get me wrong, I love the new styles and I like a girl to be hip to what's going on fashion-wise, but only as it relates to her. I like to see how she interprets the styles to fit her look and her personality. Also, I am totally knocked out by thoughtfulness. By this I mean remembering little dates that were important to just the two of us. Or remembering my favorite dessert; and you know, I enjoy doing the same thing in reverse. I guess I'm just a big sentimentalist at heart!

WHAT HAPPENS TO YOU WHEN YOU FALL IN LOVE? HOW DO YOU REACT?

Well, because my concept of love means making a commitment to one person for your entire life, I wouldn't say I've ever been truly in love. However, I do believe there are degrees of love and different kinds of love—like the love for animals, the love of your family and the love of nature, etc.

What I think you're asking is how I act when I fall for one girl. This happens all the time to me, because so many things catch my eye. When I like a girl very much, I find myself thinking about her even in the middle of a confused scene on the set. Right when I should be concentrating on work, here I am daydreaming about this girl.

I know I smile a lot more when I'm "in love." I mean, I'm a pretty happy guy and I usually have a smile on my face, but when I get in one of my "love" states, people around me laugh at the continual big grin on my face. Whenever I'm "in love," the whole world is beautiful and I think that someday one of my "in love" moods is just going to go on forever.

I know now how much untrue material appeared under the guise of news about my life. Because I didn't have time to read all the fan magazines, I knew little about what was coming out in print at the time.

In contrast to all the publicity and attention I received when "Brides" first started, my personal life was anything but exciting. I was still emotionally wounded from my breakup with Lynn when I started meeting fan-magazine contest winners for what they labeled "Dream Dates." Unfortunately, the contest winners were usually twelve years old!

Except for work, I almost completely isolated myself from girls old enough to date. For the first year of "Brides," I felt extremely lonely. For a long period of time, I rarely dated at all. My lack of confidence was coming from within.

Girls my age might have been giving me every kind of positive signal known, but I wasn't catching them. The girls who were writing in were about ten to fourteen years old—too young to date. Even the letters from older girls couldn't help. It's hard to translate a letter from Alaska into a possibility of romance. Nor was I going to call a girl in South Dakota for a date!

As a result, I found it difficult to meet girls who were old enough and whom I did want to date. So I spent a lot of time at home—alone.

When I did meet women I wanted to ask out, at the store or in the building where I lived, it often helped that they recognized me. Then again, my celebrity status could work against me, too. I've often wondered, "Is this girl interested in me because it's me—or because it's HIM—that image?" A lot of times it's been difficult to tell.

My success made me happy, but I never knew why people were looking at me or giving me the time of day. To counteract that, I've always worked hard to make dates like me. I went out of my way to be nice and make sure that I wasn't selfish so that they felt special.

At show business functions, I frequently made appearances with budding starlets whom I had never met before. If I needed to attend the Grammy Awards, for example, my "date" was set up by Jay Bernstein, who handled my public relations. As a Hollywood business arrangement, blind dates are a common practice.

Typically, I took down the pertinent information, I picked up the starlet, we attended the function, I took her home, and I went home. Strictly business. From a publicity standpoint, I needed to be seen with someone new. It wouldn't have looked good then for me to be in a serious relationship. The fans liked the fact that I was single. I didn't want to let anyone in too close then, anyway.

Also, my career required me to be seen at certain functions. When someone like Gregory Peck calls you on the phone and says, "Bobby, we'd like you to be on the bill for the Frank Sinatra farewell party," you don't say no.

It became a case of "Water, water, everywhere, and not a drop to drink." I was constantly "dating" and didn't have a girlfriend! The contest "dates" were just business for me, too, but I knew it meant much more to the contest winners. Actually, the contest winner "dates" were flattering. At least these girls were excited to meet me!

In addition to her reporting duties, Ann Moses also served as the liaison for *Tiger Beat*'s contest winners. Ann accompanied the contest winner and her family to the "Brides" set in the morning around ten-thirty. We made introductions, and I gave the winner signed albums and photographs as souvenirs.

With Tiger Beat *editor Ann Moses.*

I tried to be respectful of the work those girls had done to win one of those contests. They must have worked hard. Writing the best essay or whatever they had to do to win meant they were highly motivated. I felt proud of them.

I also knew that winning the contest was important for them. I wasn't going to brush them off and say, "Well, this is the lucky winner, see you later." She obviously had to jump through a number of hoops to reach that point. I wanted to make sure the winners had as good a time as possible.

I introduced my "date" to everyone on the set, from the wrangler who trained the horses to Bob Claver, our executive producer. I tried to arrange my schedule to be able to spend time with her, and show her and her family around. I pointed out the "Brides" dormitory, explained how Clancey's boat worked on wheels, and posed for a series of giggly photos.

Then we went to lunch at the Yankee Pedlar, a Burbank restaurant, at about twelve-thirty. The management treated me well. I often did interviews there, and the chef knew my favorite dishes. They made the greatest potato pancakes with sour cream as a special side dish for me. I loved it. Then I didn't eat dinner.

Before we left the set for lunch, I tried to make arrangements for my guests to see how a scene was filmed when we came back. The producers, Bob Claver and Paul Witt, accommodated me because they knew that having contest winners on the set was helping the show.

Every moment I spent with the contest winners was chaperoned. Usually, the mother or both parents accompanied my "date"—a completely protected situation for us all.

I always insisted that Ann or some representative from the magazine attend the luncheon. Ann's participation helped break the ice for everyone. Most of the girls were extremely demure and shy, and I had to do most of the talking. That could be difficult, especially if I had a long day going on. Sometimes, as it turned out, I spent a lot of time talking to their mothers.

Before the luncheon ended, girls usually asked me to sign mementos for their sisters or girlfriends.

"Can you write one for Pam and one more for Kelly because she'll kill me if I don't bring her one."

That armed the girl to go back to her friends and say, "Look what I have for you." Then her friends, in a sense, became part of the "date." I understood how that worked, how girls socialized.

They liked to read about me in the magazines, watch me on television, and listen to me sing. They wanted my autograph, my photographs, and pieces of my clothing. But "Dream Date" contests were about the "Teen Idol."

I began to long for a real date for Bobby.

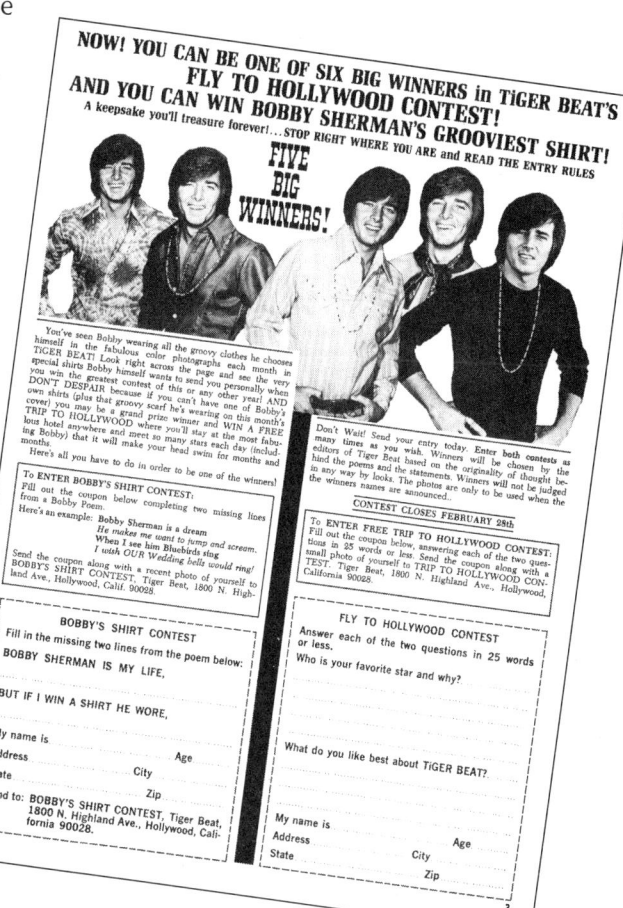

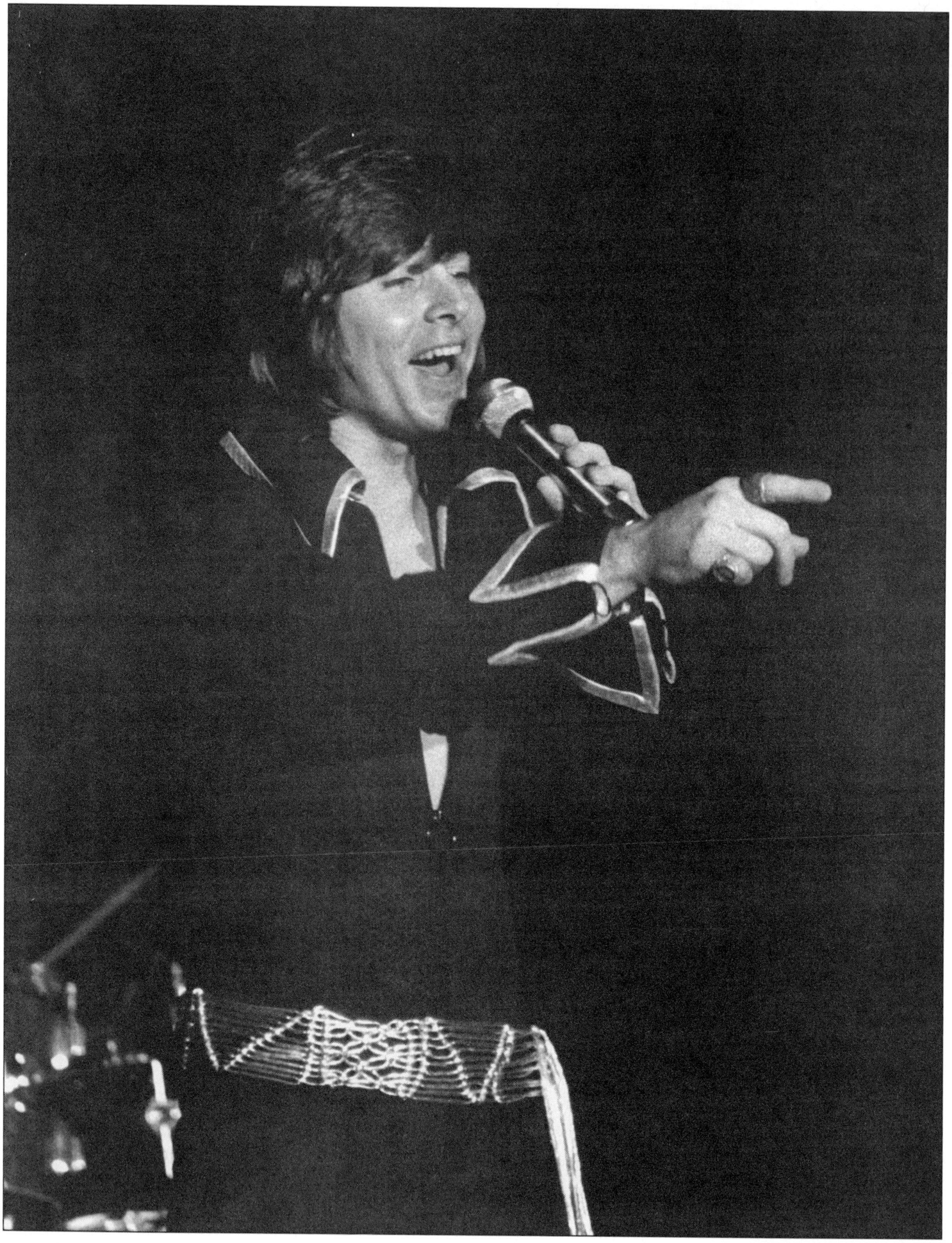

9 Concert Tour Tales

Ward

Bobby had a young audience, and we wanted to make sure that he was accessible to them. So we tried to keep the ticket prices down. At the time, that meant four- or five-dollar tickets.

Before each concert, Ward used to come back to the hotel and describe the layout of the theater for me. At the concert we did for Milwaukee's Octoberfest in 1970, he just said, "This is a huge place with a sea of people."

In the open air on that warm night, I was amazed by the sight of 150,000 screaming people.

Because of the unusual size of the audience, a fence separated the stage from the crowd. Throughout the show, girls tried to climb it. Some almost made it over, but each time security would remove them.

Finally two little girls got all the way over the fence and started toward the stage. Usually, I liked to reach out and touch the kids, but I couldn't reach over the fence. So I thought I'd go over to where these girls were coming up and shake their hands or give them a hug. As I neared them, the fans were screaming.

"GO! GO! GO!" they yelled in support.

The girls actually were getting there; they were succeeding.

Then one of the security guards apprehended one of the girls and took her back.

"BOO," the crowd jeered in response.

The other girl made it close enough to reach me. I came over to grab her hand, but she grabbed the sleeve of my shirt instead. Another security guard put his arms around her to pull her away, but she wouldn't let go of my shirt.

Because of the crepe material, my shirt didn't rip. It just stretched longer and longer and longer until I had a fifteen-foot sleeve. Finally, the girl let go. I had to pull my sleeve back enough that I could manage it. I frantically tucked and folded, tucked and folded.

I tried to hold the sleeve with my hand for the rest of the evening. The trouble was, if I moved wrong it would unravel to a mammoth length. Every time I waved to the audience, I'd have to reel in my fifteen-foot-long sleeve, like a fly fisher going for the big catch.

In spite of the fact that we had fun on our concert tours, we constantly dealt with crowds, heat, exhaustion, and, most of all, hysteria.

Right after the success of "Brides" and "Little Woman," the concerts kicked off the next wave of exposure. Promoters across the country started calling to request bookings.

Ward

The promoters rented the hall and arranged for the advertising. In Bobby's case, they didn't need to spend a lot of money for newspaper ads because local radio stations advertised the concerts. In exchange, their disc jockeys would be the ones to introduce Bobby. The stations received promotional credit, such as "WKBW Presents Bobby Sherman."

Bobby helped by calling the radio station and doing interviews, and the record company donated Bobby Sherman albums as giveaways. The stations also ran contests for free tickets, and the winners would meet Bobby during intermission.

The promoter made deals like that with the radio station, hired the hall, and then paid Bobby his fee.

Of course, Mike Belsen, Bobby's agent at the time, would try to put together a geographically reasonable weekend. We wouldn't want to fly to Seattle, Albany, and Tallahassee, for instance, because of the distances involved.

When we first started touring, Sonny Jones, our road manager (who worked with Bobby on "Brides"), would go in ahead of us and rehearse a local band to accompany Bobby. That became too unreliable, so we started traveling with a drummer and a lead guitarist and filled in with local musicians. Little by little, we built up to an entire group—a seven-piece band.

The first concert, in 1969, took place in the Anaheim Convention Center, where about 15,000 fans attended each of two sold-out shows. I had a great opening act, a then relatively unknown Steve Martin, who performed his balloon act to an impatient and unappreciative audience. All during his act, the fans kept yelling, "We want Bobby. We want Bobby."

I had witnessed some of that wild response on "Shindig." I was prepared for it, but I didn't expect it to be so massive. I found it all mind-boggling because I was watching 15,000 kids go berserk. I thought the response was just a fluke at the first concert. Then it happened every place I went—Detroit, Seattle, Buffalo.

At the start, when I had only one or two hits, I sang other people's songs. I always ended the concert with "What'd I Say?" because it was a crowd pleaser. The song also symbolized my first big break in show business.

I could have been singing about anything. I've said it many times: I could have lip-synced a Supremes record in concert. The kids wouldn't have known the difference, because they were screaming so loudly!

After the first concert at Anaheim, we created a security manual of precautions that had to be taken. We gave the security notes to Disneyland when I was booked to do a concert there, but they ignored them.

Disneyland had sold out a special attendance evening so that only 18,000 people could be admitted to the park. However, when the capacity crowd showed up, most of them streamed into Tomorrowland to see me perform. We almost had a riot on our hands.

The Disney people didn't know what to do. Ward had warned them that their crowd control setup wasn't going to work. They said, "Don't tell us about crowd control. Last week we had Ferrante and Teicher." Ward just said, "It's not going to work." Halfway through the first song for the first show, kids swarmed the stage.

While I was trying to sing the first chorus of "Easy Come, Easy Go," some poor kids passed out from excitement. They were handing kids up past me to take them out of the park. More kids passed out, and others scrambled up on stage.

The Disney management finally listened to Ward, and they worked it all out. They ordered employees to rush over from different parts of the park. That looked funny to me because you're not supposed to see someone in Adventureland costumes over in Tomorrowland and vice versa. It's a Disneyland taboo.

We performed the second show with no problems, and the Disney people seemed satisfied. At least, they asked us back again. The next concert sold out as well—but by that time they knew they needed security at the stage. By then, I knew Bobby Sherman fans could go ballistic.

I learned to expect crowd hysteria, but why it happened still puzzles me. I always found the audience's reactions fascinating, particularly when I noticed a pattern.

Radio stations that promoted the concerts held contests for ten front-row seats. The winners had passes to come backstage before the show and meet me. Invariably, they would come back with their parents and with their albums for autographing.

I'd greet each one of them and say, "Hi. What's your name?"
(In a tiny voice) "Brenda."
"Hi, Brenda. How are you?"
(Tinier voice) "I'm fine."
As many times as we did this, the girls were the same. Very shy. Very demure. I would sign their albums and say, "Well, I hope you enjoy the show."
(Tiniest voice) "Thank you."

It was the same scenario with all the winners. Then I'd say, "You have front-row seats. So, I'll be looking for you." Out they'd go.

"AND NOW, WHAT YOU'VE BEEN WAITING FOR . . . BOOOOBBBBY SHERMANNNNN!!!!!!!!"

I'd spring out on stage singing "Easy Come, Easy Go," look down at the first row, and see those ten contest winners up in front, hysterically screaming, crying, and jumping up and down. A mere ten minutes before, they had been sweet, adorable little angels. Now they were going completely out of their minds.

After their trip backstage, the contest winners returned to join their peers possessing a special knowledge that the rest of the audience did not have. Their hysteria seemed greater than anyone else's because I had shaken their hands or given them a kiss on the cheek; I imagine the excitement felt a lot more tangible for them. When everyone else started screaming, the contest winners were leading the madness.

I thought this would have been a great thesis had I continued my work in child psychology. What is that mass hysteria, that contagious something? It was remarkable.

One night, I learned how much I had become accustomed to hysteria. We were booked into the theater of the Broadmoor Hotel, an old-fashioned resort in Colorado Springs, Colorado. The Broadmoor guests were an older audience, and the kids that did show up must have been taught to be polite and quiet.

"I don't understand. I can actually hear myself, even though the house is full," I thought, completely puzzled. I performed extra hard to work up the kids. They stayed polite just as long as they could stand it. Finally, they started rushing the stage, and I felt better.

Even though we expected kids to rush the stage, we never knew what new component might add to our security concerns. When we played at a fair in Detroit, the heat gave us more to worry about.

Ward

The weather was terribly hot and humid, and the girls were crowding in around the stage. We always tried to have some kind of an open area in front since we feared the little girls could end up crushed against the stage. Somehow, the perimeter failed and girls were, indeed, in danger of being crushed. To make matters worse, they were fainting from heat prostration.

The people backstage said, "There's no way we can take them out through the crowd. When we see a girl faint out front, we'll have to lift her up to the stage and take her out through the back."

So when the first three little girls fainted, security lifted them up on the stage. Of course everybody else in the front row then figured out, "THAT'S THE WAY TO GET ON THE STAGE! I'LL JUST FAINT!" Suddenly, there were kids laid out all over the stage! It looked like Night of the Living Dead! *Once they made it up on the stage, they'd come to life and start chasing Bobby.*

More than anything, the fans wanted me to notice them. If they could reach the stage, they would. If they could attract my attention by throwing a teddy bear, they would try that, too. Somehow, certain items became "official" things to bring to the concerts.

At one of the first concerts *Tiger Beat* covered, pictures of stuffed animals strewn across the stage started the idea. I certainly never said, "Boy, I can't wait to get some more stuffed animals." Collecting presents actually created logistical problems at concerts, because everything we received had to be removed when we left. I would never dream of leaving a gift behind, but we couldn't carry it all with us either. We gave the little animals to children's hospitals, so at least they had a home.

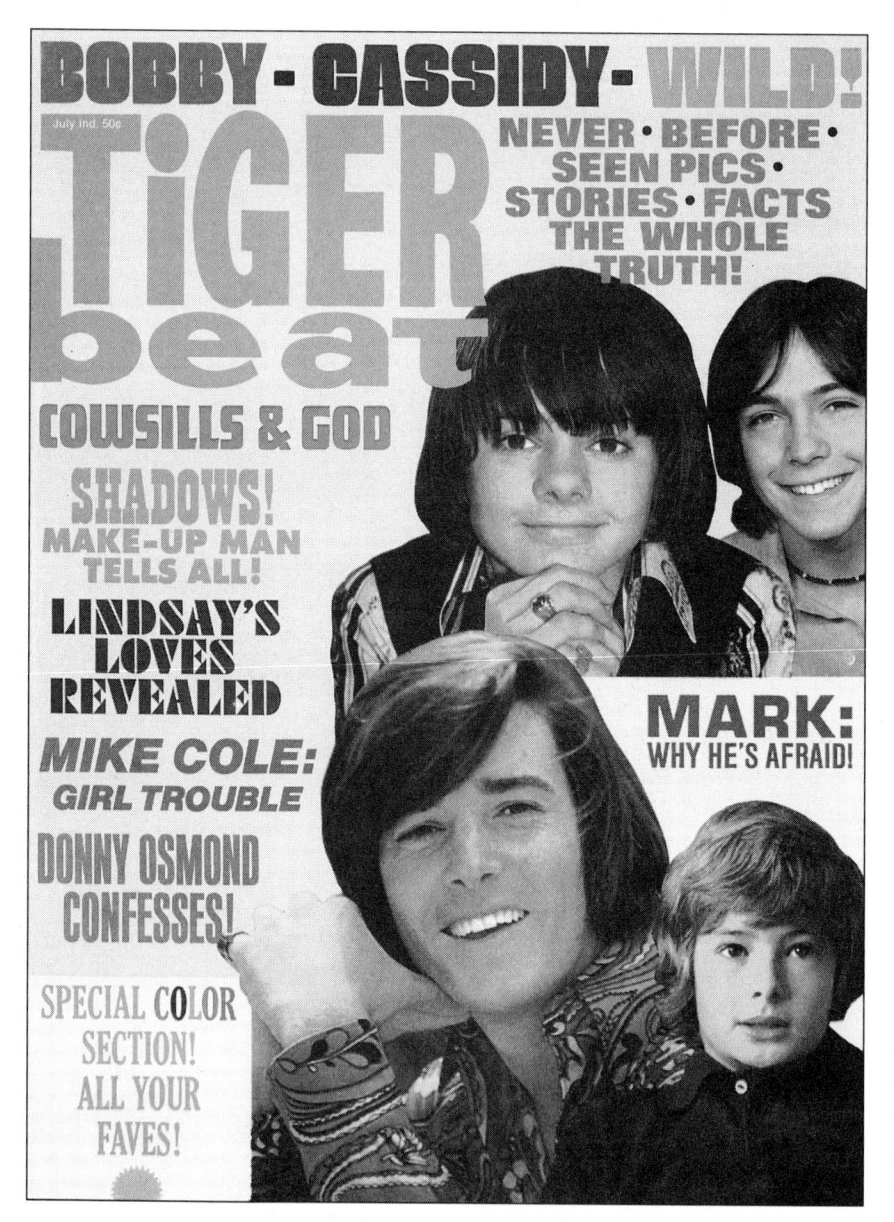

It wasn't the presents, but the emotions behind them that touched me deeply. When fans said they loved me, they meant it with all their hearts. They weren't attending just any concert; they were attending a Bobby Sherman concert. That's all they focused on for weeks.

On stage, I could see only about three rows back because I was staring into a Super Trouper, a big blinding spotlight. Beyond three rows back, I just saw flashcubes. Some kids showed great innovation, though. They brought "We Love You Bobby" or "Will You Marry Me?" signs and lit them up with flashlights. They were pretty clever.

The marriage proposals from twelve-year-old kids were just a fantasy and I understood that. If I had said to one of those young girls, "Hey, I'm going to take you up on that," I think she might have fainted. I knew those were the thoughts behind the signs, but I was there to entertain them—not to take advantage of them.

Actually, the role I often took on was that of older brother rather than boyfriend. The median age for fans who attended my concerts was ten to twelve. Every now and then I'd run into a clique of fans who were seventeen, eighteen, or nineteen, but that was a totally different situation!

The concerts marked a special time in my life. On any given night, I might sing in front of fifteen or twenty thousand kids. Half the fun of it for me was seeing them. The audience watched me, and I watched the audience.

In spite of the crowds and the chaos, I had a one-on-one relationship with my audience. Often, a parent was commandeered to take a whole group from a neighborhood. The kids outnumbered the adults by a margin of five to one.

Regardless of the numbers, I was still with them as individuals, and they felt they were with me. A camaraderie developed in that we were all there together. They knew me and I knew them. We were having fun and that was the intent.

On one occasion, though, there was a setup to catch me doing something wrong. I have no idea who instigated it, but a fourteen-year-old girl was somehow going to try to gain access to my hotel room. Then a police officer was supposed to come in and say, "What are you doing here with a minor?"

Catching Bobby Sherman in questionable circumstances with an underage girl would have made the headlines. However, she never made it past security. Busting me would have been a big coup because I had earned an "all-American innocent" reputation. I knew just one hint of scandal would have destroyed my career—along with the faith of many fans.

In a few cities, older girls hung out with the band, often because they wanted to reach me. I attended parties thrown by the band on only a few occasions. First of all, I was simply too tired. Second, I never wanted to be in a potentially compromising situation. Although the girls at those parties did seem older, I sometimes noticed they had beer in their hands, and I didn't want trouble. So I stayed for a brief time only.

Sonny, our road manager, understood the need to protect me, and he helped keep me out of anything even remotely improper. Sonny was a sweetheart of a guy, genuine and dependable. Sadly, he died a few years ago from complications caused by smoking.

Sonny worked on the "Brides" four days a week. Then, on Fridays, he went to our next concert site and set up arrangements for the weekend. Ron Boutwell, who handled merchandising at the concerts, also joined us on weekends. Ron sold Bobby Sherman posters and souvenir books. He did well for himself with that business, later going on to do merchandising for KISS, Police, and the Osmonds.

After the first couple of months touring, we had our entourage of eleven in place: seven band members, Sonny, Ron Boutwell, Ward, and myself.

Ward

Most of the time, Bobby was shooting "Here Come the Brides" during the week; so we could do Friday-night concerts only at nearby locations. Usually, we would play a Saturday night and a Sunday matinee and still have him home in time for filming on Monday.

The poor band, on the other hand, was driving from town to town. We flew in and out, but the band would be piled in their little Volkswagen vans driving from one place to the next.

The band had two or three vehicles that formed a caravan to the concerts since we had so much equipment to transport. I rarely saw them except on stage.

Because we tried to make the songs on stage sound as close to the recordings as possible, I didn't need to practice with the band very often. We rehearsed only when we added new songs to the

With Ward (at left) and Sonny Jones (at right) on tour.

show. We wrote the song order on the heads of the drums. That way, I could just walk back behind Freddy Alwaeg, our drummer, to see where we were.

Freddy was extremely talented. A lively, animated performer, he ended up attracting a fan club of his own. Not too long ago, I ran into him, and he jokingly asked, "When are we going out on the road again?"

The question-and-answer period of the show always led into the song, "I'm Still Looking for the Right Girl," because a girl would inevitably ask, "Are you married?" And I'd say, "No, I'm not married, and do you want to know why?" Then we'd go into the song.

As time went along, we added songs from my albums, and, of course, we highlighted the hits. My favorites were "Easy Come, Easy Go," "Julie, Do Ya' Love Me?," "Cried Like a Baby," and "Jennifer."

I did think a number of the songs we put on the albums were good. "The Lady Is Waiting," was a romantic song. I liked "One Too Many Mornings" by Bob Dylan, too.

As long as we had at least one hit on an album, the record company stayed happy because that's what sold the album. I felt happy because I could include songs of mine that I wanted to use. I chose the songs for the albums, and I almost always recorded songs I wanted to sing.

The exception was "I'm in a Tree," which was from a Broadway show Metromedia had financed. They wanted me to record it as a favor to them, but it was awful. The day I recorded it, Ward stood there along with Dick Bogart, our engineer. I just looked at them, shaking my head.

"They've got to be kidding here," I said.

The song, about what life would be like in a tree, was written as a straight soliloquy. I had nowhere to go with it, so I tried to make it funny, adding some dialogue. I did it for them, but I hated it.

I had no talent for picking out million sellers. The only song I felt sure was going to be a hit was "Easy Come, Easy Go." After that, I stopped trying to guess what would be popular. When "Julie" came out, it just took off. "Julie" became the fastest climber we ever had. Both the single and the album just skyrocketed to the top of the charts.

Overall, I ended up with four gold singles and five gold albums. I keep them framed on my living room wall. One day, just out of curiosity, I took one of the gold records out and put it on the record player to see what it sounded like.

A Homer and Jethro song blared back at me.

And then it dawned on me. They just take an old master from somebody that's not being printed anymore and they goldplate it. They put my label on someone else's album. At that time, they were still stamping out my records.

The more records I made, the more concerts we performed. We learned to be efficient with our time. We also began to understand what kind of audiences we were playing to and all the details involved in the machinery of the concerts. Experience was our best teacher.

On the day of a concert, everything went like clockwork. Ward would go to the theater earlier in the day and make a sketch of the layout of the stage. Then he'd come to my hotel room and go over any special information I needed. Because I was confined to my hotel room, I rarely had the opportunity to see the theater or stage before the concert. Ward's diagrams were invaluable in terms of knowing what I would be dealing with.

To avoid a public scene, when we left the hotel for the show, we generally went down in a service elevator. Some of them smelled pretty rank because they were used to transport garbage. I rarely walked through a hotel lobby. I went through a kitchen or through some less public route. Then I stepped into a waiting car, and we went to wherever the theater was.

Generally, we arrived at the hall after the band had played as an opening act for about forty-five minutes. That way, the audience was already inside. Sometimes kids stood around outside because they didn't have tickets. That made me wince. I wondered whether they had tried to buy the tickets and the show had been sold out, or whether they simply couldn't afford a ticket. They often were stationed in different spots and any time they saw a car, they'd run after it.

If there was a way to drive into the theater, we drove in. Security whisked me out and took me to my dressing room right away. I always arrived at the theater dressed for the concert.

The backstage areas were typically anything but glamorous. Corridors to the dressing rooms or out to the stage were usually painted gray or industrial white, bathed in the dingy glow of fluorescent lighting.

The dressing rooms ranged from almost elegant to merely functional—but always overflowing with gifts. Bouquets of flowers scented the rooms, and mountains of gooey baked goods awaited me.

Sometimes, the promoter and the promoter's family wanted to say hello, so I greeted them on the way in. Ward and the security people kept things moving along.

Meanwhile, I could hear the screaming going on in the theater. I'd try to take a minute and collect my wits. After looking around, Ward would come back to check in with me. He would tell me how the house looked in terms of attendance and what radio station needed to be acknowledged. Most important, he reminded me what city we were in, a tiny detail to which I often was oblivious.

During intermission, we met the contest winners from the radio stations. After that, I waited just offstage. If it was a proscenium, Ward took me to a point where I couldn't be seen, and then the disc jockey would introduce me. Later on, though, we cut the introductions. The poor guys would have a chance to say only the introductory words, "AND NOW . . ." and the audience would explode.

During those few minutes before I went on, the noise was so overwhelming I couldn't hear anything. I couldn't talk. I could hardly think. Through gestures, I would check things out with the band. A lot of times, Freddy or Sonny would signal to me just before I walked out on stage. Thumbs up. "This is a good audience."

I had to start the adrenaline going so I could stay out there and give the audience the best show I could. I'd already be in high gear and ready to go.

The band would start playing "Easy Come, Easy Go," and I'd wait for it to vamp a bit because it heightened the energy that was going on in the audience. For those few minutes, while I listened to the band, I was waiting for the right moment to go out. I could sense when the moment should be. When I felt the excitement build to a pitch, I walked out onstage.

Once on stage, I gave the band cues about when I wanted to go into a vamp, stop the vamp, keep going, or stop the song.

Usually, some fans found a way past security. Once one of them came up on the stage, I wasn't going to ignore her. If the distance seemed too great, I reached down to shake the girl's hand, or, if she was close enough, I knelt down and gave her a kiss on the cheek. The moment that happened, everybody wanted to try. Then the fans stormed the stage.

Sometimes we had to interrupt the show because the fans were jamming the aisle, creating a fire hazard. Someone would come out and say, "We're going to have to stop the show unless you all go back to your seats." That threat always worked.

During the hour I was onstage, I never stopped moving. Within the first few minutes, perspiration turned my costume into a steamsuit. Still, I kept going, as I siphoned energy from the kids. Their excitement energized me.

"What'd I Say" was always the last song. I'd divide the audience down the middle and they would yell against each other. We kept vamping that until I felt they were exhausted—or I was. Then I'd give the peace sign a couple of times, blow kisses, and off I'd go.

The band was still playing and everyone thought I was coming back out for an encore. Instead, I went directly to the car, and we left immediately. The band kept playing for a few minutes to make sure we were clear and then it was announced . . .

"Bobby has left the auditorium."

The only time I ever remember not having a great time during a concert was once in San Diego. I had thrown my back out a day or so before. I worried that I wasn't going to be able to give a good show because I was in a lot of pain. But the fans pulled me through it. Once on stage, the pain was forgotten as my energy level increased.

After the concerts, my adrenaline levels must have been off the scales. I was constantly moving on stage; I then raced into the car to leave, and we hurried back to the hotel.

It was like being a fighter. If you're a good fighter, the adrenaline's up before a fight. You walk out and you've been trained to do twelve rounds. You throw one punch, and your opponent's down—and you've still got twelve rounds of energy in you. That's what it seemed like. I'd give an hour-long show, but I always tried to have enough energy for an hour and a half.

Ward

I always stood at the side of the stage from which we would leave, so Bobby didn't have to think about which side to make his exit.

> *Ice, cokes, and towels were the only things we asked for in the dressing room. When Bobby came off the stage at the end of the show, I would have two towels ready in the back seat of the car. He was hot and sweaty, so we'd have one dry towel and one towel dipped in ice water from the ice that had melted around the cokes.*

Usually, I wound up back at the hotel at a decent hour because we didn't want to keep the kids out past ten o'clock. Back in my room, I'd turn the television on and lose myself in whatever was on. I'd watch shows like "I Love Lucy" reruns and let the energy burn itself out. Then, I'd order something light, like hors d'oeuvres from room service, have a drink, put my feet up, relax, and let my mind go blank.

During that time, I also came down from the noise I had experienced. I knew my ears had been overloaded. The aftereffect of the screams and the amplified sound on stage was like being in the middle of cannon fire. The ringing subsided gradually within that hour and a half. By 11:30 P.M., I was ready to crash. Then I slept like a baby.

The effects of the noise were cumulative. After doing the concerts for a year, I found myself tone-deaf to certain frequencies. When the fans screamed at concerts, they screamed at a certain pitch, decibel level, and frequency that went right through me. I could almost cut it, the sound became so thick. I don't know how it sounded in the audience, but from my perspective on stage, all those screams directed at me came across as the world's largest loudspeaker.

I have permanent hearing loss from the noise at concerts. The band had to turn up the volume so that we could hear what we were doing. In response, the kids screamed louder, so then the band juiced up more until our amps were all up on ten.

I heard it all from the front and the back of the stage, and the noise level was painful. On a recent physical for the police department, they did a routine check of my hearing. When I asked how it was, all they said was, "Could be better!"

Still, the positives far outweighed the negatives. I loved being with the audience. I truly enjoyed the level of performance, the rush from being at the center of it all. In spite of the physical toll the concerts took, the pleasant aspects of touring introduced me to absolute luxury.

The promoters wanted me to be happy. I always said I didn't require a limousine. At the very least, however, we could count on a big, comfortable sedan.

Travel became as smooth as possible. We never walked through airports or checked bags like everybody else. Everything was always prearranged. I was whisked right onto the plane or into a holding area such as a VIP lounge.

Plane trips meant a rest for me. When we flew on airlines, we always traveled in first class. I looked out the plane windows, daydreamed, and wrote song lyrics.

For lodging, I often had suites or even presidential suites. In the hotels, we kept our people together as much as possible. Ward usually had a room next to mine, and we had security nearby. We tried to make sure that the rooms on either side of me were for our traveling group, because girls sometimes tried to rent them. Precautionary arrangements taken care of, our thoughts usually turned to room service. I especially loved the Riviera Hotel in Atlanta. Designed like a two-story townhouse, my suite contained three bedrooms, with a bar and a living room downstairs. It was absolutely beautiful and boasted outstanding room service. In addition, the management couldn't have been more accommodating.

Every now and then, we'd find something unusual that made going to a particular city more special. I liked the Tower East in Chicago because it offered room service from the Chicago branch of Maxim's of Paris, located on the first floor of the hotel. The suites were beautiful, but it was the food that brought me there. Eggs Benedict. I could taste them on the flight in. I purposely passed up a meal on the plane just to have eggs Benedict when I arrived there.

Ward

Ordering room service there was like eating in the restaurant. The maitre'd would arrive with the menus. Waiters came up to the suite and served the meal in courses. It was wonderful.

Sometimes it wasn't the food but the cultural differences that made a place memorable, as on our tour of Japan.

I had done a television commercial for a Japanese company, promoting a then-new bubble gum called Haris Bon, which had a liquid center. The commercial had been running on Japanese television, as was "Here Come the Brides," so we had a large following there.

We played several Japanese cities, including Tokyo and Kyoto. I felt good about the concerts. The Japanese audiences started out acting very polite, but I found I could work them up if I tried.

Between shows, I watched Japanese television for entertainment. I had nothing else to do. Television shows were not in English, so Ward and I amused ourselves by watching American shows dubbed in Japanese.

Seeing Jeremy Bolt stuttering in Japanese was a highlight, I must admit! I was flipping channels when we happened onto a sumo wrestling tournament. A whole new art form materialized for me.

Our translator explained the art of sumo wrestling, an extremely stylized form involving two unusually heavy men. It's very involved and ritualistic. I found it fascinating, and we started watching every available match. I missed the sport when we came home.

Ward

We couldn't go sightseeing because Bobby was always recognized in Japan. So we became engrossed in watching the sumo tournament. We learned who the favorites were and developed favorites of our own. It was like the World Series there!

By the time the tour ended, we had become such fans we were extending the intermission during concerts so we could see the end of the match before Bobby went on.

"Intermission's almost over," the promoter would say.

"Okay. Okay. Just give us two more minutes," Bobby would plead.

The wealthy businessmen who brought us to Japan wanted to show us the traditional Japanese style of entertaining at a geisha house. I learned the business geisha houses are not brothels. The idea is to be entertained and pampered, have wonderful food, and play parlor games.

I was the guest of honor at an important dinner at one geisha house where we took off our shoes and sat on the floor. The traditionally garbed women who served us brought food and hot towels and tried to make pleasant conversation, albeit in Japanese. It was late and I was hungry.

The room was filled with Japanese diplomats and businessmen. I'm sure this dinner cost thousands of dollars. I was trying to be gracious and very conscious of not doing anything to offend anyone, as courtesy is highly valued in Japan.

What no one knew is that I hate seafood.

Needless to say, the first course was raw fish. Everyone waited for me, as the guest of honor, to begin before they could start eating.

I started moving things around on the plate to make it look like I was doing something. To my dismay, the next two courses they brought out also were fish. Finally, the fourth course emerged, a nice noodle soup—or so I thought.

I was starving. I was ready to take a big gulp of my soup when Ward caught my eye and shook his head, "NO."

I looked at the soup again and realized that the noodles had little eyes.

The "noodles" were unborn baby eels, a great delicacy in Japan.

So I filled up on tea and sake. I'd had virtually nothing to eat. When it came time to play parlor games, easy icebreakers along the lines of "paper, scissors, rock," nobody proved more animated than I was! They thought me a good sport. Nobody knew I was looped!

The larger the city we visited, the more freedom I had. New York is like Los Angeles. New Yorkers are used to celebrities. I could walk down the streets and not have a problem, but if I ended up near the arena where they were expecting me, chaos erupted. The diehard fans usually congregated near the arena where I was performing.

If a fan saw me, alone or with a friend, she would be cool. If ten or twenty or thirty fans saw me, however, the whole atmosphere changed. It became much more difficult to handle. I could always tell by their reactions whether the situation had a potential to get out of hand. If I said, "Look, don't worry. I'll be happy to sign autographs for everyone, so there's no need to push," they would calm right down. That worked fine for small groups, but I did worry about kids' safety at the concerts.

We had only one bad accident in the three years we were on the road. The proscenium for one of the stages we used could be lifted. As a result, space underneath the stage opened when the stage rose.

We had done everything we knew to do. We warned everybody, and we had extra security. In spite of all our precautions, however, inevitably, the audience rushed the stage. They ended up squeezing one little girl right under the stage, breaking her leg. We went to the hospital where she had been transported to see that she was okay. I gave her albums and some other presents, but the whole incident shook me. I never really feared for myself, but I sure worried for the fans.

In contrast to concerts today, our security concerns were mild. My concerts were crime-free and certainly drug-free. I wasn't into the drug scene, and neither were my fans.

As I became more and more successful, obviously plenty of money was available as well as all kinds of drugs. But I felt a sense of responsibility to my audience. First of all, I was working virtually seven days a week. I couldn't afford to get wasted, and I probably would have had an adverse reaction to it, anyway. Most important, I felt that taking drugs would have been a big letdown to myself and to my fans. For these and other reasons, I have never had an interest in drugs.

All along I had been saying, "Don't take drugs. You don't need it, you can be naturally high." If the fans were going to follow what I said, I should back up my words with my actions. I stayed away from the drug scene, and I'm glad I did.

Everything about the concerts seemed fast and furious. It was more like a nonstop roller coaster, not a merry-go-round. A merry-go-round just circles in place, usually to easygoing music.

MY GREATEST FEAR
by Bobby Sherman

Of all the famous faves that ever were no fave has loved his fans more than Bobby Sherman loves YOU! That is why he is about to reach a very important decision—to QUIT touring! Why? Because he places your welfare above his career! At every place Bobby stops during tours he is mobbed by fans, and he is afraid that one day one of you will be seriously hurt by the careless few who overlook the safety of others in their excitement to get to him! Bobby is determined that this will never happen for it would break his heart. Read now in his very own words why he feels he must QUIT!

In contrast, what I felt with all the constant ups and downs and fast curves was like a rocket-powered roller coaster.

Very seldom did I have the luxury to sit down, put my feet up for a couple of days, and reflect on what was going on. Literally, Ward had to come up beside me, point, and say, "This is what you're doing next." In the middle of the excitement, I felt happy but somewhat dazed. I didn't have the opportunity to enjoy it until the chaos began to taper down.

To the fans, the memory lingers on. They saw the merry-go-round. I saw the roller coaster.

Now that I look back on those times, I'm glad I took that ride.

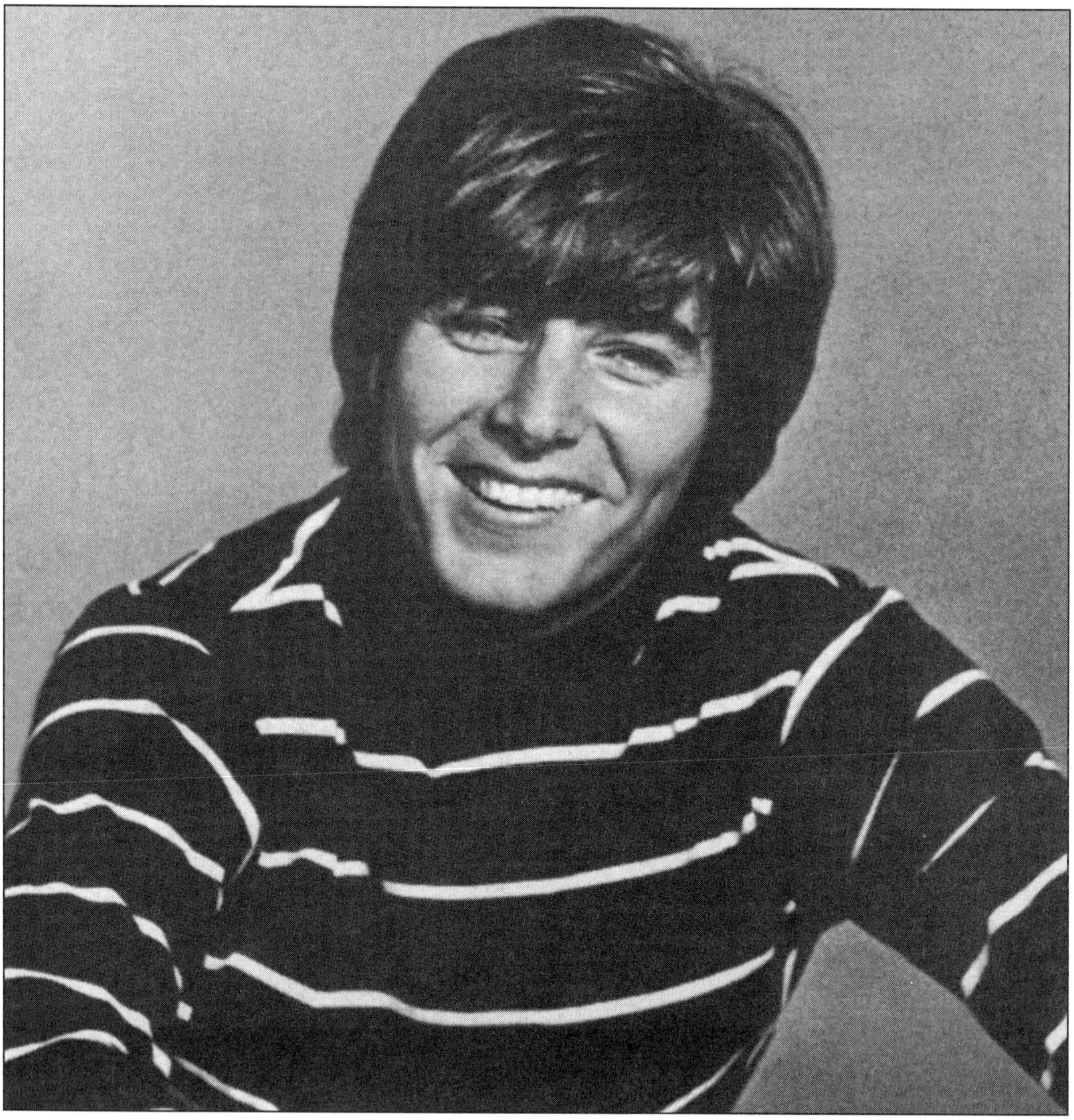

10 The Groovy Fans

On "Shindig," I was Bobby Sherman, just the house singer. The record buyers at that time were teenagers, but they weren't necessarily MY audience. They were the "Shindig" audience. On "Brides," however, the fans who liked me instantly became my record-buying audience. Because of them, my records quickly became top sellers.

Fan magazines used my photos for their covers. My likeness decorated lunch boxes filled with bologna sandwiches and Twinkies. Mothers cried over spilled cereal after kids cut out my records on the backs of cereal boxes, and giant posters of me plastered the walls of pink-frilled and decoupage-decorated bedrooms across the country.

Ward

Ed Justin was in charge of merchandising for Columbia Pictures. If a manufacturer wanted to make a Bobby Sherman lunch box or poster, Ed would license them for a royalty on sales. He had worked with me on "The Monkees" and understood the teen-idol phenomenon. He knew the kind of manufacturers who would be interested.

Bobby had the right to approve what merchandise bore his name and likeness. The Monkees didn't, but I had learned my lesson by that time. We drew the line at pillowcases and underwear.

I soon learned that the fans bought not only my records, but ANYTHING with my name or picture on it. With the concerts came souvenir books, comic books, and, of course, love beads.

When fans sent in the love beads, I let *Tiger Beat* take pictures of me wearing them, which brought still more beads. The same thing happened with the "Bobby Sherman choker" when I was doing "Getting Together." I considered the chokers a little effeminate, but I found out later that a lot of guys wore them. The choker became a fashion statement. Like earrings now, it was a unisex style.

Charles Laufer, discussing love beads sold in *Tiger Beat*

The love beads started with the Monkees. Then we repeated with Bobby. In those days, the magic price for kids for mail order was one dollar.

I never thought of myself as a trendsetter. I mostly concerned myself with the work I was doing. To be honest, in my personal life I never gave clothes or accessory items much thought at all. Fans sent me many of the items I wore.

Aside from what we collected at concerts, I received thousands of handmade gifts. Fans sent me everything from scrapbooks filled with carefully clipped and pasted articles about me, to necklaces made of bubble-gum wrappers, to rings made from a bent spoon. I could tell they had invested huge amounts of time in creating these gifts.

The fans also developed a mini-art form. Girls brought giant banners to the concerts. Some of those signs were quite impressive, almost half a row long. One girl might have made the banner, and five or six friends helped her hold it up. Seeing those signs out in the audience, I tried to acknowledge them specifically so that the owners of the banners knew I could see their work. I wanted them to realize that I appreciated the time and effort they put into creating something so involved.

My fans were extremely loyal. They seemed to think it was their job to write letters. Writing to me was their way of having contact. I started receiving fan mail in the early sixties when I was doing local Los Angeles television shows like "Ninth Street West" and "Hollywood-A-Go-Go" before "Shindig." I felt flattered.

In grammar school, girls used to send me anonymous notes that said "I love you." I can remember looking around, thinking, "Where did this come from?" That happened often, and I was flattered but embarrassed by it.

So when the fan mail started, it wasn't the first time I had received notes from girls. Only this time I was receiving correspondence from people I'd never met. Again, I was flattered.

It also surprised me that people would be moved enough through the medium of television to take the time to write to me. At first, I answered all the mail I received personally. I took all the attention to heart.

Several years later, I was still surprised when tremendous amounts of mail started flowing in for "Brides." When we began working on the pilot, I overheard Steve Blauner and Asa Clark, the editor of the show, talking about me.

"This kid's going to be a star."

I wondered if they were flattering me because they knew I could hear them, or if they really meant it.

Then, "Bobby's getting a lot of attention," was the scuttlebutt I heard, and I wondered what it all meant. I soon found out.

NOW! IT CAN BE YOURS!

BOBBY'S CHOKER NECK BAND!

Imagine, you can own this stunning neck band! It's black suede with gold trim! Guaranteed to add just the touch you're looking for at school, on dates, or anywhere. Each neck band is adjustable to any neck size so you can be sure to have that special choker look!

Bobby's been wearing his choker neck band for TV shows, concert appearances and constantly in his personal life. He received so many letters on where to find them that it became necessary to offer them to you through the mail!

SO NOW'S THE TIME! ADD THE 'IN' LOOK TO EVERY OUTFIT!

Bobby knows best! Please send me Bobby's Choker Neck Band. I enclose $2.00 for each band I want. Add 25¢ for postage and handling.

NAME
ADDRESS
CITY
STATE   ZIP

Send to: Bobby's Neck Band
Suite 600
1800 N. Highland Ave.,
GT1   Hollywood, California 90028

BOBBY WRITES TO YOU

Now YOU Can Have True Friends!

Hi Babe!

I see your face from the stage. You're right there in front, or maybe off to the side, and you're smiling and laughing with me, and sometimes singing along. You're happy when you're with me, though you only get to be there an hour. You're my friend and I wish I could take you home!

You'd like that because I don't think you have enough friends. If you pull at my hair or tear my clothes, then I know for certain that you don't have a boyfriend. And I also know you well enough to say that you're not happy the way you are. You'd like to be more popular! Right?

If you find yourself turning off the lights at night, laying down in your bed and tears welling up in your eyes, big wet pleas for people to care about you, to like you, to be near you so you won't be alone . . . well, please dry your tears because you have a friend who knows what it means. Me.

I WAS SHY

I used to be so shy that I dreaded going into a room alone. I didn't know how to act to the people. In fact, I avoided people and spent a lot of time working by myself at home, just so I didn't have to be around others. That's why I built that scale model of Disneyland. It gave me something to do alone.

But then I realized that other people were having fun and I wasn't. Other people had friends to care about them and I didn't. They HAD friends and WERE friends. I was neither!

Many nights I stayed at home and the tears would pour down the sides of my face. Really . . . I'm not putting you on. I actually used to sit down and really cry because I was so miserable. I couldn't figure out why someone, anyone, didn't come up to me and say, "Hi, I'm your friend. Come join me."

MUST BE WORTHY

Then I realized something very difficult to grasp when you first hear it. YOU HAVE TO BE WORTH HAVING AS A FRIEND. You have to be a full person, not a little mouse who sits in the corner of the classroom and rarely raises her hand or smiles or talks. People won't dislike you if you do that. They'll simply *forget* you. That's worse!

It takes a lot of effort from people to DISLIKE you. You really have to do something bad, repeatedly, for the dislike to stick. Chances are, you think you don't have any friends and people dislike you. Really, they just don't notice you or think about you. Change that!

I told you I was shy. Well, I decided I'd change my life. I began to sing . . . and look where it's gotten me! But at first, it was just my way of getting outside myself so people could see me.

CHANGE YOURSELF

I made a little list for you of ways you can do the same thing:
1. Be kind, honest and tactful.
2. If you can't be beautiful, be well-groomed.
3. Dress tastefully and stay slim.
4. SMILE and TALK.
5. Put all your energy into what you do.
6. Learn to dance, sing or play an instrument.
7. Think for yourself but respect rules.

And now I want you to repeat after me the following pledge:

I WILL NOT BE A MOUSE. I WILL TALK, SMILE AND LAUGH WITH PEOPLE. I WILL GO PLACES AND DO THINGS.

I think the problem with most unhappy people is that they keep to themselves, all closed up like a closet. No one wants to walk into a closet— and likewise no one wants to have a dull friend.

Tears on your pillow will be a thing of the past if you let people know you. But you have to go to them. Don't expect them to suddenly start paying attention to you. You have to lead the way!

You might not even have a chance to write to me once you've gotten out in the world and become a popular person. But I hope you'll try.

Until we're together,

Lots of love,

Bobby

About three episodes of "Brides" had aired before the first mail appeared. Apparently, a large percentage of it had to be forwarded from the local television stations. We found that the response was more immediate than we first thought. The first mail that arrived was generated by the very first show. People were instantly touched by Jeremy and Candy.

The response pleased me, but I didn't care how much mail came in. My job was to give the fans who were writing the letters

The Groovy Fans

as much "quality Bobby Sherman" as I possibly could. I made sure that I could be proud of the records I put out; I felt the same way about my work on "Brides." I wanted to do the best I could to make sure that Jeremy was presented with integrity. Period.

I will say that when I went out for concerts, I wanted to know how big an audience we had each night. The size of the audience became a barometer of my success. The letters provided additional information.

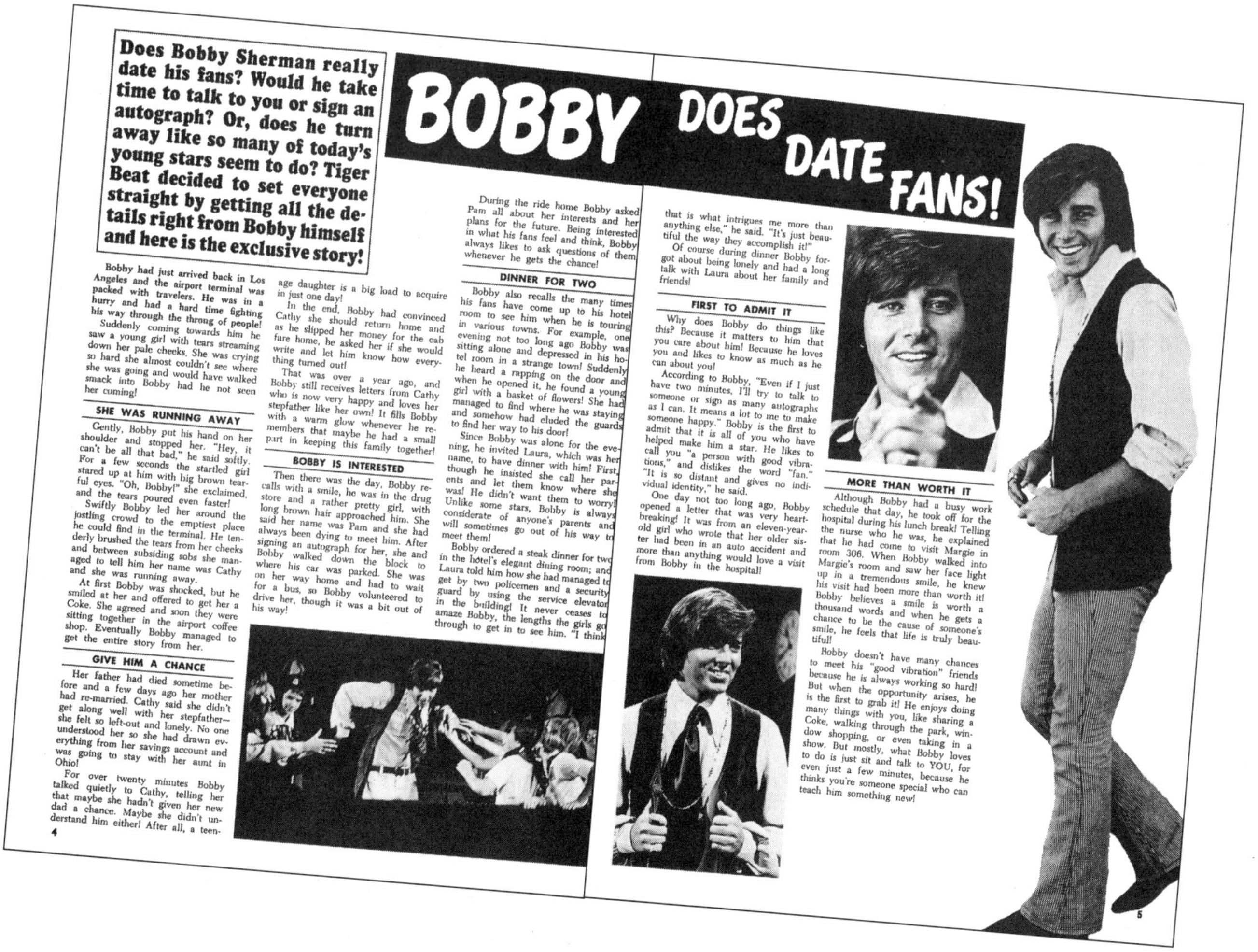

Mail had been pouring into the *Tiger Beat* offices, Metromedia Records, and Screen Gems. At one point, I was receiving 25,000 letters a week! The fans were so young, impressionable, and enthusiastic, that they weren't just writing one letter, they were writing a letter every day. Although there may have been a certain amount of redundancy, the letters certainly had an enormous impact at ABC and Screen Gems.

I could no longer answer the mail personally. Even so, quite a lot of it wound up in my hands because of hardship cases. If a fan was writing on behalf of a friend and the situation turned out to be legitimate, then I would make a follow-up call or send a special note.

I wanted to make sure all the young fans' feelings were protected, and I wanted to make sure they knew I understood their feelings. One time in Tennessee, a fan had been unable to attend the concert. Apparently, because of a car accident, she'd recently had her leg amputated. The mayor of the city heard about the accident.

As we were preparing to leave town, the mayor came to my hotel room and, to my astonishment, said he was placing me under arrest.

I said, "What???" Then he told me about this girl.

"I'm putting you under arrest. You must come and see her."

"I'll be happy to come and see her," I said. "The only thing I'm concerned about is catching our plane to fly on to the next concert."

"Don't worry about that."

So off we went, lights and sirens leading us to the hospital. The visit with a devoted fan was very moving for all of us. Then we made our way to the airport. Sure enough, the mayor had kept the plane there.

I tried to avoid having those incidents reported in the press. I didn't want publicity or pats on the back for doing what little I could in response to other people's hardships.

In most cases, the huge influx of fan mail was answered by a mailing service. That way, the fans could at least get a postcard with my picture on it.

Although I received mail from fans of all ages, during "Brides," the median age was about twelve, younger than my fans from "Shindig," who had been high school and college age. The fans for "Brides" were grammar school, junior high, and some high school students. The oldest fans were "senior citizens" of eighteen or nineteen.

The older girls usually inquired about something more than an autograph. Virtually all the mail I received had gone through other people's hands, and I only heard about some of the more colorful requests.

The vast majority of romantic letters followed the line: "I love you. I want to marry you and have your baby." Some girls of eighteen or nineteen wrote to tell me that they were ready for their first sexual experience, and they wanted me to be their lover.

I never responded to those letters. I had no way of knowing if they were a setup or what motive was behind the thought. I did understand the request, though. It made perfect sense to me for a girl to want someone older who could be in charge and guide her through a potentially scary experience. I understood, but I wasn't about to take advantage.

Most of my audience, though, was much younger and far more innocent. Part of my appeal to them came from my role as the stuttering brother who believed in "truth, justice, and the American way." I appeared even younger than I did on "Shindig." I seemed more juvenile, despite my romantic relationship with Candy.

Even though many of the fans were only seven or eight years old, they identified with Candy, too. They must have thought, "That's how I'm going to be one day," or perhaps, "Candy has Jeremy, but I'll grow up, and I'll have Bobby Sherman."

I still don't really know why the fans singled me out. Perhaps it had to do with the amount of exposure I had. Or maybe it was the fact that parents looked over what their kids were watching and buying, and I met with their approval. I embodied that boy next door they would wish for their daughters.

I know the parents were watching since I also had some interesting mail from older women. Some wanted to mother me; some wanted me to know they were divorced. Still others commended me on what a great job I was doing, essentially saying, "Hey, have I got a daughter for you!"

The deluge of attention translated into lines of waiting fans wherever I was. On tour, if kids found out where I was staying, they congregated in the lobby of my hotel. I didn't see them often because I was always sequestered in my room.

Fans found clever ways of monitoring my movements. One girl would station herself at the front entrance of a hotel, and her friend would go around back. When she saw me use the service entrance, she ran around to inform the other one. Today, they would be using flip phones.

The same thing happened at airports. If kids found out when I was arriving, they waited at the gate. They knew I always stopped to talk to them as we walked through.

Because fans constantly waited at the entrance to the Columbia Ranch, we had to develop a routine for the "Brides" set. The stage manager for "Brides" would call the front gate to ask how many kids were there. If an unmanageable group had assembled, security took me out the back. I wasn't going to drive past fans without

BOBBY TAKES YOU HOME!

Hi, Babe!

I want to show you one of my very favorite places! My mom and dad's home. Though I have my own apartment in Hollywood, my folk's home in the Valley is one place I can always relax.

I've built my own recording studio there; and I usually am there at least once a week, if only to have my mom's famous goulash for supper!

Come on along, I know you'll love this house as much as I do!

Love,
Bobby

The Groovy Fans

HOWDY AND WELCOME to my folks house in the Valley. At left, you can see me sneaking a look at you through the peep-hole in the door.

I'M NOT EXACTLY Herbie Alpert, but I can play "Carnival of Venice" if you like.

HERE I AM in my studio, which we built by knocking out a wall between my sister's room and mine.

COULD THIS BE your letter? Maybe so, because I read every letter I get and answer as many as I can!

ZITAR is what you call this Indian instrument, unlike a sitar. Just the same it takes hours just to tune it.

I DO MOST OF my writing either at the piano or on the guitar if I'm not at home. I write all the time.

JUST TO MY LEFT you can see one of the football trophies I won in high school.

THIS IS SILLY, my mom's little poodle, and as you may guess, we call her Silly because she is!

(Continued on page 36) 35

BOBBY TAKES YOU HOME
(Continued)

I'D LIKE YOU TO MEET my mom and dad, who are the grooviest people I know! We're very excited here because we just got our first look at "The Secret of Bobby Sherman" book from Tiger Beat. It's really neat!

I GET A LOT of my phone calls made here while I'm waiting for dinner. Sometimes I even call some fans!

WHEN ANNIE MOSES came along with Tiger Beat's photographer Kenny Lieu, I finally had a chance to show her my model of Disneyland that I'd told her so much about. Pictured here, I'm showing her the Main Street section.

AN INSIDE VIEW of my recording studio. This is the control panel that looks like the inside of a jet plane!

36

stopping—I couldn't do that. I was brought up to have respect for people. We had to arrange whether or not it would be manageable for me to make the stop.

Kids waited outside every day, even in the rain. I went out of my way for them. If I saw someone waiting to meet me, standing in the rain, I had to say hello. The fans' reactions touched me. They seemed to appreciate the fact that I wasn't aloof and didn't have an attitude. That's why, to this day, the fans I met somewhere along the way remain fans. That feels good. It says I did something right.

Some of the fans displayed amazing inventiveness to meet me. One girl had herself boxed and delivered to my hotel! I didn't see her (she didn't make it past security), but I heard she had folded herself up to quite small proportions, creating a sort of jack-in-the-box effect when the package was opened. My fans lack nothing in ingenuity!

They were also very organized. When they took pictures, they made agreements that if one missed seeing me, she could obtain pictures someone else had taken. They had their process very well thought out. Through the years, the fans explained to me how it all worked. The fans weren't worldly then, but they were smart. Long before computers created online information, they had their own networks in place.

Debra, a fan and longtime friend

I started writing to pen pals in 1968. My first pen pal was in one of those magazines; I don't remember whether it was Tiger Beat *or* Fave *or* 16, *one of those. They had pen-pal columns where you wrote in saying, "These are my interests." So I started out writing to a few people.*

When I'd hear from them, we'd pass around what we used to call "friendship books." You start a little book, and you make it for somebody. We would put a picture of Bobby on the front. So I would start it, and I'd pass it on to one of my other pen pals. They would pass it on to somebody they wrote to. The very last person sends it back to the person it was made for.

As you got these friendship books, you would go through them and see if there's somebody that's a Bobby fan that you weren't writing to. That's how it all sort of grew and grew.

I wanted to write everybody because everybody had bits and pieces of information that I wouldn't normally get. We swapped gossip in letters. "Oh, did you hear such and such about Bobby?" You wanted to write to as many people (as possible) so you wouldn't miss out on anything.

At one point I wrote to 250 people. I've met probably about a hundred of the people that I've written to over the years.

It's very interesting to observe thirteen- or fourteen-year-old girls today compared to the same age group in the seventies. It's fascinating to see how the times can change the way kids grow up. In the seventies, thirteen- and fourteen-year-old girls were much more innocent. Today, girls seem to go from being born to puberty,

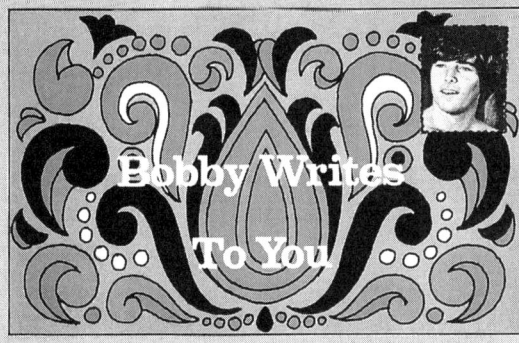

Bobby Writes To You

How Important Are Looks?

Hi Babe,

I've been sitting here at my desk reading some of my mail and I see that a lot of letters are kind of in the same vein. You think that because you aren't Peggy Lipton or Elizabeth Taylor or even the Queen of your prom, no one likes you.

What nonsense!

I think the time has come for me to big-brother you a little. I wish I could sit by your side and put my arm around you and just hold you tight while I tell you this story. I can't right now, so you'll just have to read this and pretend. But do pretend, okay?

TALKIN' 'BOUT YOU!

First off, you are beautiful. You! Right there! Yes, you!

Just because you don't knock people down with your looks (and be glad you don't... those kind of girls are the unhappiest in the world), it doesn't mean you aren't beautiful. Every person has something about them that's beautiful. You do too. If you don't think so, it's just because you don't look close enough at yourself.

Now, let me tell you about what happened to me once.

When I was in high school, I used to date a very nice girl. I really liked her. She wasn't super good looking—in fact, she was rather plain. But she was nice and she knew how to talk about lots of subjects and she laughed easily—that's always important—and I really dug her.

STUPID MOVE

But one time, when we had a date, I did something really stupid. I'd asked this girl to go out with me and I knew she was kind of counting on it, even though we were just going to the show or something.

One of my friends came to me and told me that a really beautiful girl, the most popular girl in the class, liked me and wanted to go out with me but I never asked her and she didn't know why.

Well, I was knocked out. I couldn't believe this girl would want to go out with me. So I called her up and before I knew it, I was telling her I'd pick her up at 7:30 and I just couldn't believe it.

Then I remembered my other date and I called her and said I couldn't go because I wasn't feeling well.

I picked up the popular girl that night and we went to the show and out to dinner. But then a terrible thing happened.

THERE SHE WAS

We were standing in the theater lobby getting popcorn when all of a sudden I realized I was looking right at Sue, the girl I'd broken the date with. Sue had gone to the show with her brother so she wouldn't be sitting home on a Friday night.

Well, I didn't say anything except "hello" because I couldn't. Sue had seen me with Vicki and there was nothing I could do.

It would have been different if Vicki had been really neat but unfortunately, she wasn't. She seemed to think that her beauty was all she needed in life and once I got over my fascination with her looks (and that passes pretty quickly), I thought she had a pretty drippy personality and frankly, she wasn't much fun.

A REAL HEEL

Sue didn't date me very much after that. I can't blame her. I was a real rat. Besides, she found another boyfriend who didn't do foolish things like I'd done.

Unfortunately, I didn't learn my lesson right away. I did the same thing to other girls a couple of more times. But finally, one day it hit me that the most popular girls aren't really the neatest at all.

Now, I shy away completely from girls who appear to be really too great for words because once I take them out, I invariably find they aren't. I look inside a girl before I even consider dating her.

So if you aren't the most beautiful girl in your class, don't worry about it. Work on your personality. Be kind and be quick to laugh. Smile a lot and do the most with what you have.

Guys will love you for it!

Until we're together, lots of love,
Bobby

as if there's nothing in between. There's a sense now of being instantaneously grown-up that wasn't there in the seventies.

If I was as popular to thirteen- and fourteen-year-olds today as I was then, I could walk right by them and they'd contain themselves. They're not as excitable as they were twenty-five years ago. Today they're much more reserved and in control.

Jaynie Pulliam, a fan from "Here Come the Brides"

When you're thirteen or fourteen, that's the essence of who you really are before society adds on layers of who you're expected to be in different situations as you grow up. For hundreds of thousands of girls, that's the point in their lives where Bobby made an impression. He became intrinsically connected to who we really are. He's a part of our youth—the good part we can always connect to.

Being thirteen or fourteen is pivotal to the rest of your life. It's a fulcrum between being a child and experiencing the first breath of adult life. You're starting to grow up and starting to think about what it's going to be like to be an adult. Meanwhile, all the hormones are kicking in.

I've been very lucky. I had a career that involved me with young fans. It made me, in one sense, a big brother. Maybe because of my experience with Lynn's two children, I understood them better.

I knew what the fans wanted. Somewhere in the years between childhood and dating, girls looked for an ideal fantasy boyfriend. For the thirteen-year-old kids, it was a very delicate time. Most of them probably didn't yet have an inkling about their own sexuality. So, we all grew up together.

Debra

[As kids], there was something, some attraction that you knew was there but you couldn't identify it as, "Oh, that's sex appeal," because you didn't really know what sex appeal was all about. It's like, you wanted to be close to Bobby, but you didn't know what you would do when you were close!

For the even younger fans, I was an integral part of their upbringing. I certainly served as a part of their entertainment package. Because of that, the fans had a commonality. Their interest in me created something they could use to relate to their peers—and, apparently, it still does.

Lori, a fan and friend, discussing taking Bobby to her tenth high school reunion in 1988

It was the most exciting thing to me because I got back at all the cheerleaders and all the girls that were not nice at all, and here I walk in with Bobby Sherman. It was such an honor.

Everyone looked and then did a double-take. I had these girls swarming at my table. I'd go to the bathroom and my girlfriends would say, "You better run and get out there, Lori," because these girls were swarming around Bobby, asking him to dance, asking him if he would sing.

We had the most fun because it was just special. I thought, "How much better can it get?"

When fans think back on those times, they think about their friends and the myriad events happening in their lives then—and I'm really happy to have been a part of that. The point is that I wasn't promoting anything that might have been the least bit harmful for them.

Roxanne Berry, a fan, discussing the finer points of being a preteen and noticing Bobby on "Here Come the Brides"

It's the first time somebody zings you in a way you didn't know you could be zinged.

He was a very, very important part of my young life. The dynamics were interesting. He was your boyfriend alone when you bought the magazines and watched the show—until you went to the concert. Then he was everybody's boyfriend and that was okay. Then when you left the concert, he was yours alone again.

In 1969, you couldn't see the paint in my room under the pictures that covered my wall. My cousins and I used to go to my grandmother's house because she had the only color television in town to watch "Here Come the Brides." She gave us huge bowls of ice cream but we hardly ate them; we'd just sit and stare. My grandmother would say to my grandfather, "The girls like that boy."

There we were, eleven and twelve, sitting there with our stupid hair, with the sides pulled up trying to do the Bridget look. We had no idea, of course, that she had eighteen million wiglets, and we've got six strands sticking straight up, and it's just not curling like it's supposed to. But we tried. That's what Jeremy liked, so we had to do it.

After Bobby, there was never anybody I liked quite as intensely. I liked David Cassidy, but there was never anything as fascinating as there was about Bobby. There was something about him. I could never put my finger on it. Obviously he was cute. He was talented. He really could sing a song. I don't know what it was, but he touched a chord, and you really cared about this guy.

As a group, I'm very proud of my fans. I think they turned out well. I'm also proud of the fact that they elected me to be their big brother, or whatever.

I still receive all kinds of fan mail, but the tone has changed. It's not marriage proposals from women now. Often, I receive requests from autograph collectors, and a lot of people want signed album covers. The letters are more thoughtful, and the writers often reminisce about the "good old days." It's nice to hear they're still remembering me.

Dian Kauble, a fan from "Shindig" and "Here Come the Brides," in a letter to Bobby

I don't know if you'll ever get this letter, but I wanted to let you know that you jogged my memory as I ran across a CD the other day. It was just there looking out at me and brought back a lot of nice memories of when I was a teenager, and you were the hottest thing around.

Even though we're all grown-up with families of our own, it's still nice to remember the way it was.

I have accomplished some things in my life that I'm proud of, but I'm most proud that so many of my fans have grown up to be caring and responsible family people as well as good citizens. If I had something to do with that, then great, I did a good job. I have yet to have a fan who's written me from jail! They turned out to be well adjusted and started focusing on the right things.

Dian Kauble

Maybe I saw something in Bobby that was something I looked for in my husband.

I grew up in El Paso. When Bobby's first album came out, "Little Woman" was being played on all the radio stations. It was a big hit, but you couldn't buy it anywhere in my town. I had to special-order this album through one of the music stores. After that point, I guess he became more recognized, so it was easy to get the albums.

I was in the music section of a store one day not long ago and I thought, I'm just going to take a stab at this, and it [a Bobby Sherman CD] was sitting right there on the front of the row looking at me, so I grabbed it. I thought, "YES!" I took the CD home and showed my husband.

"Look what I found!"

"Oh no," he said. "Here we go again."

When the records hit, the fans couldn't go anyplace without my being in their faces or their ears. The publicity campaign was unbelievable, and it reached a larger audience than I knew.

In recent years, I've received more mail from grown-up men than I did during the concert years from boys. Now the mail from men acknowledges that I was their favorite performer, and they ask for autographs and photos. Back then, guys just didn't do that. A guy wasn't going to write a fan letter to another guy. I'm glad the times have made us more open-minded.

When I was doing concerts and later the show "Getting Together," some of my fans were young men who styled their hair like mine and wore the same kinds of clothes I wore. They told me they took pride in the fact that people remarked on how they looked like me. That's what they were aiming for. I understood that because I did the same thing with Ricky Nelson.

I found that emulation flattering. I had a positive influence on someone else's life.

Dena

Bobby and I were working in the park on a beautiful October day. As we talked, a girls' soccer team began to gather nearby, and I saw his attention shift. The girls were all about thirteen or fourteen and were greeting one another and giggling.

At first, he looked at them and seemed to be analyzing what they were doing—almost as a reflex. It was as though some part of him immediately went on alert. Some twenty-five years ago, that same group of girls would have descended on him in a heartbeat. Now, he could stand fifteen feet away and remain in the background.

I had already thought of the irony of the situation when he turned to me and said, "There would have been a time that if I had stood here with that group of girls, it would have been a mob scene. This is kind of nice."

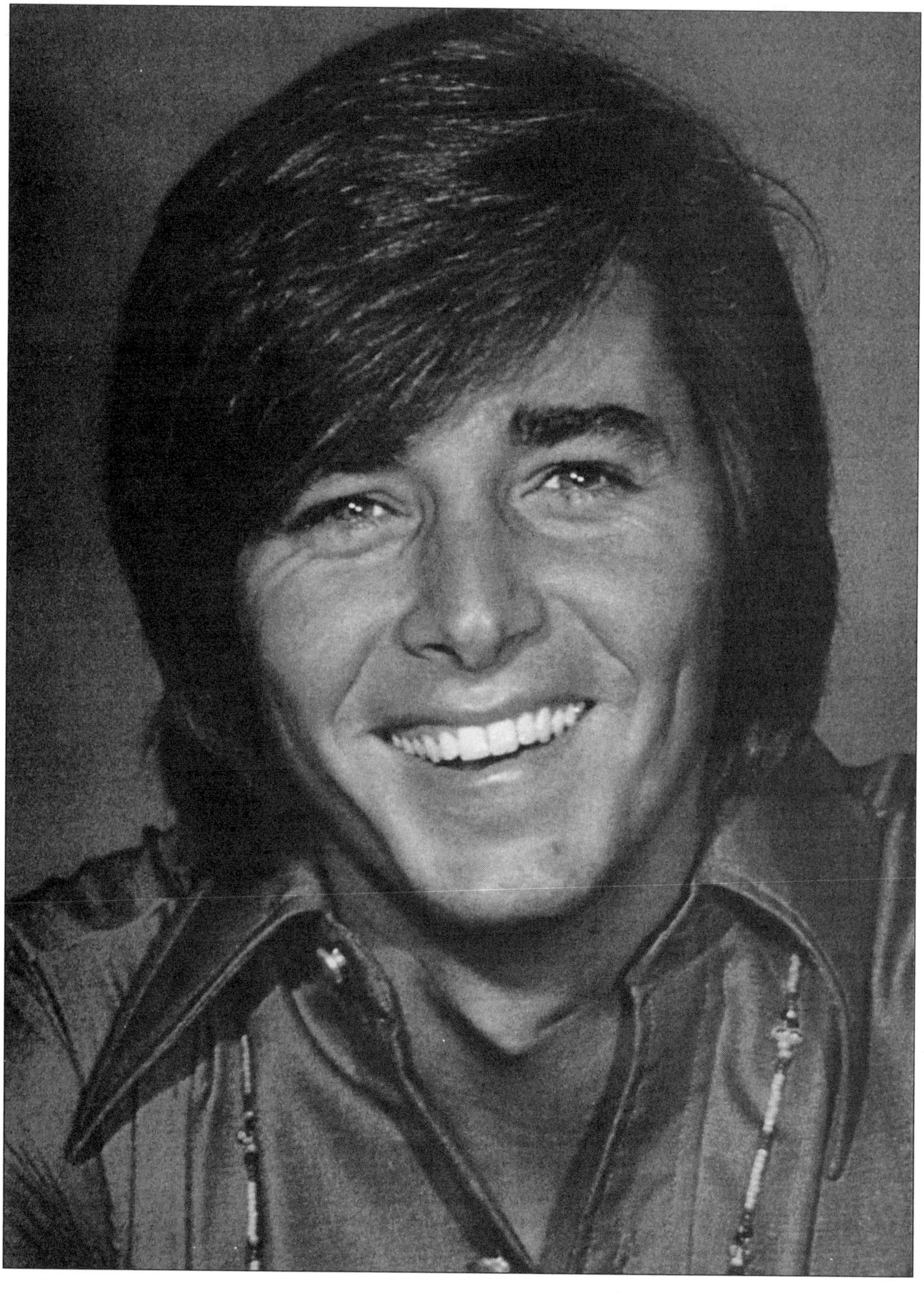

11 "The Partridge Family"/"Getting Together"

My whole body ached.

Every movement seemed like wading through molasses. Every muscle felt tense. How was I going to loosen up and dance?

I was preparing for a song with the wonderful group the Fifth Dimension. The song was "Feelin' Alright." But I wasn't.

We were filming "The Bobby Sherman Special" in May 1971. I was trying to be up. Instead I was down—fighting a losing battle with the flu. I felt awful the whole time we were working. During one of the biggest show business moments of my life, I kept resisting the desire to curl up into a ball under heavy blankets.

The show, which combined a filmed montage, live-audience interaction, and a performance with the Fifth Dimension, should have been a pleasure. "Here Come the Brides" had been off the air for about six months, and I had been constantly busy with concerts and guest appearances.

There were two days of filming and two days of rehearsal at the NBC studios in L.A. The scenes with me swimming in the pool and pushing a little girl on the swing were all filmed at Griffith Park in Los Angeles. Then a studio audience came to NBC, and we taped a dress rehearsal and an actual show. We used bits of both, together with the scenes we had filmed. In the final version, and through the magic of television, I didn't look sick at all.

Ward

Both ABC and Screen Gems wanted Bobby to do another series. But first, he did the TV special, which did very well. Bobby's costumes look kind of funny in retrospect, but at the time we thought they were cool.

In spite of the rust-colored, tie-dyed jumpsuit I wore on the TV special, Screen Gems wanted to work with me again. Several projects had come and gone while Ward and I looked for the right one.

Ward

The director, David Winters, staged the Monkees' concert tour. David had gone on to form a television production company called Winters/Rosen. He approached me and said, "We could sell a half hour special to ABC sponsored by Dr Pepper." That became "The Bobby Sherman Special."

Screen Gems was upset that another production company had sold a Bobby Sherman vehicle. Bobby and I had worked for them for years. Hadn't we ever heard the word loyalty? How could this have happened?

I said, "Your expertise is sitcoms. You've never done a variety show. If Bobby's going to do a variety show, he's going to do it with somebody who knows how to do a variety show."

They said, "Well, okay. But we want to do a show with Bobby, too."

So we said, "We think it should be a situation comedy because, first of all, that's what Screen Gems is really good at, and second, it's half as much work for each show because it's only half an hour."

We didn't want to call it "The Bobby Sherman Show." We wanted him to play a character. Bobby's best comedic skills are reactive; the ability to seem like a nice guy doing his best while all kinds of craziness is going on around him.

The result was "Getting Together."

I was at my folks' place one day when Ward came over with the pilot script. "Getting Together" was going to be a spinoff from "The Partridge Family."

I read the script and liked it. It was good, light comedy. I thought it was something that my fans would enjoy.

My character, Bobby Conway, was a young, struggling songwriter who had linked up with an eccentric lyricist named Lionel Poindexter. Bobby lived in an antique shop, drove a hearse, and cared for his preteen sister.

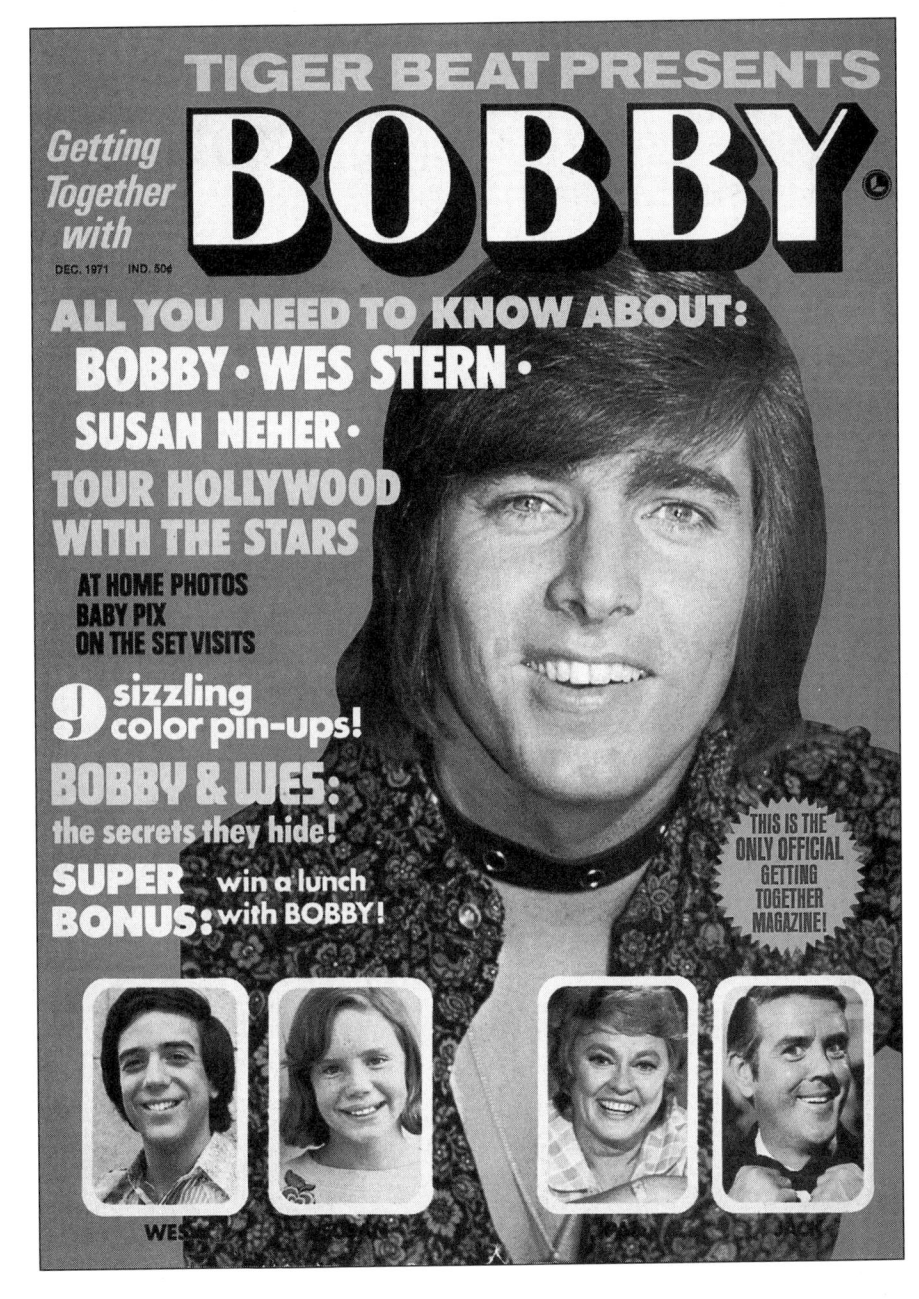

The story was contemporary enough for my fans, and it was a transition from Jeremy and the 1800s to the present day. Still, like Jeremy, the character of Bobby Conway was me.

Bobby Conway wanted to succeed in the music industry. He was a nice guy who found himself looking after everyone in his path. He did his best to pursue his dreams while dealing with everyday responsibilities. I knew him the same way I had known Jeremy.

Once I made the decision to do it, everything happened very quickly.

Ward

Bob Claver, who was the executive producer of "The Partridge Family" and Paul Witt, who was one of the producers of "Here Come the Brides," came up with the concept for "Getting Together."

In those days, Screen Gems was the sitcom factory. They had shows such as "Father Knows Best," "Bewitched," "I Dream of Jeannie," and "Hazel."

"Getting Together" allowed Bobby to use his music, but we didn't want it to turn into an excuse for a variety show. We were trying to have him taken seriously as a television actor.

I was also hoping that we could sell a variety show as a summer replacement series. That way, Bobby would be on in two different formats: as an actor in a situation comedy in the winter and a singer on a variety show in the summer.

So it was decided that Bobby wouldn't appear singing his songs in "Getting Together," but that his character should be in the music business—which explained his long hair.

Making "Getting Together" a spinoff from an episode of "The Partridge Family" seemed to me to be a good way to launch the show. Earl Bellamy directed the pilot episode, and we had eight days to shoot the entire script.

I had met David Cassidy before because our sound stages had been right next to each other. When we were finishing the last season of "Brides," they had started filming "The Partridge Family."

I had seen David on several occasions, but just to say "hi" in passing. We didn't hang around together; we were both busy and didn't have time. We both knew who the other was but that was about the extent of our association.

Ward

David Cassidy didn't much like the idea of the spinoff. The first day on the set, I heard David on the phone to his agent complaining about it. It was an uncomfortable situation.

"How could you have allowed this to happen?" David was saying. "This isn't a 'Partridge Family' episode at all. It's a pilot, and I don't have anything to do. I don't understand why, on the show I'm starring in, all of a sudden Bobby Sherman has more to do than I do. . . ."

From his point of view, who wouldn't feel that way? To assuage David, Screen Gems gave him a share in the profits of "Getting Together" and the news appeared in the press.

The next thing that happened was that Jack Cassidy, David's father, appeared on "The Tonight Show," and, of course, one of the questions was, "What about all this hoopla surrounding your son becoming a teenage idol?" He said, "Well, there's good things and bad things. My son has no private life. He started out as a serious actor, and he doesn't want to turn into Bobby Sherman."

Super Statistics on Bobby Sherman

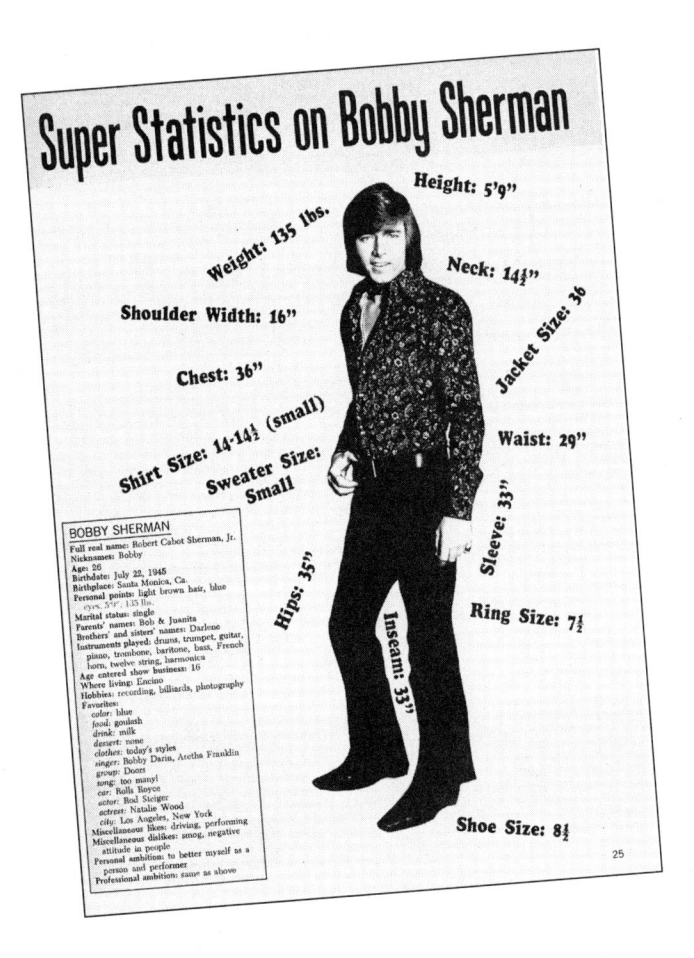

- Height: 5'9"
- Weight: 135 lbs.
- Neck: 14½"
- Shoulder Width: 16"
- Jacket Size: 36
- Chest: 36"
- Waist: 29"
- Shirt Size: 14-14½ (small)
- Sweater Size: Small
- Sleeve: 33"
- Hips: 35"
- Ring Size: 7½
- Inseam: 33"
- Shoe Size: 8½

BOBBY SHERMAN
Full real name: Robert Cabot Sherman, Jr.
Nicknames: Bobby
Age: 26
Birthdate: July 22, 1945
Birthplace: Santa Monica, Ca.
Personal points: light brown hair, blue eyes, 5'9", 135 lbs.
Marital status: single
Parents' names: Bob & Juanita
Brothers' and sisters' names: Darlene
Instruments played: drums, trumpet, guitar, piano, trombone, baritone, bass, French horn, twelve string, harmonica
Age entered show business: 16
Where living: Encino
Hobbies: recording, billiards, photography
Favorites:
 color: blue
 food: goulash
 drink: milk
 dessert: none
 clothes: today's styles
 singer: Bobby Darin, Aretha Franklin
 group: Doors
 song: too many!
 car: Rolls Royce
 actor: Rod Steiger
 actress: Natalie Wood
 city: Los Angeles, New York
Miscellaneous likes: driving, performing
Miscellaneous dislikes: smog, negative attitude in people
Personal ambition: to better myself as a person and performer
Professional ambition: same as above

Working with David was just the same as working on any show. It was work. We were polite to each other, we knew our lines, we did our jobs and left.

Fans waited for the pilot episode with the two of us, debating which one of us they liked better.

I never felt any direct competition with David, although I was often asked if I did. In terms of fans, there was a David Cassidy camp and a Bobby Sherman camp. Maybe after the announcement that Patti and I were married, some of my fans drifted over to David. I don't know.

David wound up experiencing some of the same difficulties that I did. Being a teenage idol or bubble-gum idol makes it difficult to be taken seriously in other contexts. So you work that much harder. It took him a long time, as it has me, to accomplish some of the things that we wanted to do. He's appeared on Broadway two or three times. That's pretty good.

I was really impressed with Shirley Jones. Aside from the wealth of experience she brought to the show, she was a sweet lady. She made the whole experience very pleasant for me.

The rest of the "Partridge" cast were also a very professional bunch. Susan Dey was extremely nice and obviously very talented. Danny Bonaduce was as he appeared, kind of a cocky, funny little kid. Brian Foster, who played the young drummer, was a big fan of mine. I was always carrying him around and kidding with him. Suzanne Crough, who played the youngest daughter, was adorable, too.

In the end, some footage of the pilot didn't air on the March 1971 episode of "The Partridge Family." Some segments had been reserved to demonstrate to ABC where the show was going. Apparently, it went well. ABC gave us the green light, so we went right to work on "Getting Together."

I had met Wes Stern, who played my partner Lionel, for the first time in Jackie Cooper's office at Screen Gems. I had read with two other actors, but we were looking for a particular chemistry.

The other two actors were fine, but then Wes came in and did his bit. Right away, the chemistry seemed to work. He was like a sheepdog. You wanted to pet him.

I felt he was perfect for the part. Jackie Cooper, Paul Witt, and Rene Valente, head of casting, asked me, "What do you think? Who do you feel more comfortable with?"

I hadn't planned to voice an opinion, but when Wes left, I said, "I think that's Lionel."

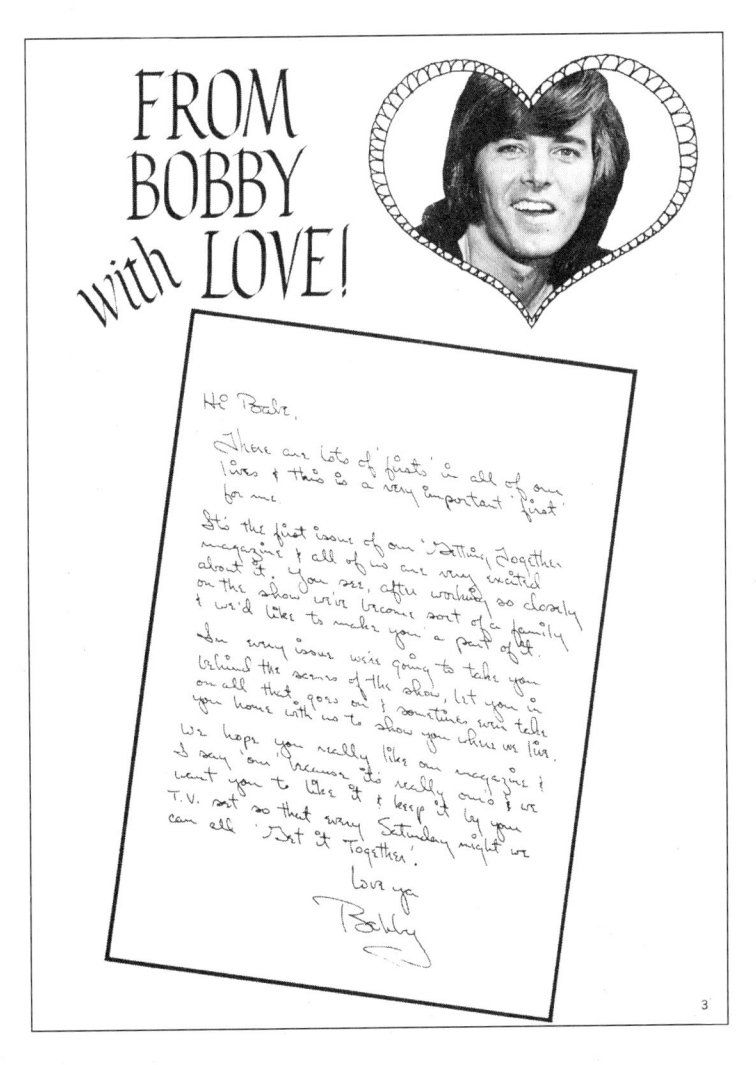

"Getting Together" began on September 18, 1971. Paul Witt, Lou Antonio, and Bob Claver, all of whom I had worked with on "Brides," directed episodes. We had skilled directors, and I really liked the music on the show, particularly one song called "Jennifer," about Susan Neher's character, Jennifer, my little sister on the show. I didn't write it but I wish I had. Even though it wasn't a hit single, it received a lot of airplay.

As time went along, I added lines or jokes, contributing what I thought Bobby Conway would have done. So many of the right elements for a hit show seemed to be there, including some dynamite guest stars: Cindy Williams, Penny Marshall, Rob Reiner, and Stuart Margolin.

Our regulars, Pat Carroll, Wes Stern, Jack Burns, and Susan Neher, formed a solid ensemble. By the time the show ended, Wes Stern and I were good friends. He was quiet, but extremely likable. When a show goes off the air, the cast goes their separate ways, and you lose touch with each other. It is one of the saddest things about doing a series.

Susan Neher, who played Jennifer, was a little sweetheart. She was a fan and very shy at first. She was about twelve years old when the show started and had to have a tutor on the set. For someone so young, she was very professional. She's in her mid-thirties now. It's amazing to me that so much time has passed.

Pat Carroll, who played my landlady, and Jack Burns provided a lot of laughs. Unfortunately, I wasn't around enough to be able to socialize with them. We didn't have the time to build the kind of rapport that I had experienced with the cast of "Brides." The pace was too fast and furious. A lot of the "Brides" camaraderie developed during the second half of the first year. "Getting Together" lasted only one season.

In retrospect, the only reason we ran into trouble was that we were up against "All in the Family," a colossal hit for CBS.

Ward

ABC scheduled "Getting Together" at what, at the time, was a good time slot—7:30 on Monday nights.

At the last minute, after all the schedules had been announced, CBS moved "All in the Family" opposite "Getting Together." It was not that they had anything against Bobby, but this was a very competitive network environment. "All in the Family" had come on as a midseason replacement the previous year. It was not yet a huge hit, but it had created an awful lot of controversy and talk.

"Getting Together" was a good show; it was well produced, well written and directed, and expressed some moral values.

The problem was that the parents, the adults of the family, would be in their living rooms watching "All in the Family" on their color sets, which had the little Nielsen ratings boxes on the back. Meanwhile, the kids—who outnumbered the parents in most cases—would be up in their rooms watching "Getting Together" on black-and-white televisions, which didn't have Nielson boxes attached.

The kids didn't have a voice to say what they were watching if the telephone rang. Because of the response we received when the show went off the air, I believe we were holding our own in the numbers of people watching.

When the network decided to cancel "Getting Together," the fans contacted all the ABC television stations around the country. The kids were very upset because they liked the show. They wrote in, they formed picket lines, and they were very vocal about their feelings.

To be honest, I'd go home and watch "All in the Family," too. I already knew what was happening on my show. Still, mail was up, and kids were watching. If we had stayed on for a second season, I believe the show would have continued to do well, and we would have held our own. Sometimes things happen for the best, though.

At that point in my life, I was wearing down fast. Between being on the road and doing the show, I couldn't relax. I was starting to fall apart physically. My bout with the flu in May was a precursor to what I was dealing with by September. By then, I really felt the pinch. I was going twenty-four hours a day, and I wasn't sleeping right. I began to find the workload overwhelming.

I had to be on the set by 6:00 A.M., which meant getting up at 4:30 A.M. "Getting Together" used the same stage as "Here Come the Brides." Going to work at the same place was a double-edged sword. On the one hand, it felt comforting and familiar. On the other hand, it seemed unsettling and sad.

It was odd to see different sets on the stage where I was used to seeing the dorm and Lottie's place. It made me melancholy.

When I arrived at 6:00 A.M., I'd go to makeup and then to wardrobe. I'd check my call sheet for the day to see what scenes I was doing. Much of the routine was strikingly similar to the way I had worked on "Brides."

Next, I'd meet the people who were going to be in that week's episode. Then we rehearsed and shot the master and the close-ups—and did that all day long until six-thirty or seven at night. In between, there were interviews and lunches off the set, lots of press coverage. The pace was grueling.

In addition, I felt the pressure of carrying the show myself. Most of my records were out by then. A seemingly endless stream of merchandising carried my name.

I was twisted in knots because I could no longer gear up for such exhausting days. Toward the end of the show's run, when it got to be five o'clock, I'd ask the prop guy to make me a bourbon and 7-Up so I could unwind.

Actually, there was a time at the very end of "Getting Together" when I knew it wasn't going to go anywhere. The ratings were down, and we weren't likely to be renewed.

Metromedia and the concert promoters were trying to take advantage of the time we had. Consequently, the pace became even more fast and furious than it had been during "Brides." The interviews were nonstop. The schedule for my concert tours was going crazy. My energy and drive finally gave way.

To tell the truth, I was happy when it all stopped.

Just after the end of filming "Getting Together," the concerts started tapering off. Then "Getting Together" went off the air. The last episode was telecast on January 8, 1972.

All of a sudden, I had a sense of relief that I finally had some time for myself. That meant freedom for the oddest things. I could walk out in the yard and make a decision about moving a plant from one spot to another. I finally had an opportunity to enjoy a home life.

By the time "Getting Together" was ending, I had home fires to tend. I was ready to settle into domestic tranquillity.

> Hey! Get your friends together and play this groovy new "Getting Together Game!" It's an exciting, action, thrill, and fave-filled funthing we call . . .
>
> ## LUNCH WITH BOBBY GAME!
>
> This terrif Tiger Beat game was designed just for you and your friends to see what it's really like to live in Hollywood and to know your faves personally. And what could be better for a Bobby Sherman luvver than to be invited by Bobby himself to have lunch with him in his dressing room trailer on the set of his new TV show, "Getting Together?"
>
> Well, that's the incredible invitation you have right in your hand when you start out from Tiger Beat's offices at 1800 North Highland in the heart of Hollywood. But Hollywood is an unusual town, so you'll find that just his personal invitation is not enough to get you into Bobby's presence. All kinds of crazy fun things can and do happen, so whoever gets there first has proven that she has a lot of plain old-fashioned good luck! The rules are easy to follow.
>
> To set up your game board, (pages 42 and 43), just glue it to a piece of cardboard, measured to size. To begin, each player needs a marker or a "man" like in Monopoly or similar games. Anything will do . . . buttons, coins, just so that each player has a different marker of her own. You'll also need one di (half of a pair of dice).
>
> ## EASY RULES
>
> Any number can play. Each player must have a marker. All players begin at the Tiger Beat Offices (Space #1).
>
> To find out who plays first, and how each player takes her turn, each player rolls the di once, remembering her number. The girl with the highest number goes first. In case of tie, the tying players roll again. The rest of the players take their turns clockwise around the board.
>
> To leave the Tiger Beat Offices, players must roll a one or a six. They cannot move until they do. If two players land on the same GREEN square, the player there first is "bumped off" and must return to the Tiger Beat Offices to begin again.
>
> When a player lands on a square that has a number, the player must follow the instructions written on the square.
>
> If two players land on the same square (other than the six green squares) the first one there is "bumped off" and must move back to the nearest PURPLE square.
>
> To reach Bobby Dressing Trailer, players must roll the exact number they need. For example, if a player is three spaces away from the trailer, she must roll a three to get in. If she rolls a higher number, she still cannot move until she rolls the exactly right number. She must wait her regular turn between each try.
>
> There's room for only one guest at Bobby's lunch, so the first girl there wins the game, and Bobby! Have fun, and good luck!
>
> GAME APPEARS ON PAGES 42 AND 43.

LUNCH with BOBBY GAME

START: Pick up your invitation from Bobby and your Studio Gate Pass from Ann Moses at TiGER BEAT office.

1. You have luck finding a taxi! Advance two squares!

2. You discover you've lost your Gate Pass and Invitation. Return to TiGER BEAT offices.

3. Heading for Bobby's Valley home, you see FRANK WEBB who gives you a ride to Ventura Boulevard in the heart of the Valley.

4. Spot DONNY OSMOND at a record store. He invites you inside to listen to new albums! Fun, but cost you time and 1 turn!

5. DANNY BONADUCE gives you a ride on his Vespa motorcycle direct to Bobby's house! Advance to Bobby's house!

6. Spot MRS. SHERMAN'S Beauty Shop. Have your hair done. You now look super, but lost time. Roll di and go back that number of spaces.

7. See WES STERN having lunch. He directs you to Columbia Ranch. Great! Advance 4 squares!

8. Ran out of taxi fare. Walking takes longer. Skip one turn.

9. SUSAN NEHER and her mom give you a lift to NBC STUDIOS in Burbank where Susan is taping a TV special. Advance to NBC!

10. TITO JACKSON gives you a lift to WARNER BROTHERS STUDIOS. Advance to WARNER BROS. STUDIOS.

11. Playing with ALLY and GOOFY at Bobby's house was a ball! But you're late! Skip 1 turn.

"The Partridge Family"/"Getting Together"

13. Spot DAVID CASSIDY at THE YANKEE PEDLAR. He gives you an autograph and directions to COLUMBIA RANCH. Advance 3 spaces!

14. An ice cream man sells you a Popsicle but gives you wrong directions by mistake. Go back to WARNER BROTHERS STUDIOS!

12. At an intersection you see a real Sheriff showing JACK BURNS how to direct traffic! You stop for an autograph. Roll di and go back that number of spaces.

BOBBY'S TRAILER! You made it! And best of all there's Beautiful Bobby himself, standing in the doorway, waving and smiling and inviting you in to lunch. Congratulations!

15. You buy a map of Movie Stars Homes! PAT CARROLL'S home is on it. What luck! Advance to PAT CARROLL'S home!

27. "GETTING TOGETHER" producer thinks you're cute & asks you to audition for a part. Advance 2 spaces!

16. You are totally lost! Go back to SHERIFF STATION for directions!

26. On the "GETTING TOGETHER" set you giggle during a take. The director yells cut angrily. Bad girl! Go back 3 spaces.

17. You see SHIRLEY JONES parking at a supermarket. Have fun talking with her but now you're really late. Go back two spaces.

18. You run into SUSAN DEY shopping. Asking about her beauty secrets took too long. Lose 1 turn.

25. Oh, no! Now you're lost on one of the many sets at COLUMBIA RANCH. Roll the di again, but move back that number of spaces.

19. On a street in Burbank you see CHAD EVERETT filming "Medical Center" on location. You stop to watch, losing valuable time and 1 turn.

20. A record store displays a giant BOBBY poster. The owner gives you one free! You're so lucky, take an extra turn!

24. At the COLUMBIA RANCH the guard is very careful. You have to convince him your invitation is for real. Stay here until you roll a 1, taking regular turns.

23. You find a lucky penny! Good for you! Advance 3 squares!

21. You spot the COLUMBIA RANCH on the other side of the Ventura Freeway but you can't cross safely. Lose 1 turn.

22. At Burbank's Pickwick Stables you see KURT RUSSELL grooming his horse Raquel. You take a ride. Go back 3.

43

Bobby Writes To You

AN EXCLUSIVE NEW TIGER BEAT COLUMN

Hi Babe,

Well, this is my first column where I really tell you about the things I think about most. This month I'd like to talk to you about love.

Love is a subject that's on everybody's mind today. Love isn't everywhere, but more & more I see signs of love wherever I go. If you have some ideas on how we can all spread love, write to me here at Tiger Beat & let me know. Until we're together,

Love,
Bobby

12 Girls, the Press, and Patti

A knock on the door came late one evening in 1969.

Through the peephole, I could see Diane, a neighbor in my apartment house. We had struck up a casual friendship, exchanging greetings in the elevator or in the lobby.

As I opened the door, I realized Diane wasn't alone. Her friend Patti Carnel emerged from the shadows behind her. Diane said she was locked out of her apartment and wanted to use the phone to call her sister. I showed Diane to the phone, but I couldn't take my eyes off Patti.

Patti had an almost angelic look; blue eyes, long auburn hair, and a gorgeous figure. She looked so pretty and fresh that I was immediately attracted to her. We chatted while Diane used the phone, and they left after only a few minutes, but Patti's image stayed with me. She was a knockout.

Patti walked into my life on April 1, 1969. Since my breakup with Lynn I felt the need to protect myself from more heartache. I couldn't show the feeling Patti had awakened, and she gave me no encouragement at the time. But soon afterward, I happened to see her in the lobby. She had been dating someone, and I overheard her telling him she was no longer interested in seeing him.

I saw my chance and I took it. Heartache or not, this girl was too special to let get away.

Patti

After I met him that evening, within a week I got a phone call from him, and he invited me to Easter Sunday dinner with his family. I was flabbergasted.

When I first met him, because I knew Diane liked him, I wasn't looking at him in any other way than just somebody my girlfriend liked. I didn't want to intrude. It was like, "That's her territory, I'm not going to even think about anything." When he asked me out, I was taken aback at first. Then I thought, "He seems like a really nice guy."

Of course I got very, very bad reactions from Diane. I was in a quandary. I was asking my mother, "Well, he's asking me, but Diane's the one who likes him." She said, "Yes, but he obviously is not asking her out, he's asking you out."

At the time I started dating Patti, I was seeing a couple of other girls. Then I got so busy with concerts that I couldn't keep up a dating book. I soon didn't want to.

If it had been six months earlier, I still would have been immersed in the pangs of my breakup with Lynn. When I met Patti, it was absolutely the right time for a new relationship to begin.

At first I was on the road so much that I barely had time to see Patti. Nonetheless, she intrigued me. Being with her seemed right.

She didn't watch television much, so she wasn't really aware of me as Jeremy. She seemed to find out about who I was from her girlfriend. She liked me for me and wasn't impressed by all the hoopla.

I couldn't explain the impact she was having on my life. Although Patti was physically stunning, something else was going on that I couldn't figure out.

I don't know if that's the point at which I began to say to myself, "I'm in love with her," but I found myself thinking about her a lot.

Patti didn't know how pretty she was, and that prettiness could have very easily led her into trouble. Her naivete worried me, and I felt extremely protective of her. She had no transportation, for instance, and wanted to learn how to drive, so I paid for a driving course for her. Then the driving instructor was making advances to her!

Nonetheless, she got her license, and I even let her drive the Rolls. So what did she do? The first time she took it out, she rear-ended another car. I settled with the guy she hit for $300, and I

I took this shot of Patti in 1977.

bought her a car of her own. I couldn't help it. She could do no wrong in my eyes.

A lot was going on in her young life, and I was watching her grow up. When Patti and I were first seeing one another, she told me she was eighteen. I was almost twenty-six. One day she asked me to pick her up from school, and I realized it was high school! She was seventeen, but close to turning eighteen and about to graduate. I had to set some limits.

I told her, "We really don't need the hassle and I don't want to make your folks upset with me." As a result, we backed off a bit from the relationship for a few months, but stayed in touch.

By the time she turned eighteen, I was busier than ever. Whatever time I did have free, though, I wanted to spend with her.

Patti

I was going to high school and my boyfriend would pick me up in a Rolls-Royce! It was so funny. A lot of my girlfriends held me in awe but I wasn't awesome. It was just the way it was. People began to become aloof toward me, I guess, because I was being courted by a celebrity. The way people looked at me was different.

I was seventeen when I met Bobby. I was too young to know who I was. Bobby had to be not only a boyfriend but a father to me as well.

My role with Patti changed from moment to moment. Even though I was seven years older, and I took on certain responsibilities for her, we behaved more often like a couple of kids. I was always inventing things for us to do.

One morning, when I was at the apartment by myself, it was raining. I didn't have to go to the set that day, and I was happy to sleep a little bit later. I just stayed in bed and listened to the sound of the raindrops' gentle dance on my window. I enjoyed it so much that I took my blanket and pillow, opened the sliding door, and slept on the floor near the overhang to hear better. It felt so peaceful. It was so nice.

I tried to duplicate that effect one time for Patti and me. I created a tape loop, which I ran through the tape machine. The tape must have been twenty feet long. I looped it around a piece of furniture and threaded it back through the recorder so that the tape played continuously, creating the pattering sound of rain. Then, I pitched a tent on the living room floor. Patti and I went inside the tent and pretended that it was actually raining, as if we were out in the wilderness. I liked experimenting that way. It was fun and romantic.

We had to plan very simple dates because I couldn't go out without being recognized. It was much easier to stay home. All I wanted to do was relax and Patti afforded me that possibility. She wanted to kick back and have fun, too.

I bought my dog, Dopey, about that time. She was such a cutie, but she could also be a real terror. I don't know how many times I had to reupholster the edge of the couch thanks to her, but she kept my spirits up.

Patti

Bobby was usually tired and just wanted to relax. We loved to play board games. Monopoly. Yahtzee. In fact, we'd play Monopoly with real money. He used to return from the concerts with a suitcase of money. It was such a kick. He made me laugh like crazy.

When I did enjoy a day off, I often cooked dinner. I bought thick, juicy chateaubriand steaks and marinated them in sweet-and-sour sauce. I cooked the steaks on a little hibachi on the terrace of the penthouse, and we drank Dom Perignon champagne together.

We were suited to each other. We both enjoyed quiet evenings and getting together with friends like Lou and Lane Antonio. I became friends with Lou during "Here Come the Brides" when he had directed and appeared in a number of episodes. His wife, Lane, owned horses so she and Patti hit it off. Before we were married, I bought Patti a horse. That helped her to occupy her days when I was gone so much.

When Patti and I went out, people remarked what a great-looking couple we were. Girls gave me their phone numbers, and guys made passes at Patti. I couldn't blame other men for trying. I certainly understood if a guy wanted to date Patti. After all, I did. Although I was used to girls approaching me, it did surprise us both that people would make advances right in front of us.

Patti

Girls would throw themselves at him. I'd just sort of sit there and yawn and say, "Let me know when it's over."

At first, the fact that girls were constantly coming on to me bothered Patti. She didn't know how long our relationship was going to last. She worried about whether the next pretty girl that came along was going to win me over. She was especially concerned when I was out of town doing concerts. She had no way of knowing how isolated I was on the road. Finally, I talked to her about it.

Patti in her riding habit, 1978.

"Time is going to show you that I'm not that loose, and I'm not that hungry to jump around," I told her.

I know there were times long before we were married when she felt very blue. She wanted more of a commitment, but I wasn't ready for those responsibilities. We met just as my popularity was cresting and too much was going on around me. Between 1969 and 1971, "Brides" ended, the concerts continued, and "Getting Together" began.

As time went on, we both wanted to have a more permanent relationship, and we also both wanted to have kids. There wasn't anybody else in the world that I wanted to be with more.

Fortunately for me, her parents approved of me. I still think fondly of her family. They trusted me and believed more was going to come of my relationship with Patti. They were right.

At some point, I knew we were going to get married and she did, too. We could tell when we looked at each other. It was just a question of time and the best opportunity. Perhaps subconsciously, all my actions were moving me in that direction.

In January 1971 I bought a house. In its present form, it's a fourteen-room ranch-style hideaway surrounded by an acre of foliage. Back then, it boasted fewer rooms and a much different landscape, but I instantly fell in love with it.

Like the time I bought my Rolls, I simply told the real estate agent, "I'll take it." When Ward heard this, he asked why I hadn't let him negotiate the price. I said, "I didn't want to negotiate; I wanted to buy it." Sometimes I'm my own worst enemy when it comes to things I want. So, without realizing it, I put down some deep roots.

Soon after I bought the house, tragedy struck. The street outside my driveway is extremely busy. Dopey darted out into the street one day and was killed by a passing car. I found myself sitting on the curb, sobbing. It was an awful day.

Not long afterward, Patti bought a pair of bloodhounds, which I named Wally and Goofy. I thought they were adorable, and the feeling was mutual. I loved romping with them but I soon found that they were virtually uncontrollable. They grew so big and were so exuberant, they could knock me down. I gave them their own separate living quarters, a "dog house" complete with carpeted interior. It was quite splendid—until they chewed it up.

I gave up on building homes for the dogs and started work on a recording studio in my house. It was the start of many additions that I would build through the years.

By the summer of 1971, I was wearing thin from constant work, but I had a house, two rambunctious dogs, and a relationship with Patti that I wanted to hold onto.

I said to Patti, "I think we should get married."

Patti

The proposal was out at the pond at the house. There's a little fish pond out there. I can't pinpoint the exact day or time. We just always talked about being married.

He could be so charming sometimes. One of the things he

would do is have special cheeses and champagne.

I dressed up in this long, sort of southern belle dress. I had a big straw hat on with a ribbon. We were just sitting there and that's when he said it more directly than ever before.

"I want you to be my wife."

He gave me a really pretty engagement ring, a marquise-shaped diamond.

It was a big diamond. Her wedding ring was simpler, more refined. We picked it out together. She gave me a ring as well, a gold-leaf design. From the time we actually decided to get married, everything happened very quickly.

I wasn't confident enough about our plans to make any announcements at that point. In concerts, I had always said that when I did marry, the fans would be the first to know. When the time came, however, the circumstances prevented me from announcing it when I wanted to.

If I had announced our engagement and then, two months later, the wedding didn't happen, we would have been terribly embarrassed. Then the media attention would have changed from *Tiger Beat* to the *National Enquirer* with all the scandal magazines discussing what went wrong. The next thing I knew I'd have been on the tabloids in the checkout lines. I didn't want that kind of speculation about my life.

Also, the people in my business, at the agency and the record company, said, "Don't say anything right now until we have everything organized." They wanted to create a media blitz of "Bobby Got Married!"

Patti and I were married at Our Lady of Grace Catholic Church in Encino on September 26, 1971, with the reception afterward at the house. I asked Lou Antonio to be my best man. A group of about fifty family members and friends attended the wedding and reception.

There we stood, the best man and I, in the front of the church. I was wearing a regular black tux, surrounded by flower girls and bridesmaids. But nothing about the scene was sinking in. As the wedding music began, I still wasn't feeling terribly caught up in the romantic aspect of the wedding itself. Standing off to the side of the altar, I just looked at Lou, feeling shaky.

"What am I doing here?" I asked him.

The bride and groom.

It was just a fleeting moment of panic; Patti told me later that she had felt the same thing.

Then, while I was standing at the altar, Patti emerged from the shadow of the church entrance. She was absolutely radiant. She wore a long white dress with a gorgeous train. She looked just incredible, a beautiful angel in white.

Suddenly, she was all I saw.

The guests, the bridesmaids, the priest, everything else melted away. The shakiness evaporated. I knew I was doing the right thing, right that moment.

The ceremony was over. We had really done it—we were married. Then I knew we were together.

That whole weekend was spiritual in the sense that, without saying it out loud, I realized that this was my wife. A lot of emotion goes with that realization. I don't mean baggage, but a lot of feeling in terms of respect. We both knew then that we had a responsibility to each other. I took it seriously, and I know she did, too.

Our wedding day, September 26, 1971.

We didn't take our honeymoon right away. I was still finishing "Getting Together," and it just wasn't the right time. Still, that weekend was special. We had made a transition.

That doesn't mean our lives suddenly took a serious tone. We still had a lot of fun.

Money was no problem, and when I had time off, we would do whatever we wanted. We loved going to Santa Barbara for the weekend. But often we would do nothing, just go out in the yard and walk around.

Best of all, we were attracted to each other. Even if we weren't touching each other, we were still making love.

The groom on his wedding day.

To me, making love is not the act of sex. Making love is AFTER you've had good quality, fire-brandishing sex. That's when the two of you begin to make love. Afterward, you cuddle, you do things

Sunning at Bass Lake, California.

together. Then you add a deep, caring bond to the whole interaction. Making love is an ongoing thing. The person you love can be sitting across from you, and you can still be making love. Patti and I were best friends, and we were always together. It was a constant adventure.

After we were married, Patti developed a group of friends who shared her interest in horses. We gave small get-togethers with people that we liked. To entertain, we added a theater room to the house.

Because we outfitted the house with so many amenities, we didn't need to go out to have fun. We weren't Hollywoodites. She didn't like that social scene any more than I did, so we were compatible.

Some of our getaways were especially happy times. On one trip we rented a Winnebago, went up to Mammoth Lake, and hung out there for three or four days. We met some police officers and their wives vacationing there, and we water-skied with them.

I had just bought my sixteen-millimeter camera, so I took pictures of Patti saying "Twinkle, Twinkle Little Star," experimenting to see how the sound and picture synced up. We even took steaks and champagne when we went camping. That's the way we roughed it!

We had a great time for a few days until more campers showed up and people found out I was there. After that, we dropped the Winnebago off at my folks' house and went to Santa Barbara where we stayed at the Miramar, the famous old hotel on the beach. Every so often we found beautiful places where we could relax.

Shortly after we were married, Patti became pregnant. We were ecstatic. But within months, our happy times became clouded. I remember vividly the day she had the miscarriage.

I was having the driveway resurfaced. So I was outside, knee-deep in black tar, when Patti appeared at the bedroom window. She began pounding on the glass. I turned around and knew immediately something was wrong. I desperately tried to remove my tar-covered boots, but it felt as though I were moving in slow motion. It seemed to take forever for me to get inside to where she was.

When I reached her, she was okay, physically, thank God. But she lost the baby. She was extremely upset about it, and I was, too. We both wanted children.

Again, it was the wrong time to make any kind of announcement.

I didn't think Patti could take the strain. The photographers would have been clamoring around the house trying to take pictures, and I didn't think that would be fair to Patti.

Joyously, soon afterward, she became pregnant with Christopher. Again, we had planned to announce the fact that we were married. As happy as we were, however, we found ourselves in a delicate situation because for the first few months Patti had to be careful not to exert herself. The doctor said, "You might not want to announce anything at this particular time, mainly for her." I agreed.

For the months that Patti was pregnant with Christopher, I didn't do much of anything except grow a mustache and look after her. "Getting Together" was off the air by this time, and I did only one guest shot on "The Mod Squad" during that whole nine months.

The fact that I could be home so much worked in our favor. Although we had help, Patti needed some TLC because it was a frustrating time for her. I tried to be at home as much as possible. We went to Lamaze classes because I wanted to be sure I was prepared.

We added on to the house, building the library, the maid's room, another bathroom, and what turned out to be the boys' room.

As the months passed, I let Patti coordinate a lot of the construction because it kept her occupied. She had a friend who was learning to be an interior decorator, and part of her friend's school project turned out to be decorating our house. It gave Patti a reason to go out and shop. She'd say, "Guess what I bought?" and I'd say, "Oh my God! We've spent how much?"

Patti has very good taste so it wasn't like, "What has she gotten me into?" In the library I still have a turquoise blue couch she picked out. Christopher was on the way, we were putting the house together, and she seemed content. I was happy too.

The only sad note during this time was our decision to part with Wally and Goofy. They were sweet, but they had grown too big and rambunctious to play gently with babies. Although I hated to see the dogs go, Sonny Jones had a ranch with plenty of room for them to frolic. It seemed to be for the best.

In their honor, I created Wally and Goofy Music, my two music publishing companies, so that at least they live on in name.

After Patti had been pregnant for seven months, we finally went on our honeymoon. At that point, the doctor said it was okay for her to travel. So we took a cruise to Hawaii and Kauai, stayed for a couple of weeks, and flew back.

It was a strange time for me because it was the first time I ever remembered sitting back and not doing anything for a couple of weeks. I guess it was all settling in: I was married; I could take days off; and I was about to be a father.

On my birthday in Kauai, I put my head on Patti's stomach, and Christopher kicked me in the ear. It was a unique birthday present. I said, "Thank you very much."

Finally, the great day arrived. That morning, Patti had gone in to take a bath, and she didn't know that her water had broken while she was bathing. We did know she was starting to get contractions. I was trying to time them.

"Something's not working out right. The water hasn't broken yet? Let's go see the doctor," I said.

I raced her over to the doctor, and he said, "Get her to the hospital. She's dilated five centimeters."

"Do I have enough time to take her there?"

"Yeah, you should be okay."

But he didn't bother to tell me what Patti was going to be like as we were driving to the hospital.

She was starting to yell.

We had almost reached Hollywood Presbyterian Hospital when we came to a crosswalk with an old man shuffling across the street.

Patti was yelling, "Hurry up. Get your butt across the street." She was going on and on. I was shocked and amused, but I didn't want to laugh because this was serious. I didn't want her to have the baby on the street.

I maneuvered around the old guy and took her into the hospital. They put her in a wheelchair and led her into the delivery room. I gowned up and the doctor said, "Are you ready?" I nodded and followed behind him. I was prepared for what I needed to do. I wasn't prepared for the way I was about to feel.

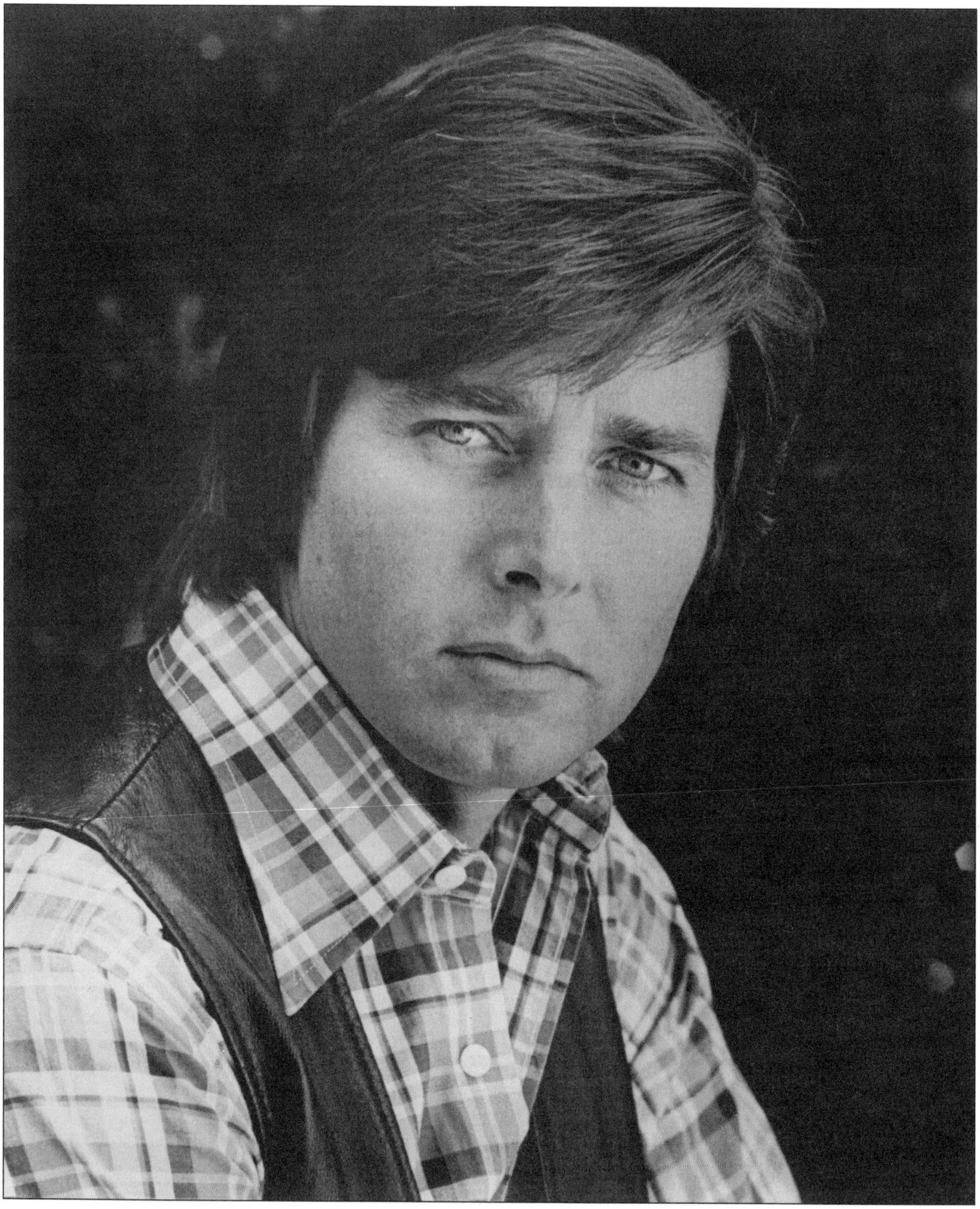

13 Christopher and Tyler's Dad

"Shallow breathe. Shallow breathe," I said in my best calming voice. I was acting as Patti's coach.

She continued screaming.

"It's going to be okay. Everything's going to be fine," I kept telling her.

"You think it's going to be okay? You think this feels okay?" Patti cried. "Why don't you try lying down here and having some of these contractions?"

I couldn't argue with that.

For hours I stayed right by her side, alternately feeding her ice chips and rubbing her shoulders. I didn't want her to be in pain, but there was so little I could do to comfort her.

Christopher Noel Sherman was born December 13, 1972, weighing six pounds, twelve ounces. I counted his little fingers and toes and exhaled. I was tremendously relieved that he was healthy and that Patti was okay.

That's when I first felt like a father. I felt scared. I felt responsible. I felt exhilarated. I felt completely at peace.

Just after Chris was delivered, I came back around to Patti's side. The emotion of the moment swept over me. I leaned down and kissed Patti's cheek.

"And then there were three," I whispered to her.

With Chris at Disneyland in 1974.

I don't even think she heard me, but I remember saying it. I hadn't rehearsed it. It just came to me. Tears came, too. I had never been happier.

A week later we publicly announced that we were married, that we were a family.

I said to Jay Bernstein, my press agent, "Patti's going to be okay now. Can we formalize it somehow?"

We decided to do a news conference. I still cannot believe how many newspeople showed up at the Sheraton-Universal Hotel. I didn't realize my marriage was that much of a scoop.

I met dozens of reporters in one room and then everyone came into the next room to meet and take pictures of Patti and Chris. I tried to explain what had happened, and why we had waited.

When it came to living up to the promise to my fans, "You'll be the first to know," I had honored that as soon as I could.

What I didn't know was that girls felt jealous of Patti. I had no idea that some fans would take my marriage to Patti as a personal affront. That was the last thing in the world either of us intended.

I was simply tired of the whirlwind. I needed to settle a bit. At twenty-eight, I wanted to know what it was like to have a family life of my own.

I'm sensitive to the "secret marriage" questions now because I wasn't sensitive enough to them then. Frankly, I didn't know there was anything to be sensitive about.

From the time Patti and I married until Chris was born, there wasn't anybody in our lives except each other. Patti and I spent every day together. Then, when Chris was born, we doted on him for a long time. The same thing happened when Tyler came along.

I don't think I was as in love with Patti at the outset as I was later on when we were a family. Our relationship deepened as we began creating a life together with our children.

We had an ordinary day-to-day family life. We even found a wonderful dog.

After Chris was born, we acquired a collie and named him Boo. Because I had always been a "Lassie" fan, Boo became my favorite of all the dogs I'd ever had. He even appeared in our Christmas family portrait.

Most important, his temperament was perfect for children. Before long, everything in my life revolved around my children.

Parenthood changed our lives in ways we had not imagined. I felt completely prepared for dealing with a new baby. I thought, "How difficult can it be? It's not like he's going to get up in the middle of the night and walk around, not at the beginning anyway."

For a while, I was right. Chris slept in our room at first so Patti could nurse him, but that meant I couldn't feed him anything. Sometimes I felt useless. I changed his diapers, but then he'd just sit there. I couldn't entertain him yet. He was too new.

Then Chris moved to his own room. I kept thinking I was hearing him crying. I worried constantly. There was nothing wrong with him, but I was a nervous wreck!

I installed an intercom right next to his crib. I kept the other end on my side of the bed.

"He's going to be fine. Don't worry," Patti kept telling me. But I listened to his every little cough. Every time I'd hear a whimper—ZOOOM—I'd be in there.

I was much worse than Patti. I would make one of my dashes in to check on him, and Patti would say, "Bobby, give it a rest."

Now, as a medic, I deal with emergency situations on a regular basis. After years of training, when something does happen, I stay calm and handle the situation. I didn't have that confidence then.

In spite of the rewards, parenting is a tough job. I was learning a lot—the hard way. I found myself trying to communicate with someone who couldn't communicate back. I was trying to get things across, to entertain, to be loving.

The challenge was to grow into the role of a parent without losing my ability to be a kid. I believed that was an integral part of being a good father. I wanted Chris, and later Tyler, to be able to enjoy me as a person, a kid, and a friend, as well as being their dad.

Just as I was beginning to get the hang of disrupted sleep patterns and diaper changes, Patti surprised me with some news: she was pregnant with Tyler.

Tyler Carnel Sherman entered the world on February 9, 1974, weighing seven pounds, eleven-and-a-half ounces. Chris was fourteen months old.

Chris's delivery had been a little more eventful because it was the first time for all of us. When Tyler was born, knowing what was going to happen helped me feel prepared. I was even able to take pictures of the delivery. It was exciting and I could enjoy it. By then, I was an old pro in the baby world.

Having two babies was twice the work in a lot of ways, but it was also twice the fun. That fourteen months' head start made Chris the bigger brother, but as Tyler grew older, they drew closer and closer together, not just in ability, but as friends.

The same fourteen months had also taught me much more about being a father. I was more attuned to what each new day would bring in Tyler's development.

By then I was semiretired. The world knew I was married, and I was content with the way things were going. I had done the film, *He Is My Brother,* with Keenan Wynn, and Ward and I produced a movie, *The Day the Earth Moved,* with Jackie Cooper and Stella Stevens.

One day I was sitting on the couch with Tyler. He was less than a year old and couldn't talk yet. Patti was with Chris in the boys' room. I was holding Tyler on my lap, looking down at him and talking to him. I had just started building my third and most ambitious Disneyland model in our backyard.

Father's Day 1974 in Hawaii with Chris and Tyler.

    I was saying things to Tyler like, "Pretty soon, you're going to have a street just for you at Disneyland. And it's going to be so much fun, and we're going to have a golf cart that goes all around. . . ." He was looking at me and listening to me, but I could tell he was not quite with me yet. So, I kept talking and talking, and all of a sudden, there was this FOCUS.

    He has beautiful blue eyes, and I could just tell, all of a sudden, there was this click "ON," like an abrupt arrival of consciousness. It was as if he was saying, "I'm here." He knew it. I knew it. He looked right into me. I had held him and talked to him all the time since he was born, but still, there had not been that connection.

    From then on, whenever we would do something, I'd always check Tyler to see if that contact was still there. It never went away.

    For the first two years of Tyler's life, I stayed busy working on my model of Disneyland. I wanted to do something special for the kids. I had thought of building them a treehouse, but I was worried that they would fall out of it. So I decided to build something much more ornate as well as safe.

    I planned a one-fifth scale model of Disneyland's Main Street. I started just before Tyler was born, and he was two and a half when I finished. Day after day I worked with the wood. I couldn't make bricks small enough, so I simulated a brick effect by hand-routing plywood. It was painstaking, but it worked.

Patti would bring the kids out, and I'd give Chris a little block of wood so he could hammer something and feel that he was working.

I don't think that the kids really enjoyed Main Street until they were older. Then they were able to have birthday parties and play there.

During that time, Patti and I met Marlon Brando. He came over to the house for dinner with Patti's best friend, Jill Banner.

I found him to be a very private man, a loner. At first, I was a bit in awe of him, but then I decided he was an okay guy. We spent time together when the girls went off to chat. I found he was extremely bright and full of surprises.

One night when Patti and Jill were off on their own, he and I ended up in my recording studio. To my amazement, he played the congas—and he was actually pretty good. I still have the tapes.

The boys on Main Street.

Christopher and Tyler's Dad

One outing we had together turned out to be unexpectedly funny. Patti was jumping her horses in competitions, and Jill wanted to see her compete at the Pomona Fair. She urged Marlon to come, too. He didn't want to go but finally agreed, provided he could wear a disguise.

He made himself up to look like Claude Rains in the film *The Invisible Man*. He had completely bandaged his head, leaving only holes for his mouth, nose, and eyes.

Best of all, he went to buy a hot dog, and he managed to smear mustard all over the bandages. It was funny but gross. Even he got a chuckle out of it.

Although the Disneyland Main Street wasn't up yet, I was working on the facades and he liked those. One building had a little ceiling fan in it, and he was intrigued with making the ceiling fan work. It never did, but it was a good idea.

Except for the concrete base on which the Disneyland model sits, I designed and built every facet of it. Twenty-nine building facades, the tallest one reaching ten-and-a-half feet, make up the fifty-by-fifty-foot model.

Dressed up for our big party to unveil my Disneyland Main Street model.

The project became so big, both in its size and the energy it required, that I started to be overwhelmed by it. I wanted to give up more than once, but Patti wouldn't let me.

Patti

I respect the fact that he did finish it. It was a labor of love. He was always fascinated with the architecture of Main Street Disneyland.

He would take extensive pictures of the buildings—the corbels, the cornices, the paint jobs, the colors. He would put the slides of the pictures he took on the big screen and then measure them according to scale. This is how meticulous he was. Why, I don't know. But it was something he wanted to do.

We had 250 people over for a "Street Completion Party." It was done in a "Gay Nineties" theme with straw hats, costumes, popcorn machines, and balloons all over.

One of the guests was Walt Disney's daughter Diane, who came with her husband to see what I had done. I'll never forget watching her walk around the bend near the pool and seeing Main Street. Her face lit up.

"My father would have fallen in love with this," she said. "Oh God." I thought, "That makes it all worthwhile."

In addition to the work on Disneyland, I was completely changing the landscape of our one-acre yard. Originally, there was just a nice lawn, and orange trees. It was pretty. But, at the same time, it didn't have Disneyland, and it was too manicured.

I wanted the look and feel of the setting from the forest scenes on "Here Come the Brides." I planned out special items like the waterfalls and the pool. I surrounded the pool with rocks and painted the interior azure so the effect is that of a lagoon.

I had a couple of specialists work with me on different areas using exotic plants to make a forest setting. I created a jungle feeling around the palm trees. After that, I just let it grow. If a tree fell, that's where I wanted it to be. I thought, "God did that, so I'm going to leave it alone."

The Disneyland Main Street is in the middle of the yard, with the forest all around. A track goes in a circle around the perimeter.

Now, riding in the golf cart around the perimeter track, we have earphones with special effects and music. As we drive along, we pass Disneyland, go around the bend, and arrive at the western section. Then we come on the cemetery where it's dark and the sign says, "Enter at your own risk." At night, eyes light up and you can hear growls. Then, there's thunder and lightning, and it starts to rain.

Patti, Chris, and Tyler with Chemineau.

Christopher and Tyler's Dad

Even though the boys had their own little amusement park, I don't think we spoiled them. They had their chores to do and rules to abide by. Throughout the year we didn't shower them with expensive toys. I admit, though, that I went overboard when it came to their Christmases. I felt it was important for me to re-create what I believed in when I was their age. I wanted them to have that same magical experience.

Christmas 1975.

Chris Sherman, drummer of the rock band "Whatever"

When Christmas came around, we got what we asked for. I got a beautiful set of drums when I was twelve or thirteen. I still have those drums. They're still the ones I use.

At Christmas, I'd dress up in a Santa outfit. Patti would bring the kids out, look around the corner, and say, "Watch out, he's gonna turn around. Get back in bed quick." They'd scurry back in bed. Then I'd go outside and throw some pebbles on the roof to sound like the reindeer were taking off.

Next, I'd run into the bedroom, climb out of the Santa outfit, and jump into bed, pretending to be asleep. Within seconds, Chris and Tyler would thunder in to give me the news.

"Daddy, Daddy, guess what? Santa was here!"

"You're kidding. And I slept through it."

For years, they believed in Santa only because I carried it out for so long.

Christmas 1977.

More than anything else I tried to provide them with the ability to dream. As they grew older, even though they realized there was no Santa Claus, they always remembered what their dad did to make them believe it.

When they have kids of their own, I hope they'll remember the freedoms they had growing up: that it's okay to think and to dream and to play.

Chris

I know I love him, and (someday when I have kids) if my kids love me as much as I love him, that would be great. That's all I could ask for.

For a long time, the boys wanted to be Ninjas. I had built them a target on which they practiced throwing Ninja stars, but they invariably missed and hit the garage door. The door still has holes in it. I'm so sentimental that I won't cover up the holes. It reminds me of when they were little kids.

With Chris at Yosemite in 1976.

I used to hold "Encino Olympics" that I made up for the two of them. There would be a swimming competition and a shooting competition. One year one would win and then the next year the other one would win. I had trophies made up, so they could say, "Oh, this is the Encino Olympics trophy I won. I came in second," even though there were only two of them. I was giving them food for thought to start their own creative processes.

As a child, I had created Frank, but they didn't need to create imaginary friends. They had each other. There was a time they were so into watching television that I feared I might lose them creatively so I worked at making up games to show them how to make their own fun.

Chris

He'd come up with games that would keep us entertained for hours. He'd take all the pillows off the couches and set them along the coffee table, making tunnels for us to go through.

He'd put a blanket across two chairs and set up a tent for us to sleep in. Then we'd go to the Disneyland Hotel, and he'd make up a game where he'd buy us a helium balloon. We'd stand at one end of the room. He'd let go of the balloon, and Tyler and I would run to catch it. Whoever got it won.

We'd play tackle. He'd hold two pillows, and we would just run at full speed right into him. We'd go to hotels, and he'd make up some sort of baseball or football game that we would play with crumpled-up paper.

It seemed to me that he was having at least as much fun if not more than we were.

Chris's first day of kindergarten, 1977. Tyler's along for moral support. Groovy lunch boxes!

I hoped to give them the ability to think and to create and not let anything be unattainable. I let them see the ideas I've had, and how I carried them through. I'm happy to say they seem to be proud of the things I've done.

It's interesting now to watch them take their friends through different parts of the house, showing them the forest and Disneyland. They relish being able to show not only that their dad has a sense of humor, but that they tolerated it.

Chris has picked up my humor, the way he delivers a joke. He's impish.

Chris

I took about six months of music lessons, and the rest was just listening to other bands.

My dad got me my stuff and just let me go. He gave me a few pointers here and there, but I think he wanted me to develop by myself, my own style.

Christopher and Tyler's Dad

I've got all my dad's CDs, and I play them regularly. They take my mind off things when I'm sitting there doing laundry or whatever I have to do.

I enjoy his music. It's good-natured, and it makes you happy when you listen to it.

Tyler was the first one to play the drums and have a natural sense of rhythm. It was uncanny how good he was. I said, "He's going to be a terrific drummer, there's no doubt." And what happens? He turns out to be a gifted keyboard player and composer, and Chris turns into one of the best drummers I've ever heard.

Tyler Sherman

I was playing drums and experimenting with different instruments. I had a feel for the drums first off, and then I went to piano. I've stuck with piano ever since age eight or nine. Then I got into synthesizers doing my own music.

If I hadn't been around my dad, I wouldn't have had any idea what a synthesizer was or what they did. He pretty much started me out. He would put me in the studio when I was a baby while he was doing his music. He would sit me down, and I would fall asleep to the music.

Chris, in a 1988 fashion show.

Tyler, 1995.

For two or three Christmases in a row, Tyler wanted a new keyboard. Chris wanted new drums or an addition that would go onto what he had. Buying them equipment was expensive, but I was happy to do it. To this day, they've stayed with music on their own.

I give Patti a lot of credit for raising the boys. I knew she'd be a wonderful mom, and she has been just that.

It wasn't until Chris was born that Patti started realizing who she was. She didn't like my being in show business, and she longed to live somewhere much more rural.

But I had my studio here, and we had a wonderful home. I couldn't figure it out. Somehow, what we wanted started taking us in different directions, and we grew apart. We weren't enemies. We still loved each other, but, through the years, our expectations of each other changed.

Patti, Tyler, and Chris at the stables, 1977.

As time went along, Patti's needs and her desires about how she wanted her life to be started shifting. I was going through my own changes, and there was conflict. It wasn't hateful or spiteful, it was just two people going down different roads.

Toward the end of the marriage, we weren't really sharing anymore. We merely negotiated things, and it wasn't fluid. I felt I was talking to someone who had her own agenda, and I wasn't included in it. She probably felt the same way. Finally, the marriage came apart.

Patti and I lived together for eighteen months while we waited for a court date for the divorce. During that time there was no plate throwing. The kids never saw anything negative. Through it all, we stayed friends.

When she moved out, everything that belonged to her was packed up. The kids and Boo were in the car. I opened the gate, gave the kids a hug, and watched as the car drove away. I closed the gate and that was it.

It was the darkest period of my life.

The day I watched them leave was the beginning of a lot of awful days. The house seemed like a big echo chamber. I couldn't sleep. I'd wake up because I'd have dreams about Chris and Tyler.

I kept saying to myself, "This situation is going to correct itself. It's all going to be okay." I didn't want to feel that sense of absolute loss.

My divorce from Patti was finalized in January 1979, after seven years of marriage. Chris was six and Tyler was almost five.

I was feeling sorry for myself, and I think the only salvation I had was that I was able to have the kids on weekends. I had to be okay for them. For a long time, though, I was simply pretending.

Then Patti and the boys went to Europe for three months.

At first, I didn't think much about it. The trip was an opportunity for Chris and Tyler to see other countries. The day I took them to the airport, it dawned on me that I wasn't going to see my boys for three months. The only reason I had remained glued together was for their weekend visits.

I watched the plane take off. I did a lot of praying that they'd return safely. Then, on the way home, the thought of how long three months without them would be sunk in.

I went crazy.

I started drinking badly enough that I rarely went out. I wouldn't accept offers to do a lot of things. If I had to work, I got it together long enough to do what I needed to. Otherwise, I shut down. It was a very dark time.

One particular day, I drank a lot of Scotch. The next thing I remember, I woke up under the pool table. I don't remember how I got there and that scared me.

For about a month I didn't know what time of day it was. I didn't know what day it was. It was far worse than my breakup with Lynn. When she and I had broken up, I was devastated but I worked.

When the kids left, it wasn't just a romantic relationship that was out of my life, it was my children, part of my soul.

The feeling of losing my boys was so overpowering that I didn't have any other hurt zones left. Nothing compares with the feeling of having your children taken away from you.

People thought I was on vacation someplace, but I was home. Half the time, at night, I didn't even turn on the lights. I wouldn't watch television because I'd see something that might remind me of them or that would somehow set me off.

So I had two choices: go off the deep end or start to work and do something. Create something.

I began to create projects around the house. I built a rock wall. I expanded my studio.

I hit on the idea of creating an arcade for the boys. I turned their bedroom into a mini amusement park with pinball machines, a miniature bowling alley, an electronic chess game, and other fun things. My energy started returning as the time for their homecoming neared.

The first weekend the boys came home from Europe, I felt like I was whole again.

The kids loved what I had done for them.

When they were with me, it was quality time. We rented movies. We played. They couldn't wait for the weekend, which was

My boys.

all I needed to know. Any time they could spend extra time with me, they couldn't have been happier. We went to Disneyland often.

In fact, they loved the arrangement because they had two houses. When they spent time with me, they had freedom. Patti was a good mother, but she was strict. During the weeknights when I didn't have them, she was the one who had to say, "Okay, you both have to do your homework, etc." She had to play both roles.

I could be "the Disneyland Dad." And our lives moved on from there.

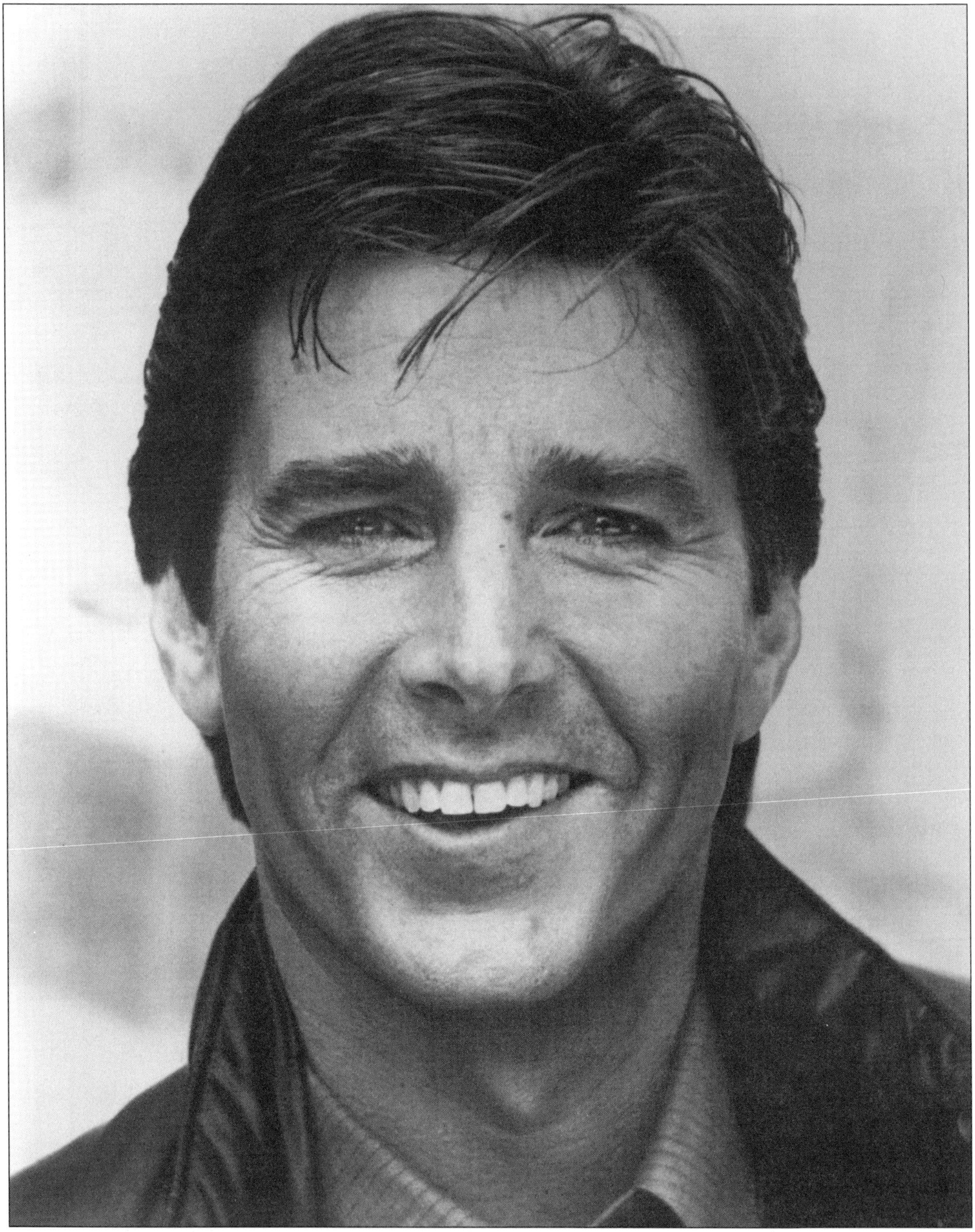

14 TAC-5 and the LAPD

Proposal by the Bobby Sherman Volunteer EMT Foundation, endorsed June 26, 1995, by Alan R. Cowen, Chief of Paramedics, Commander, Bureau of Emergency Medical Services, Los Angeles City Fire Department

The Bobby Sherman Volunteer EMT Foundation is involved in creating a pilot program to solicit Emergency Medical Technicians, provide them with equipment, communications, and backup, and schedule their presence to provide emergency medical services and triage at community and nonprofit public gatherings.

This proposed program will vastly improve the delivery of emergency health care services to the public and provide significant relief to the overburdened public emergency medical system.

Nearly a decade in the emergency medical system has taught me, time and time again, that many events involving large crowds lack medical backup.

On Saturdays and Sundays in Los Angeles, for example, soccer matches and other recreational sports draw crowds that fill the parks; players break limbs, suffer heat exhaustion, and experience life-threatening emergencies, but there's often no standby medical personnel present.

If somebody suffers a knee abrasion, he or she ends up

> *calling 911 for a paramedic unit. Meanwhile, a heart attack victim might have to wait for that ambulance while the paramedics bandage a knee. It's a waste of manpower and a drain on the system.*
>
> *The foundation's plan is to provide medical standby emergency services at all types of nonprofit events. There are thousands of certified EMTs (Emergency Medical Technicians) in Los Angeles county alone, only a small percentage of whom are actually employed as medical providers at any one time. Volunteer medical standby work sharpens their skills by providing valuable experience.*
>
> *Starting in the San Fernando Valley in California, we plan to provide first aid vehicles, portable first aid stations, and a central facility to coordinate volunteer efforts.*
>
> *I believe we will have enough success within the first year that the program will go citywide. Our next goal is to have it go statewide and then nationwide.*

Although I've been a certified EMT since 1988, my interest in first aid began years before.

As I drove to the Columbia Ranch during "Brides" and "Getting Together," I often passed car accidents and wished that I knew how to help.

Accident victims would be lying in the road and observers would stand near them with their arms folded, looking grim. It wasn't that they didn't want to help; they just didn't know what to do. I shared everyone's feelings of helplessness.

I couldn't spare the time to take first aid classes then. After I became a parent, though, I wanted to know more about first aid.

As a toddler, Tyler seemed accident prone, but it was only because Chris was fourteen months older and more coordinated by comparison. Tyler was not clumsy. In fact, his misadventures in his attempts to keep up with his older brother were kind of cute. One incident, however, motivated me to learn first aid.

When Tyler was about four, he fell off his drum stool and hit his head, which started to bleed. Patti always panicked at the sight of blood.

Tyler wasn't badly injured, and I stopped the bleeding and bandaged his head. I knew then I wanted to be ready if anything worse ever happened.

I picked up a Red Cross first aid pamphlet. I read more and more. By the time I took an actual first aid course, it was a cakewalk.

Finally, I became so adept that the Red Cross asked me to lend a hand as an instructor. I was delighted. I began assisting in classes and then took the Basic Life Support course. Next, I took Advanced First Aid.

I thought my first aid training would stop there. Then, in the late eighties, I met Chief Alan Cowen, the chief paramedic for the city of Los Angeles.

I set up a meeting with Chief Cowen because I had an idea for TAC-5, an acronym for Traffic Accident Communication. The "5" is synonymous with the symbol for a hand, which universally means help.

Chief Alan R. Cowen

Bobby had on a black turtleneck and a very sleek, very well-tailored black sport coat with black pants, and at once I realized it was Bobby Sherman the singer. The meeting with him could not have been more pleasant. He had enthusiasm, and he was a very dear man. He had empathy for people.

He was excited about the project he was doing. He proceeded to give me a whole rendition of what he intended to do. He had it well planned, and I was struck by his individualism and his courage in wanting to get this thing accomplished to help people. There was little in it for Bobby Sherman but a whole lot in it for the public.

Chief Cowen liked my idea, but it was probably a little too ambitious. It put volunteers on the roadways searching for drivers in trouble. There were too many jurisdiction problems, and it wasn't the most efficient use of our volunteers' time. I began to look for other ways to apply the concept.

In that process, I became friends with Chief Cowen. I was impressed with his professionalism, and we seemed to be kindred spirits.

He told me I had a flair for first aid training and encouraged me to take an EMT course. I had no idea what an impact the training would have on my life.

Chief Cowen

Bobby's the kind of spirited fellow that emergency people should be like. He's not only capable, but he also has about him a sense of compassion. He represents life and its journey in one of the clearest universal messages, and that's the message of kindness. He is probably the most generous man I have ever met.

I took the basic course to become an EMT in 1987 and earned my certification. The training films with the blood and guts didn't bother me, but there was always that little bit of a doubt about how well I would react in a major emergency. I discovered the truth quickly enough.

I was on duty with my partner when we came on a car that had spun out of control on the freeway. By the time we reached the vehicle, the driver was hysterical. While my partner tried to calm the young woman down, I checked the car. Protocol dictates that we check in cars for toys or clothing items that might indicate the presence of a child.

Through the driver's window, I glimpsed what appeared to be the flesh-colored legs and shoes of a doll. When I checked more closely, I discovered not a doll, but a little girl on the floor of the passenger's side. Her head was pressed between the passenger seat and the door. She had not been wearing a seat belt and had apparently hit the door handle in the spinout. She had a hematoma, a huge knot on her head, and was unconscious. She wasn't breathing. Her chin was pressed so far into her chest that her tongue was cutting off her airway.

I stayed calm. My training had taught me what to do. I managed to open an airway and began to administer mouth-to-mouth resuscitation. I put the first breath in and was about to start the second one when I saw her take a breath.

It was the best moment of my life!

As an EMT, the challenges I met became more and more severe, but I knew each time what I was supposed to do. Possessing knowledge gives you a different perspective. You immediately assess a situation with more authority.

When someone is hurt, I immediately go to work. It's like acting when someone says, "Okay. Ready. Action. You're on." It's when you're all finished and your patient is released or moved up to the next level of care that you can sit back and reflect.

At that point, you acknowledge what you did right and look for the things that you could do better next time. If it's a traumatic situation, you start shaking a little bit. The shakes go away after about the first year of emergency medical services (EMS) work.

After that, you handle the situation and say, "Okay, now where should we go for lunch?" If you can't develop that ability to separate your emotions, then you'll quickly burn out on the job.

Not long after I had become an emergency medical technician, I was working in the Emergency Room at Northridge Hospital. A man brought in his wife, who was hemorrhaging. She had undergone an operation a week or so before and had gotten up and walked around too soon. She had started to go into tachycardia, an excessively rapid heartbeat.

She was lapsing in and out of consciousness as the nurse and I searched for a vein to start a saline solution. All our attention was focused on stabilizing her.

Meanwhile, her husband kept looking at me. Eventually he saw my name tag but he didn't say anything. At that moment, he was too worried about his wife.

After we got a good line going, we were able to bring her vital signs back up. Her color started coming back to her, and she began to revive.

A few minutes later, she felt better and had regained some strength. When he knew she was okay, her husband pointed to me.

"Honey, guess who this is," he said. So I knew he'd found me out.

She still couldn't really focus but she stared at me for a moment, and her eyes grew big.

"Bobby. It's Bobby Sherman. You're kidding. Oh my God. I must look a mess. Oh gosh. I don't have any makeup on."

WHAT BOBBY SEES WHEN

• **ARE YOU SHY?**
I think generally I am. I don't know if I can say things. I am a very out going and free thinking kind of person, but still, I'm rather withdrawn and I keep to myself. Like if I'm with a whole crowd of people I'll get a little bit uncomfortable. I don't mean like when I'm performing. When I'm performing I know what I'm supposed to do and then it is automatic and I really enjoy it. But I think, generally, when I'm around a lot of people and I have nothing to do I get uptight only because I kind of feel my element is a little better said when I am performing.

• **ARE YOU INTELLIGENT?**
How can I answer that? I would say no, but the fact is that I am ... because I built the recording studio and I am building a new one on my own and because of some of the things I have put together and some of the things I do is enough of an indication to me that I am supposedly intelligent.

But on the other hand, when I took my three IQ tests, after the first one, they wanted me to take it again because they thought I was cheating. They wanted me to take the third one because they thought that I was lucky. After the third one, they realized that I didn't belong in the grade I was in. They were going to advance me to a whole different kind of thing, but I didn't want to go. I didn't want to give up football.

My opinion is valid in relationship to what is supposedly the truth because I don't impress people. Like on "Music Scene" ... I got nothing but compliments from people who saw the show, but when I saw it, not that I thought it was bad, but I didn't think it was good either. It was a question of saying, "I wonder how the other people thought it was?" I'm so objective that I lose scope of being able to say what is right and what is wrong. I don't want that to enter into my mind ever when I'm performing because when I perform it's real and I *feel* it at the time.

• **ARE YOU HANDSOME?**
No, I don't think so. I have no opinion of how I look. Like sometimes I will comb my hair one way and think I look all right then, but I don't put it on a graph and say I'm handsome today in comparison to yesterday when I was grubby. There are times I feel I look better than I do at other times, but I don't put it on any graph that coincides with handsome, average and ugly to the rest of the world. I have never been able to be a judge of that and I don't want to be.

• **DO YOU HAVE A SENSE OF HUMOR?**
I think at times I do, especially when it's not my own sense of humor that I am trying to satisfy as opposed to when I am trying to make other people laugh or tell a joke. I have more concern about another person getting a punch line or a joke or enjoying myself.

When I try to entertain myself, I don't think I am very good at that. I cringe a little bit, like when I was doing "Music Scene" and I finished my number ... I was walking up the steps and I hit the step and it looked like I tripped and I kind of laughed, but on the other hand, when I thought about it, I cringed. I think I laughed and thought, don't make that mistake a second time.

• **ARE YOU KNOWLEDGEABLE ABOUT WORLD AFFAIRS?**
Yes. I don't think I could sit down and give an educated argument or synopsis on world events. I just don't have all the facts about every situation. However, there are things I do deal in, but a bit of work and times goes into it as far as finding out facts about life and what the situation is. Like the McCartney death rumors ... I started doing a lot of research on it. So I think I can talk about that as opposed to talking about what Nixon's speech was about even though I heard the jist of it. There are some things I am not up on. I think I could be, but time doesn't allow.

HE LOOKS IN THE MIRROR

• **DO YOU THINK YOU ARE CONCEITED?**
To be honest with you, I would like to think not. I think I have been and it was so totally and quickly squelched and smashed to bits that I dismissed it because it was a waste of time and not getting anything accomplished.

I kind of wish, in a way, I had a touch of it so sometimes when I get depressed or overly shy because of what's inside of me that I could overcome it, but I don't have that ability. I've got a long way to go and a lot of things I want to do and I desperately don't want to be out of the picture again, like one show ending and the waiting so many months for another. Not that I am being ungracious ... it's something I feel I have a lot to say about.

When time lags I get impatient. I think there are such things as "stars" and I think that right now I am so far away from being one that I am not going to even try to anticipate where I am on the scale. I think the reason I am in this business is so I can do something and entertain and feel a sense of accomplishment as opposed to the monetary or spiritual thing.

• **ARE YOU HEALTHY?**
Yes. I get colds now and then, and I did have a case of ptomaine poisoning once. Outside of that I have never been seriously ill.

• **ARE YOU A NAME DROPPER?**
I think I come into contact with a lot of big names and sometimes I will be talking to someone and I will think of what someone else has said to me and I'm "dropping a name." Maybe people have a right to think I am a name dropper, but I don't think I am. I don't use "names" to get into places or impress anybody. If it's a part of a conversation or useful for explanation, that's different.

• **ARE YOU A DEDICATED FOLLOWER OF FASHION?**
No, I don't think so. I guess taste will put certain combinations of things together, so in that way I am. But I don't go out and buy things because they are "in." I never went out and bought a Nehru suit because it didn't agree with me, but on the other hand I wear turtle necks, vests and bell bottoms because I like them. So if the fashion is "in" and I like it, I'll be strong on it.

• **ARE YOU A GOOD MUSICIAN?**
Yes. I think I am good on certain things. On other things I'm just average, but I think overall I have the concept of what music is about. I am a good producer in conjunction with being a good musician because even if I can't play it, at least I know how I want it to sound. It doesn't really matter if I want to have something played that nobody but I can play or if I am trying to get a certain idea across to the musicians then I will do it so they can hear what I'm talking about.

• **DO YOU HAVE GOOD MANNERS?**
I get by. I think more than I am aware of. I'm more aware of people than manners. I will generally adjust to the atmosphere of the person and the situation and conduct myself accordingly.

• **ARE YOU A GOOD DANCER?**
I think the only way I can answer that is to say I'm adequate. I will go along with the trend, but I think I usually just react to the song more than I do the "right" thing.

• **ARE YOU A GOOD DATE?**
I like to think so, but I really don't know. I try to have fun, but if the person I'm with is in a very serious mood I try to adjust accordingly. I just try to relax and have a good time. I don't think I'm very demanding ... I look for communication.

• **ARE YOU THE MARRIAGEABLE TYPE?**
Yes, I am, I think it will happen someday. I don't know about right now. I do think I'll be ready when the right girl comes into my life who really means something to me.

• **ARE YOU A LOVER OF CHILDREN?**
Yes, not too many though. Say you have four kids and you say you love them all the same ... well I can't agree with that. Each one is an individual with separate problems and personalities, so you react to each of them differently. So if, I have only a couple of children, I feel I can devote more time to them.

• **ARE YOU A SPORTS ENTHUSIAST?**
When it comes to football I really am. I really like it and do enjoy watching the game.

• **ARE YOU A DAYDREAMER?**
I think that's how it all started!

"Don't worry," I said. "You've been through a lot. You look just fine."

We sat there and talked until her strength returned. Before she left, she asked me for an autograph.

Being recognized by fans is always a heartening experience. When they see I'm a medic, they're proud of my efforts. I consider this work a way of giving something back to them as well as to the community.

Learning a new skill adds to the services I can provide. As a beginning EMT, I learned sign language, for example, because I had to deal with many people who were either hard of hearing or could not hear at all. It makes people comfortable, even if you're bad at it or slow. They appreciate that you've taken the time to learn something for them.

I've continued to add to my skills through the years. In 1991, I became an instructor for the American Heart Association and began teaching EMTS as well. My involvement simply kept growing.

By 1992, I'd been with the emergency medical services system about five years. The Los Angeles Police Department knew about me because I had donated my time for the Baker-to-Vegas 120-mile marathon, which annually brings in law enforcement participants from across the country. The police department asked me to provide medical services for the event. I was honored.

Butch Rager, retired LAPD police officer

He had applied to be a specialist reserve, and part of the process is that we do a background interview.

I was given a package [a personnel file] of somebody named Bobby Sherman. I started looking at it and said, "I'll be damned. This is the guy that my sister had all the posters of, all the records of." I thought, "He's a celebrity, I'm probably going to get him on something—drugs or a dirty background of some sort."

He came in and he was just so nice and so friendly. I thought, "Boy, I'm going to feel guilty doing this guy, but I have to do what I have to do."

He sat down, and we talked about this and that 'till I thought he was pretty comfortable with me and I was comfortable with him. Then I hit him with all the questions—from his finances to his sex life. You name it, we talked about it.

After twelve years of doing this, I can tell when people are lying. He's as clean as a Safeway chicken—his whole background, his whole life has been an open book, basically. He not only had a clean background, but he's a nice guy.

They appointed me as a specialist officer, assigning me immediately to the training division, which they usually don't do with reserve officers. Since then, I've taught thousands of cadets first aid and cardiopulmonary resuscitation (CPR) and handled recertification for officers.

I am the only EMT instructor with the LAPD. Although I'm paid by the department as a reserve officer, I voluntarily sign the checks back over to them. Maybe karma really works. Unlike the checks I had to sign over years ago to sing on local TV shows, this is something that does some good. It's more important that these officers learn CPR and first aid than it is that I receive a paycheck.

From the first day, when they handed me a schedule, it's been nonstop. I love it.

With Mom.

Officer Marty Fentress, LAPD, TV, Photo, and Sound Unit

I realized what a valuable resource Bob could be for the Los Angeles Police Department. We have a reserve program that is divided into three types of reserves. We have line reserves, who are full-fledged, gun-carrying police officers; we have technical reserves, who are non-field certified; they get a uniform, they get a badge, they don't have a gun. They work nonhazardous duties like the front desk, administrative-type jobs. Then we have a group called specialist reserves, which is what Bobby is right now.

Police officers in California have to have twenty-four hours of training every two years to keep certified by the state. Of course, part of that training is keeping their CPR and first aid up-to-date. When Bobby came on board, we only had one or two police officers that were at the academy teaching. Of course a lot of their time is taken up with recruits. I know that they were overwhelmed, not only with the recruits, but with the reserve academy, which is in-service training for the field officers and the officers on the department. So, I said, "Bobby, would you be interested in helping the department by teaching first aid?" Of course his response was, "Oh, absolutely. When do you want me to start?"

The week we got him in as a specialist reserve, that next weekend he was teaching.

I spend about forty hours a month working for the department as an instructor in the classroom, but I help in other areas when I can. Because of my television experience, Marty sometimes asks me to appear on camera for training tapes and special projects. We've put together a music video called "The Thin Blue Line," about police work. I sing the title song, the proceeds of which will benefit police charities.

In addition to my teaching duties, in 1993 I started providing medical standby care for the police academy graduations and special events such as Mayor Richard Riordan's monthly bike tours.

I'm a medical officer and a supervisor. I also arrange for the assignment of certified medics for various functions like the annual Baker-to-Vegas race. I enjoy it all.

Marty Fentress

Before Bobby Sherman, we would have graduation ceremonies and there was never anybody out there in case somebody passed out or had a problem. Some of these graduation ceremonies are

TAC-5 and the LAPD

held in 90°F to 100°F weather, and we never even thought about it. It's really nice to have Bobby there, and he's there every time.

He was made Reserve Officer of the Year. That's quite an honor. It's because Bob just keeps putting in.

In the late eighties, I had started outfitting my own car, a black Daytona, with the right kind of equipment to show what could be done. It became the prototype for the medical unit I drive now.

I used what I learned from working in my first car to set up the red Daytona I drive now as a rescue unit. It carries anything and everything an EMT might need for as many as ten patients: oxygen tanks, packaged splints, rolls of bandages, bottled water, and other paraphernalia. It has emergency lights, a TV camera for documentation, and several types of radios.

Through the years, my friend Fred Miller helped me develop these ideas. Fred and I became friends when he was my EMT instructor, and we often work together on volunteer functions such as the Baker-to-Vegas races and Mickey Thompson Off-Road Races. Fred is the first to remind me just how well equipped the TAC unit has become.

With Fred Miller at the 1990 Mickey Thompson Race in Las Vegas.

Fred Miller, a paramedic with the Los Angeles City Fire Department

When I met Bobby, he already had that TAC unit basically designed. What I did was help him with the fine-tuning.

Any time you go up a level, you get to use another piece of equipment. So this poor little Daytona started off with just a little bit of first aid supplies in the car. Now it has really outgrown itself. It's at a point where it's full. I'm sure the next vehicles will be designed with a little more room in mind.

We drove to Las Vegas in the Daytona, and I'm sure that it was easier for the astronauts to get in the Apollo shuttle. I mean, you're afraid to touch anything because there are wires and everything is hooked up to something. There are dials and gauges. Everything's got a use.

In uniform.

During the L.A. earthquake in 1994, my usually too-full car was completely emptied of supplies as I responded to call after call. What started out as a tough day became a thirty-eight-hour ordeal. People were asking for help on every corner—it was an almost overwhelming and humbling experience. I wanted to help as many people as I could.

Being a medic is the most rewarding job in the world. When someone is in pain and you can help ease some of that pain and make things right, there is not a better feeling. An Oscar or an Emmy is all very well, and that's something that I would love to enjoy. However, no award could measure up to the joy I experience when I've helped somebody.

I believe that every man, woman, and child on the face of the earth should know first aid and cardiopulmonary resuscitation.

These life-saving techniques work, and you never know when you're going to need them.

> ### Dena
>
> *One day, I joined a* CPR *class Bobby was teaching. In a tiny classroom, some twenty ordinary citizens sat on folding chairs, clutching their information sheets. Each of them had signed up through the* LAPD *to learn* CPR, *not knowing who their instructor would turn out to be.*
>
> *Before the class started, I sat down in the second row in the middle. Two women next to me were looking at Bobby and then at each other.*
>
> *"Is that . . . ?" one woman said.*
>
> *"I think it is," said the other.*
>
> *No video monitor was available to show the short presentation tape Bobby had brought along. He filled in with live demonstrations.*
>
> *"Hey, are you okay?" Bobby asked, shaking a plastic dummy's shoulder as he showed the correct procedure to approach a potentially unconscious patient.*
>
> *For four hours, with only short breaks, Bobby alternately inspired, instructed, and entertained his class. I glanced around the room after two hours had passed. Everyone was watching with interest.*
>
> *In the time we sat there, students learned how to use the head tilt/chin lift to open airways; they asked questions about rescue breathing; and they memorized numbers of compressions for adult and infant* CPR.
>
> *At the end of the class, students lined up single-file to test their knowledge. Everyone in the class passed the test. Each of us walked away better equipped to help someone in trouble.*
>
> *"That's what I love about teaching," Bobby told me as we left. "If I help someone in need, that's one person I've touched. When I teach a class like this, I've instantly multiplied the good that can be done."*

I love the fact that working as a medic is real life, that it's happening right now. There are no take-twos, so you have to think on your feet. During the last nine years, there's no doubt I've become a better person, a lot more aware of my fellow human beings as a result of this work. But, also, I think it's made me a better performer. I'm certainly a lot more in control of my own faculties and my abilities to portray real thought or feeling.

Medical rescue work and teaching is the best life experience and training that I could ever have.

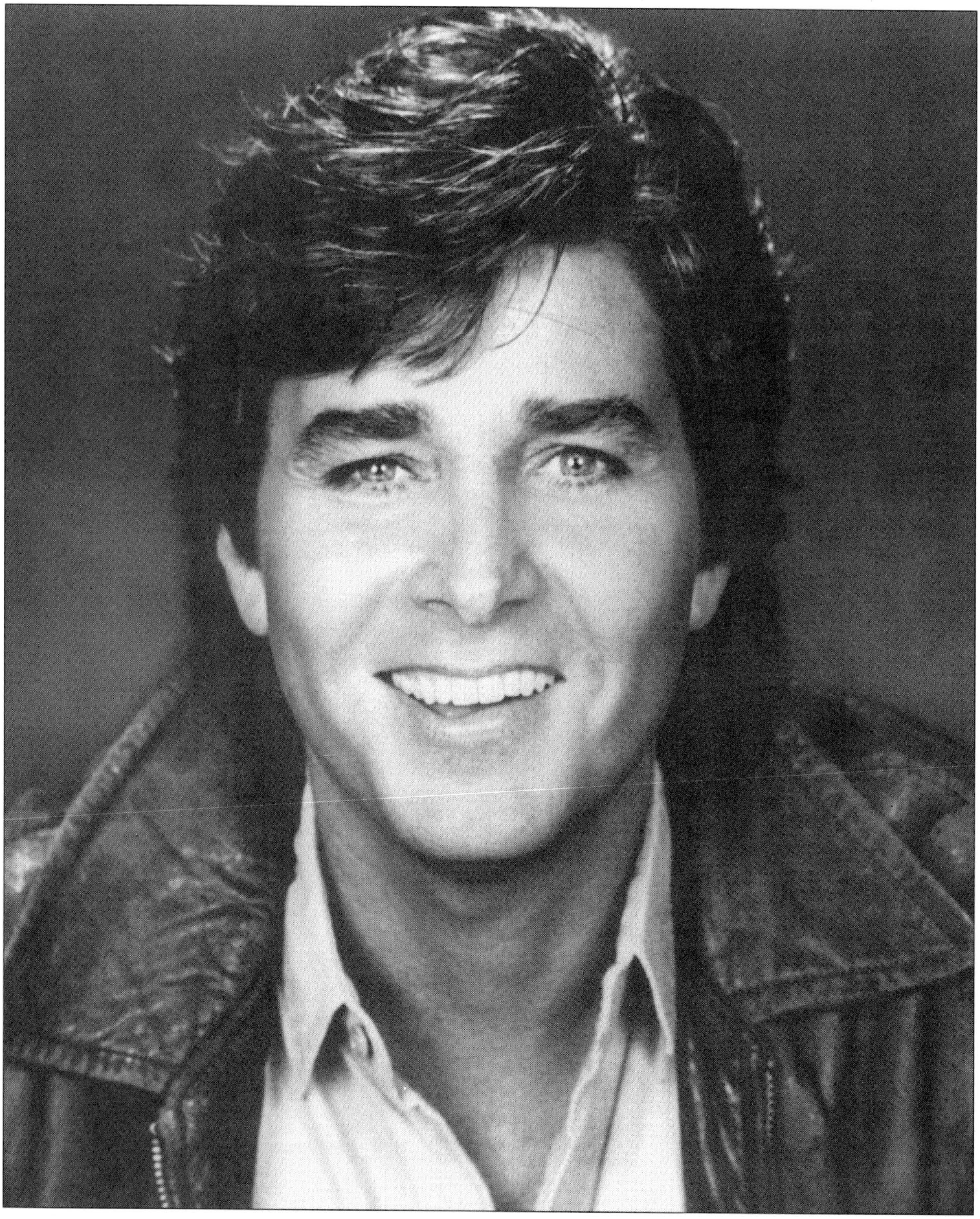

15 What Now?

Ward Sylvester

One of the reasons teenage idols don't last very long is that little sisters want their own idols. They don't want to adopt their older sisters' heroes. So, after two or three years, you get a new one.

Show business is very fickle. As the old joke goes, first it's "Who is Bobby Sherman?" Then it's "Get me Bobby Sherman." Then it's "Get me a Bobby Sherman type." Finally, it becomes "Who is Bobby Sherman?"

After my fans had grown up and were no longer looking for a teenage idol, I was still being classified as one. Even if it was "former" teenage idol, that label still followed me.

I had stayed a teen idol for so long that I became synonymous with the term. It reached the point that people were saying, "If you want to be a teenage idol, try to be another Bobby Sherman." When my popularity waned, Chuck Laufer of *Tiger Beat* admitted to me, "We would do anything to find another Bobby Sherman."

Ward

Teenage idols always have the problem of transition. How do they get taken seriously? How do they keep a career going? The most brilliant example of it was Bobby Darin, who traded up from being a teen sensation to being a legitimate adult singer. In a sense, Frank Sinatra and Elvis Presley were other examples, although their transitions were rocky and it took them a long time.

The mistake most teenage idols make is trying to demonstrate that they're hipper than their fans, which, of course, they usually are. They are older, and they're living in a very different environment. However, their peers are not the same people as their fans. To win the respect of their show business peers, they adopt the values of the community they're in rather than the community that cares about them. They end up condescending to or being embarassed by their fans and turn them off.

That's something that Bobby has never done. He's always appreciated and valued his fans. I give him great credit for that.

Overall, the whole teen-idol phenomenon was tremendously flattering. God bless the fans. Their belief in me afforded me the kind of lifestyle I wished to have. Still, it's strange how success affects your life.

Once I had achieved success, I lost touch with some of my friends. It's an odd fact of life that your fences rise as your affluence increases. The same walls I had to erect to protect my family's privacy also kept me from knowing my neighbors.

Fame didn't change me but it did change people's reactions to me. Something about fame puts people at a distance. I've often wondered whether I would have pursued a career in show business if I had known what it could cost.

Professionally, I found myself in a catch-22 situation. My teen-idol status brought in enough money that I could stay home with my family; it also frequently kept me from being offered the type of parts I wished to play. Throughout most of the seventies, I was semiretired. I kept busy raising Chris and Tyler and working on Main Street.

Of the few television appearances I made during that era, I'm particularly pleased with the "Mod Squad" episodes. In one, I played a convict who had been framed by my girlfriend's father. This straight dramatic role marked a complete departure from the work I had done previously.

Both the "Mod Squad" parts and an appearance on "Cade's County" with Glenn Ford gave me the chance to do some dramatic work. While filming "He Is My Brother," I had the chance to work with the distinguished director Edward Dmytryk, whose credits include *The Caine Mutiny*. Those roles might not have changed the way I was perceived, but at least they gave me exposure as someone other than a teen idol.

What Now?

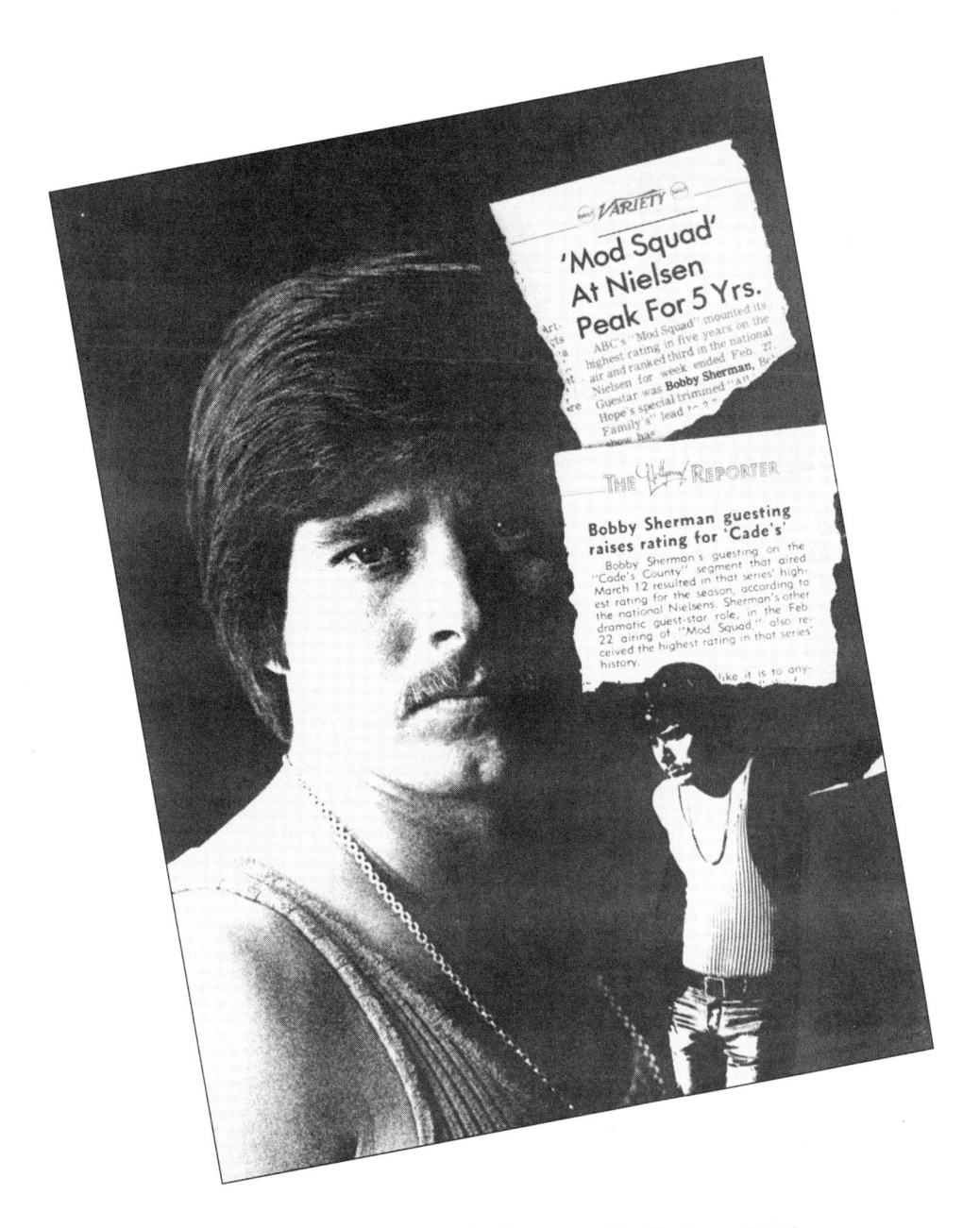

> **VARIETY**
> **'Mod Squad' At Nielsen Peak For 5 Yrs.**
> ABC's "Mod Squad" mounted its highest rating in five years on the air and ranked third in the national Nielsen for week ended Feb. 27. Guestar was **Bobby Sherman**. Bob Hope's special trimmed "All in the Family's" lead to...

> **THE HOLLYWOOD REPORTER**
> **Bobby Sherman guesting raises rating for 'Cade's'**
> Bobby Sherman's guesting on the "Cade's County" segment that aired March 12 resulted in that series' highest rating for the season, according to the national Nielsens. Sherman's other dramatic guest-star role, in the Feb. 22 airing of "Mod Squad," also received the highest rating in that series' history.

Although I still spent a great deal of time with Chris and Tyler, my responsibilities for them had changed by the 1980s. As they grew up and went off on their own paths, I had time and energy again to devote to my own career.

I made numerous television guest appearances on shows such as "The Love Boat," "Blacke's Magic," "Fantasy Island," and "Murder, She Wrote," and hosted a fall preview show for CBN, now the Family Channel. I did the film *Get Crazy* to work with Allan Arkush, who had directed *Rock 'n' Roll High School.* I also composed the music for "People Magazine on TV" and "Crimewatch Tonight" for CBS, and produced the television movie *The Day the Earth Moved*. I scored all the music for *The Day the Earth Moved* myself in my studio.

Then in 1986 a chance to do something new came with the comedy series "Sanchez of Bel Air" for Paramount Pictures Television. For its thirteen episodes, I played a character named Frankie Rondell, the proverbial obnoxious neighbor.

Frankie had made one hit record in the sixties, called "The Bop Shop." He had earned enough money from it to buy a house in Bel Air. Retired from show business, he spent his time being a nosey neighbor to the Sanchez family. Although the character wasn't based on me, I could identify with aspects of his life.

When I started the show, I had only a couple of scenes. The audience response to my role was so strong, though, that more lines were added for my character. I became an integral part of the later shows.

I was happy because I had never done a situation comedy with a live audience. At first, I went through those before-air nerves, just saying to myself, "Okay, get this down. Concentrate." Then I began to loosen up and move into the rhythm of it all. The experience stretched me, and I liked that.

Bob Claver

He surprised me more than anything on "Sanchez" because he was the funny neighbor, which is not a part you'd cast Bobby in, and he was marvelous. I give the producers a lot of credit because you would never think of him in that part.

As "Sanchez" ended, I was becoming immersed in EMS work. In hindsight, maybe the cancellation of the show was destiny. If I had pushed hard, I might have found myself in another series. But, as it happened, I got the opportunity to do what I'm doing now, so I have no complaints.

The eighties marked a period of transition for me. Events of that decade were sandwiched between my two most traumatic experiences.

Twice in my life, in 1979 and 1990, my saddest days have been caused by departures. The first time, I was saying good-bye to my children. The last time, I was saying "I love you" to my dad.

Because my dad had always been an active and strong figure, busy with the milk route and his own projects, I found it hard to imagine him incapacitated. His decline was gradual and maybe that was good. Had we lost him suddenly, I think that would have devastated all of us. He had always been unwell with asthma but when he was diagnosed with congestive heart failure, emphysema, and chronic obstructive pulmonary disease, I knew he wouldn't be in this world much longer. Especially after I became involved with the EMS system, I understood what was happening to his body. I knew he wasn't going to improve.

The most difficult thing was seeing him suffer. He hung on for so long. During the four years before he finally passed away, I'd rush him to the hospital many times.

Everyone around him was suffering, but he was suffering the most. He was unproductive and saw the effect of his illness on my mom. He hated the idea of being a burden to her. We hated watching him suffer.

As time went on, I have to admit my prayers changed. He was in such agony the last four months that I began to say, "God, do him a favor. Take him." That's what I resigned myself to pray for.

The day he died, Darl called to tell me.

"Dad's gone," she said, softly. I could tell she was broken up, but it was almost a relief.

We went to the hospital, and my sister and mother went in to see him one last time. I didn't want to. The day before, he had been sitting up and smiling and cracking jokes. I hugged him and told him I loved him as I left that evening. He was actually breathing freely, and he had color. It was a moment of euphoria before he passed away. I hadn't seen him look like that in years.

That's how I prefer to remember him.

Of all the skills my dad taught me, the greatest was how to be a father. We live on in the hearts and minds of those we love. My dad's love of music carries on through me and Chris and Tyler.

Mom, Dad, and Darl at the hospital when Chris was born, December 13, 1972.

It seems like yesterday when Tyler and Chris were four and five. It's amazing to say they're twenty-two and twenty-three. Although I didn't really stutter when I was on "Here Come the Brides," now, when anyone asks their ages, I start to stutter.

Memories of Chris and Tyler, especially when they were little, can bring out all kinds of emotions for me. I have a picture of them that I took at Disneyland in which Chris is holding Tyler's hand. They were beaming and happy. Even though it's not a sad picture, it can easily bring a tear to my eye. It takes me back to those times, which I remember very fondly. Over the years that memory becomes a little more sad, because I miss those times.

I love being a father. Once Chris and Tyler were born, I thought about how nice it would be to have a daughter, especially with the model Disneyland. It would be the world's biggest dollhouse.

Maybe it was better that I didn't have a little girl, though. Knowing the world as I do, my little girl would probably have never been allowed out of the house until she was thirty. I think I might have been a little too naive back then to know how to raise a daughter. I certainly could handle it now, though.

When Patti and I divorced in 1979, I stepped into the world of dating again—and, unfortunately, I've simply never been much of a dater. I never perfected the patter to toss off lines like, "Would you be interested in going out with an ex–teenage idol?" That doesn't seem right.

I've never approached a lady with the idea of making a score. It's just not my style.

I've had short-term relationships when I was attracted to someone, hoping that there could be something there, and then personalities clashed and it didn't work out. But everybody does that. I always stay open to possibilities for the future.

I certainly could see myself getting married again. I believe I've gained a greater understanding of myself and my surroundings than I had the first time. I feel a lot more settled and prepared for that kind of eventual commitment.

On the other hand, I don't want to be impatient. People often become infatuated and they think, "This is it." Then, two weeks later they're saying, "Well, I thought this was it." A little bit of maturity can give you a lot of insight on longevity with a relationship, because a relationship really is work.

There's an advantage to growing older. You have an idea of where you're focused and where you can go. Then you know how to cultivate the possibility of romance. Meanwhile, I'm happy with the course my world has taken.

I find my life now to be just as appealing as it was when I was doing concerts. My responsibilities have changed, but in basic ways, I haven't. I eat the same kinds of food; I enjoy the same kinds of activities. The intrinsic quality of my life hasn't changed. But the structure has.

These days I'm so busy teaching at the police academy, preparing the volunteer EMT foundation, doing standby medical backups, and making an occasional television appearance that I have to schedule everything. Tyler attends college out of state, studying music, so I rarely have the opportunity to see him. Although Chris lives only an hour away, he stays busy as a drummer with his band, "Whatever." I couldn't be more proud of them.

I am blessed. I don't know what I'll be doing five years from now, but I'm in control of my life. I could do a concert tour or a television series and that wouldn't make me less qualified to work as an EMT or an instructor. There's still the lure of landing that meaty dramatic role. I don't know if that's ever going to happen. Maybe it will. Maybe it won't.

I do know that being a teacher at the academy now is me. It's not a role. When I stand before a group of young cadets, I don't need the aid of props to feel comfortable, as I did when I was a kid.

But some things never change. When I teach a first aid class, I still have to keep moving.

I remember learning that somewhere before.

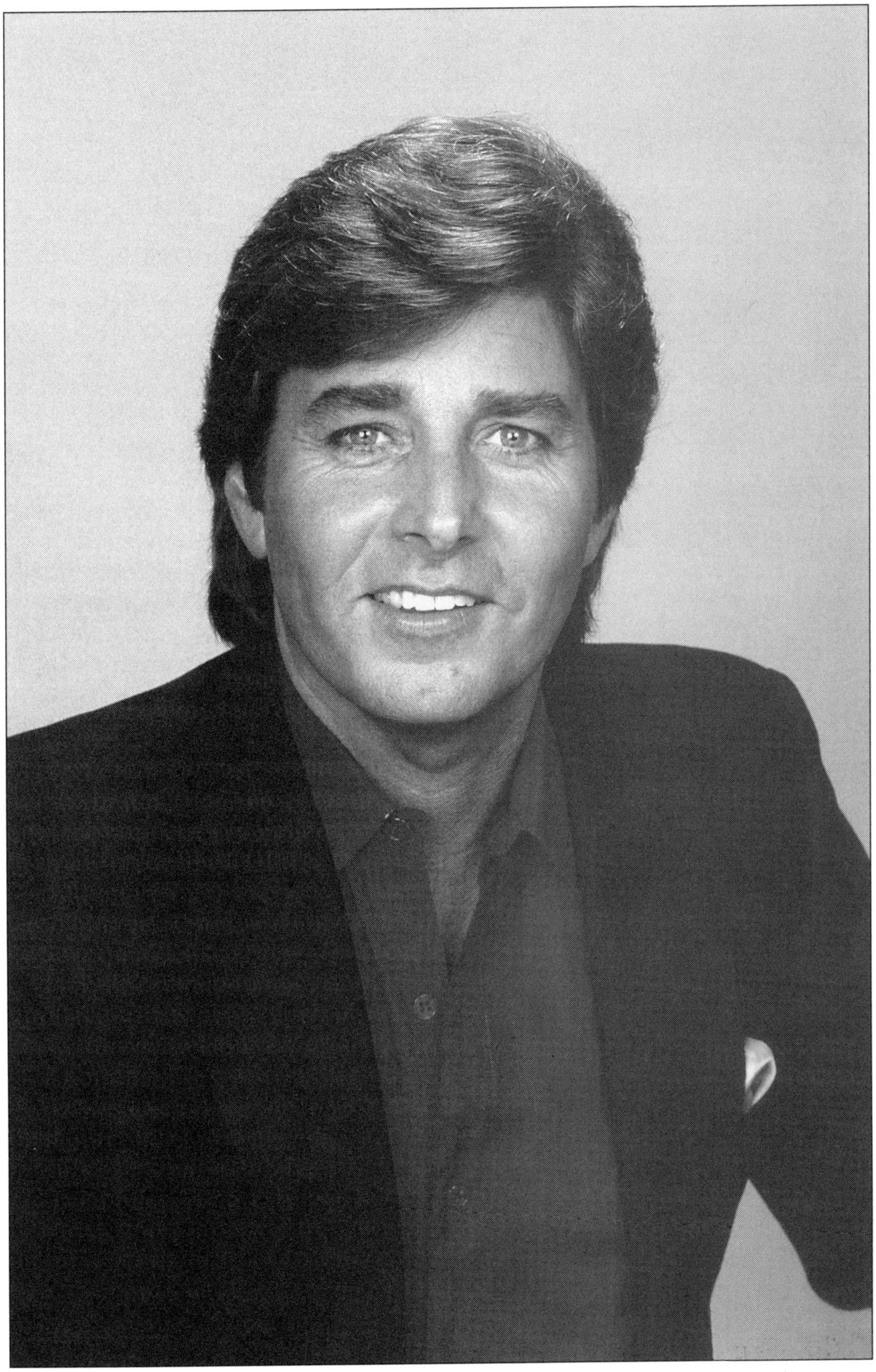

Discography

Singles Released A/B Sides:	Label	Year
"Judy, You'll Never Know"/"Telegram"	Starcrest	1962
"I Want to Hear It from Her"/"Nobody's Sweetheart"	Dot	1964
"You Make Me Happy"/"Man Overboard"	Decca	1964
"It Hurts Me"/"Give Me Your Word"	Decca	1965
"Hey Little Girl"/"Well, All Right"	Decca	1965
"Anything Your Little Heart Desires"/"Goody Galum-Shus"	Parkway	1965
"Happiness Is"/"Can't Get Used to Losing You"	Cameo	1965
"Cold Girl"/"Think of Rain"	Epic	1967
"I'll Never Tell You"/"Telegram"	Condor	1969
"Little Woman"/"One Too Many Mornings"	Metromedia	1969
"La La La (If I Had You)"/"Time"	Metromedia	1969

"Easy Come, Easy Go"/"Sounds Along the Way"	Metromedia	1970
"Hey, Mister Sun"/"Two Blind Minds"	Metromedia	1970
"Julie, Do Ya Love Me?"/"Spend Some Time Lovin' Me"	Metromedia	1970
"Goin' Home (Sing a Song of Christmas Cheer)"/"Love's What You're Gettin' for Christmas"	Metromedia	1971
"Cried Like a Baby"/"Is Anybody There?"	Metromedia	1971
"The Drum"/"Free Now to Roam"	Metromedia	1971
"Waiting at the Bus Stop"/"Runaway"	Metromedia	1971
"Getting Together"/"Jennifer"	Metromedia	1971
"Together Again"/"Picture a Little Girl"	Metromedia	1972
"I Don't Believe in Magic"/"Just a Little While Longer"	Metromedia	1972
"Early in the Morning"/"Unborn Lullabye"	Metromedia	1972
"Mr. Success"/"Runaway"	Janus	1974
"Our Last Song Together"/"Sunshine Rose"	Janus	1975

Albums	**Label**	**Year**
"Bobby Sherman"	Metromedia	1969
"Here Comes Bobby"	Metromedia	1970
"With Love, Bobby"	Metromedia	1970
"The Bobby Sherman Christmas Album"	Metromedia	1970
"Portrait of Bobby"	Metromedia	1971
"Getting Together"	Metromedia	1971
"Bobby Sherman's Greatest Hits, Vol. 1"	Metromedia	1971
"Remembering You"	Phase One Productions	1976

Discography

Released on CD:	**Label**	**Year**
"The Very Best of Bobby Sherman"	Restless Records	1991
"The Bobby Sherman Christmas Album"	Restless Records	1991

Metromedia Albums Reissued on CD:

"Bobby Sherman"	K-tel International	1995
"Here Comes Bobby"	K-tel International	1995
"With Love, Bobby"	K-tel International	1995
"Portrait of Bobby"	K-tel International	1995
"Getting Together"	K-tel International	1996
"Bobby Sherman's Greatest Hits, Vol. 1"	K-tel International	1996

Bobby's greatest hits appeared in different versions on the following two releases:

"Bobby Sherman's Greatest Hits, Vol. 1" from Metromedia:

Side 1	**Side 2**
"Little Woman"	"Cried Like a Baby"
"La, La, La (If I Had You)"	"Spend Some Time Lovin' Me"
"Easy Come, Easy Go"	"The Drum"
"Seattle"	"Waiting at the Bus Stop"
"Hey, Mister Sun"	"Getting Together"
"Julie, Do Ya Love Me?"	"Jennifer"

and "The Very Best of Bobby Sherman" from Restless Records on CD:

1. "Little Woman"
2. "La, La, La (If I Had You)"
3. "Easy Come, Easy Go"
4. "Seattle"
5. "Hey, Mister Sun"
6. "Julie, Do Ya Love Me?"
7. "Cried Like a Baby"
8. "The Drum"
9. "Getting Together"
10. "Mr. Success"
11. "Runaway"
12. "Our Last Song Together"

Bibliography

Sources for further information:

Goldmine's Rock & Roll 45RPM Record Price Guide
by Neal Umphred. Krause Publications, 1994

Osborne & Hamilton's Original Record Collectors Price Guide
O'Sullivan Woodside & Co., Phoenix, AZ 1983

The TV Collector
   Published by Stephen W. and Diane L. Albert,
   P.O. Box 1088, Easton, Massachusetts 02334
   Vol 2 No. 66 and 67
   ("Here Come the Brides" special issues)
   Copyright 1993

Index

"All in the Family," 164–66
Alwaeg, Freddy, 125
American Heart Association, 208
Anaheim Convention Center
    concert, 119–20
Arnaz, Lucie, 60
Avalon, Frankie, 72

Belsen, Mike, 118
Benet, Brenda, 66
Berry, Roxanne, 151
Births
    Bobby Sherman, 2, 4
    Christopher Sherman, 185
    Tyler Sherman, 188
Blank, Bob, 32, 34–35
Blauner, Steve, 81, 82
"Bobby Sherman Special, The"
    157–58
Bobby Sherman Volunteer EMT
    Foundation, 203–4

Bolt, Jeremy (character), 29
Boutwell, Ron, 124
Brando, Marlon, 190–91
Bugle, 35
Building projects
    in childhood, 20–21
    Disneyland model for kids,
        188–92

Cameo Parkway Records, 55
Campbell, Glen, 65
Carnel, Patti, 79, 171–83
    divorce from Sherman, 199–201
    meeting Sherman, 171–72
    miscarriage, 181
Cassidy, David, 161–62
Catalina, Frankie (character), 72
Charles, Ray, 66
Childhood
    bugle playing, 35
    building projects, 20–21

231

childhood accident, 9–10
dog Suzie, 16
Dragnet shows, 19
experimenting with why things work, 18
first sexual encounter, 40
football playing in high school, 42–44
friendship with Johnny Marks, 19
Gault Street Elementary School, 17
imaginary friend Frank, 15–17
La Brea Avenue home, 15
Las Vegas summers at film studio, 21–24
milk route with father, 26–29
movie making, 50
parties at home, 38
performing, 38–40
religious beliefs, 16
singing, 38
Van Nuys home, 17
Children, life with, 185
Choate, Henry, 7
Choate, Willa Mae, 7, 10
Christopher's birth, 185
Clark, Dick, 66
Claver, Bob, 81, 94, 160
Clayton, Dick, 55, 56
College, 48
Concert tours, 117–37
  1966, 69
  hearing loss from, 130
  typical day, 127–29
Cooke, Sam, 66
Cooking, 92
Cowen, Alan, 205

Dates, dream, 105–15
Dating, 41–42

"Dating Game, The" 70–71
Day the Earth Moved, The, 188
Disneyland, 31–32
  building models of, 32–38, 188–92
Divorce from Patti Carnel, 199–201
Dolenz, Mickey, 75
"Dragnet," 19
Dream dates, 105–15

"Easy Come, Easy Go," 101, 127
Emergency Medical Technician (EMT), 206–13
Emergency room work, 207

Fans, 139–55
  gifts, 140
  mail from, 142–44
  from "Shindig," 61–62
Father. *See* Sherman, Robert, Sr.
Fentress, Marty, 210
Fonda, Jane, 52–53
Football playing in high school, 42–44
Freeman, Juanita, 5–9
Freeman, Tom, 7

Gault Street Elementary School, 17
Get Crazy, 217
"Getting Together," 89, 159–67
Gifts from fans, 140
Gold records, 127
Good, Jack, 56
"Goody Galumshus," 55
Grandmother, 10
Gurr, Bob, 37–38

Hair length, 91
Hanley, Bridget, 83–88
He Is My Brother, 188, 216
Hearing loss, 130

Index

"Here Come the Brides," 29, 78–103
   stunt scenes, 97–98
"Hey, Little Girl," 65
High school life, 38
Human behavior classes, 48

"I'm Still Looking for the Right Girl," 125
Imaginary friend Frank, 15–17
"It Hurts Me," 65

Japan travel, 133–34
Jones, Shirley, 163
Jones, Sonny, 118, 124
"Judy, You'll Never Know," 50
"Julie, Do Ya Love Me?," 127
"July Seventeen," 76
Justin, Ed, 139

Kasem, Casey, 65
Kauble, Dian, 153

"La, La, La (If I Had You)," 101
La Brea Avenue home, 15
Las Vegas summers at film studio, 21–24
Laufer, Charles, 109, 215
"Little Woman," 100
Litton Industries work, 47
Los Angeles Police Department, 209–10
Love beads, 140
Lynn (first love), 76–78

Mack, Reuben, 35
Mail from fans, 142–44
Managers for show business, 49
Marks, Johnny, 19
Marriage to Patti Carnel, 178
Maternal grandparents, 3

Merchandising, 139
Milk route with father, 26–29
Miller, Fred, 211
Mineo, Sal, 52–53, 55, 59
"Mod Squad," 216
"Monkees, The" 72–74
Montgomery, Gary, 31
Moore, Clayton, 25
Moses, Ann, 114
Mother, 5–9
Movie making in childhood, 50
Musical combo in high school, 45

Noone, Peter, 66

Parties at home, 38
"Partridge Family, The" 160–62
Paternal grandparents, 11–12
Performing, beginning of, 38–40
Pierce Community College, 48
Psychology classes in college, 48
Pulliam, Jaynie, 150

Rafelson, Bob, 73
Rager, Butch, 209
Recordings
   "Easy Come, Easy Go," 101, 127
   gold records, 127
   "Goody Galum-shus," 55
   "Hey, Little Girl," 65
   "It Hurts Me," 65
   "Judy, You'll Never Know," 50
   "Julie, Do Ya Love Me?," 127
   "La, La, La (If I Had You)," 101
   "Little Woman," 100
   "Telegram," 50
   "Think of Rain," 71
   "You're Nobody's Sweetheart Now," 51
Red Cross, work with, 204–5
Religious beliefs, 16

Retirement. *See* Semi-retirement
Righteous Brothers, 64

"Sanchez of Bel Air," 218
Schneider, Bert, 73
Screen Gems, 81
Seligman, Selig, 56
Semi-retirement
    Bobby Sherman Volunteer EMT Foundation, 203–4
    as Emergency Medical Technician (EMT), 206–13
    emergency room work, 207
    Los Angeles Police Department, 209–10
    Red Cross, work with, 204–5
Sexual encounter, first, 40
Sherman, Christopher Noel, 185–88, 193–97
Sherman, Darlene, 4
    family, 56
    horses and, 25
    marriage, 35
Sherman, Juanita, 5–9
Sherman, Robert, Sr., 5–9
    death of, 219
    illness, 7–8
    relationship with, 63
    wookworking and, 36
Sherman, Tyler Carnel, 188–89, 197
"Shindig," 60–67
    audition for, 56–57
    salary, 13
Singing, beginning of, 38
Sister. *See* Sherman, Darlene
16 Magazine, 106

Soul, David, 78–79, 95
Starcrest Records, 50
Step-grandfather, 7
Stern, Wes, 163
Swackhamer, E. W., 81
Sylvester, Ward, 71, 75

Teen idol phenomenon, 215–22
Teen magazine coverage, 105
"Telegram," 50
Television programs
    "Bobby Sherman Special, The" 157–58
    "Dating Game, The" 70–71
    "Getting Together," 89, 159–67
    "Here Come the Brides," 29, 78–103
    "Mod Squad," 216
    "Monkees, The" 72–74
    "Sanchez of Bel Air," 218
    "Shindig," 13, 56–57, 60–67
"Think of Rain," 71
Tiger Beat, 105
Tolsky, Susan, 88, 96
Trumpet playing, 23–24

Usher, Gary, 65

Van Nuys home, 17
Vitalis hairdressing commercials, 71–72

Witt, Paul, 160
Wood, Natalie, 52–53

"You're Nobody's Sweetheart Now," 51